GUIDE TO

CAREER INFORMATION

GUIDE TO CAREER INFORMATION

A Bibliography of Recent Occupational Literature

by

CAREER INFORMATION SERVICE
NEW YORK LIFE INSURANCE COMPANY

Foreword by
DEVEREUX C. JOSEPHS
Chairman of the Board, New York Life Insurance Company

HARPER & BROTHERS, PUBLISHERS
NEW YORK

Library of Congress Catalog Card Number: 57-12498

CONTENTS

FOREWORD

ONE of the most welcome achievements of our time—welcome alike to young people and to all of us who are interested in their success—is the development of modern occupational literature. Within the last few decades a rich body of writing about the world of work has come into being. The great demand for this material testifies to its importance.

As we at New York Life have good reason to know, young people are immensely eager to learn what the future has in store for them. This knowledge has come to us as result of our decision five years ago to publish in national magazines a series of "Career" advertisements. These advertisements are actually 2-page articles by leading authorities describing opportunities in their own fields of endeavor.

The lively interest of parents, young people, and guidance counselors in these advertisements brought home to us the magnitude of the service we could render, and the New York Life Career Information Service has been our response. Through it we have distributed more than 14 million reprints of the 27 career advertisements so far published. We plan to extend the list and to revise the texts as necessary.

As a further service we are publishing this bibliography of recent, professionally-approved occupational writings. We believe that it will answer many of the requests for additional information occasioned by our career series, and that it will help workers in the field of guidance bring to public notice the great store of existing information. Beyond this, as a company we want to acknowledge the responsibility we feel is ours to assist in the guidance and counseling of young people. It is not a job to be left wholly to the specialists in the field, or to the youngster. All of us—parents, teachers, friends, and potential employers—owe this help to those whom we expect to carry forward our tasks.

The usefulness of this book to the young "explorer" of career possibilities has been a paramount consideration. Consequently we have grouped occupations under 52 headings, or occupational "families." An index and a system of cross references insure that all the resources of the bibliography will be fully presented. It is also planned to reprint the listings in a series of separate pamphlets.

Several specialists in career counseling and occupational bibliography have contributed to this book. We are particularly grateful to John H. Cornehlsen, Ph.D., who as Consulting Psychologist gave his general supervision to the project, and to Sarah Splaver, Ph.D., who prepared the Annotated Bibliography.

New York Life is sponsoring this book as a public service. We will appreciate whatever suggestions readers may offer to increase its usefulness. Comments from laymen and professionals will be equally welcome, for we are all partners in that most satisfying of endeavors—helping young people to make the most of the world of tomorrow.

DEVEREUX C. JOSEPHS
Chairman of the Board
New York Life Insurance Company

PREFACE

For many years the problem of finding out about jobs has faced young people, their parents, counselors, librarians, and others working with them. Many ways have been devised to help young people be more informed about jobs and their reactions to them and the world of work. Ever since the early work of people like Parsons and Kitson emphasizing the importance of vocational guidance there has been a growing trend to introduce job knowledge and job experience into the educational and developmental programs of students. These efforts often become parts of an enriched educational curriculum when knowing what people do in the community around one becomes a means of broadening horizons. Somewhere along the way students often participate in an educational unit which is aimed at acquainting them with the world of work and the sociology of occupations. This is a background on which a young person does—and is required to do—much selecting and choosing as he makes decisions related to his career future.

With the complexity of the modern world and the difficult task of absorbing an adequate background of job knowledge, the importance of reading about jobs receives renewed emphasis. In addition, this reading about jobs offers many of the merits of an independent educational discipline. It is especially valuable because it provides a meaningful introduction to the realities of economic life. In part, this is because occupational books and pamphlets are written from the point of view of the person who has a choice to make. They tend to focus sharply and thus to be more concrete in their treatment of subject matter.

The sharpness of focus is often well balanced within the classroom when the overall framework for the "unit" relates to the broad scope of occupational fields with opportunities for more detailed glimpses at specific occupations. Occupational surveys and occupational approaches to social development fit splendidly into broad social studies programs.

We should not overlook the basic appeal of occupational literature. Occupational literature has the same appeal as all good reading material: it tells about the thousands of things—both the usual and the unusual—that people are actually doing.

I think we owe a good deal to the New York Life Insurance Company for what they have done. By sponsoring the publication of lists of occupational literature, the company renders a double service. It brings authentic and interesting materials to the attention of career-minded young people and, at the same time, lends its support to parents and educators in assisting them with plans for the future. This and other services related to career planning now being offered by New York Life aid in bridging a gap between business and education. They provide the counselor, librarian, teacher, parent, and others concerned with the development of young people with an invaluable tool and service. A public service of this sort impresses me as a logical extension of a life insurance company's basic commitment to the well-being of the American family.

JOHN H. CORNEHLSEN, Ph.D.
Consultant in Career Services to the
New York Life Insurance Company

RECENT OCCUPATIONAL
LITERATURE

"READING ABOUT OCCUPATIONS"
An Introduction for Young People

As a young person today, you are probably "career-minded"—and with good reason. Yours is the exciting prospect of living in a world where work opportunities will be ever richer and more interesting.

It is primarily to help you learn more about occupations that our book, *Guide to Career Information,* has been prepared. Nevertheless, don't be surprised when you find your elders looking into it too. Parents have a natural interest in what benefits young people. Equally interested will be the general reader who likes to keep track of social and economic developments. Indeed, the appeal of occupational literature is so broad that no reader today seems excluded.

What Is There To Read? If you've just become interested in jobs and careers, the first question you ask may be "What is there to read about occupations?" First of all, there are descriptive reports and studies, and in addition there are many fine biographies of successful men and women and several series of lively fictional treatments.

You will find modern occupational literature varied and entertaining. Even formal reports and studies meet high standards of readability and general appeal. Thanks to the skill and enthusiasm of hundreds of career-guidance specialists, and to their nation-wide professional society, the American Personnel and Guidance Association, you have at your service a large body of career readings as interesting as they are authentic.

How Reading Helps You Find Out About Jobs. As you probably realized long ago, there are all sorts of ways to find out about jobs. This is true whether you are taking part in a school or community career-guidance program, or whether you are relying on your own efforts alone. One way to find out about jobs is by frontal attack: You can try your hand at part-time and temporary employment to get experience. Other ways are visits, interviews, conversations, hobbies, lectures, films, and exhibits. Above all, there is reading.

For finding out about jobs today, reading is virtually a "must." Besides what it contributes in itself, reading greatly increases the effectiveness of each of the other methods of learning about jobs. This is true in part because reading materials operate much as do souvenirs. Remember the miniature Statue of Liberty you brought home from New York? Or the picture of the bears begging food in Yellowstone Park? They helped you recall the sights you saw and the good times you had. Similarly, reading a brochure or pamphlet—or even some statistics—after you visit a plant will help you recall the jobs you saw being done, the tools and machines in use, conditions in the shops, and the products coming off the line.

3

No less important an advantage in approaching occupational information through reading is its convenience. You can read about jobs at times when personal inquiry and observation are impossible. What is more, through reading imaginatively you can picture yourself in whatever job strikes your fancy.

Suppose you are interested in a career in trans-oceanic flying. Either through your local library or by writing to an aviation association, you can obtain literature explaining the duties of flight personnel. By reading over this material, it is possible that you will learn enough of what is involved to imagine yourself piloting an air liner from New York to Paris, or pointing out the North Pole to passengers on a flight from Copenhagen to Los Angeles. Short of actually flying as a regular member of the crew, your closest approach to such experiences is most likely to be through reading.

The same is true of countless other jobs performed under special conditions. As a "scrub nurse," for instance, in the operating room of a hospital, you would be responsible for the instruments that the surgeon uses during an operation. This means that many times a day you would play a part in the saving of human lives. Certainly this is a job many girls want to know more about. However, since it is difficult to gain admission to an operating room in any capacity other than as a patient, reading and imagination must take the place of direct, personal experience.

Occupational Reading as an Aid to Career Thinking. So far the discussion has centered on the informational aspect of occupational reading. There is another.

If you've thought about careers, you will probably agree that one thing worth having is an understanding of yourself and your relation to particular occupations. As you may have discovered, it is easy to fall into a pattern of circular thinking. Remember the chicken and the egg? And which came first?

You can get into the same kind of wrangle trying to decide whether to approach jobs first in terms of what you want to do—or what you have the ability to do—or what you want to get out of life—or what you have the time, money, and opportunity to do—or what offers you the biggest reward, or the most fun! So many factors are involved that you hardly know where to begin. Often, too, soon after you have begun, you find yourself back where you started.

Reading professionally approved occupational studies should go a long way toward making effective career thinking habitual. You will learn the trick of focusing on a particular job while at the same time examining realistically both yourself and what lies ahead. In doing this, you will acquire a sense of the close relationship between career opportunities and current social and economic developments.

Using the Annotated Bibliography. When your career thinking is attuned to current developments, especially in a fast-developing technological age such as our own, up-to-date information becomes important to you. Hence your need for a compact and authoritative guide to the most recent reading materials available.

You will find such a guide in the annotated occupational bibliography to follow. Listed are more than 800 recent books and pamphlets about occupations and about career planning. The majority were published within the last two years, and none are more than five years old. The compilers kept in mind professional standards for accuracy and completeness when choosing works to be listed.

The annotated bibliographies are your guide for locating information about par-

4

ticular occupations. They will also help you gather ideas about what there is to do. You will see that the entries are arranged alphabetically by titles within occupational groupings. Annotations give the name and address of the publisher, cost, and level of reader interest, plus a concise description of the contents. At the end of each occupational group are the names and addresses of organizations offering further information.

You can use the annotated bibliography in at least four ways: (1) to "look up" a title you have heard about; (2) to find the latest sources of information on career planning and on particular occupations that interest you; (3) to gather ideas about possible jobs and careers; (4) to serve as a check-list lest you overlook worthwhile career possibilities.

Of all the uses, the last might well be the most important for you. In a work of this sort, there is a kind of "built-in democracy" operating to your advantage. Each occupation has a chance to state its claim upon your favor. Of course, you are always free to disregard the claim, but whether you do or don't, you are made to realize that with respect to each occupation a legitimate claim exists.

Career Planning. "Career planning," someone once said, "is like driving an auto through morning traffic. The man who gives thought to it will get to work sooner!"

For you as a member in good standing of today's career-minded generation, reading New York Life's *Guide to Career Information* may well be a part of the journey toward your life's work. In the distance, you feel sure, there awaits an occupation to fit your own unique combination of talents, preferences, needs, and resources. However, with so many different factors to consider, and so many different destinations on the road before you, you are probably wondering just how you will ever find your way alone to the right one.

If this is bothering you, don't let it. There are many sources of help. Your parents, for example, and your relatives and friends. They are always happy to share their experience and apply their point of view to your problems. Besides, there are counselors and counseling aids (the bibliography lists several under "Career Guidance") to help you organize your study of yourself and of careers and jobs.

What is more, over and above the many people interested in your success and ready to help you achieve it, you have working for you the energy of our expanding economy and its wealth of opportunities. All of these will contribute to make your career planning an interesting and pleasant experience.

Just keep in mind that the world of occupations is a world meant for you to live in and enjoy—and that one of the greatest enjoyments it offers is the chance to discover for yourself the particular fields where your own talents will flourish.

ACCOUNTANCY AND BOOKKEEPING

ACCOUNTANTS:

(D.O.T. Nos.: 0-01.10 through 0-01.40)

ACCOUNTANT. 1953.

4 pages—35¢; special to students, 25¢.
Chronicle Guidance Publications
Moravia, N. Y.

One of a series of "briefs," this pamphlet includes information on the importance of the job, work performed, working conditions, earnings, requirements and preparation, opportunities, places of employment, methods of entry, and related jobs.

ACCOUNTANT. Revised 1953.

4 pages—15¢ in Canada, 20¢ elsewhere.
Guidance Centre, Univ. of Toronto
371 Bloor St. W., Toronto 5, Ontario

This "monograph" defines the job, the history of the work and describes working conditions, qualifications, preparation, opportunities, earnings, advantages and disadvantages, getting started, and related occupations.

ACCOUNTANTS. *A. D. Waring*. 1954.

20 pages—25¢.
Michigan Employment Security Comm.
7310 Woodward Ave., Detroit 2, Mich.

This is one of a series of "occupational guides" and includes information on the history of the occupation, nature of the work, number of workers and their distribution, prospects, qualifications and educational requirements, earnings, and disadvantages and advantages.

CAREERS IN ACCOUNTING. Revised 1956.

8 pages—25¢.
B'nai B'rith Vocational Service Bureau

1129 Vermont Ave., N. W., Washington 5, D. C.

Included in this booklet is information on the outlook in this field, nature of the work, training and qualifications, how to get started, earnings, and working conditions.

EMPLOYMENT OPPORTUNITIES FOR WOMEN IN PROFESSIONAL ACCOUNTING. BULLETIN NO. 258.

Women's Bureau, U. S. Dept. of Labor.
1955.

40 pages—20¢.
Supt. of Documents, Govt. Printing Office
Washington 25, D. C.

The history of women's progress in the field of accountancy is traced in this pamphlet which presents a thorough coverage of the field. It includes a job definition, and contains information as to the number of women in the field, college requirements, license requirements, job outlook, salaries, job opportunities, advancement, and a list of professional societies.

EMPLOYMENT OUTLOOK IN ACCOUNTING. BULLETIN NO. 1048

Bureau of Labor Statistics, U. S. Dept. of Labor. 1952.

32 pages—20¢.
Supt. of Documents, Govt. Printing Office
Washington 25, D. C.

One of the "employment outlook" series, this bulletin discusses the development of the field of professional accounting. It lists the various areas of employment, training and qualifications, earnings, working conditions, trends, and outlook. It also lists schools offering training in accountancy.

SHOULD YOU BE AN ACCOUNTANT? *J. L. Carey.* 1956.
  8 pages—free.
  New York Life Insurance Co.
  51 Madison Ave., New York 10, N. Y.

One of a series of illustrated career booklets published as a public service, this pamphlet presents the history of the field and its importance to society, the work of "public" and "private" accountants, their earnings, advancement, drawbacks, qualifications, and training.

BOOKKEEPERS:
(D.O.T. Nos.: 1-01.02; 1-01.03)

BOOKKEEPER. Revised 1954.
  4 pages—15¢ in Canada, 20¢ elsewhere.
  Guidance Centre, Univ. of Toronto
  371 Bloor St. W., Toronto 5, Ontario
This "monograph" defines the job, gives information as to personal qualifications and educational requirements, entrance into the field, related occupations, earnings, and advantages and disadvantages.

(also see fields of BANKING AND FINANCE)

For additional information, write to:

AMERICAN INSTITUTE OF ACCOUNTANTS
270 Madison Ave., New York 16, N. Y.

ADVERTISING AND PUBLIC RELATIONS

ADVERTISING COPY WRITERS:
(D.O.T. No.: 0-06.94)

ADVERTISING COPY WRITER. Revised 1954.

4 pages—15¢ in Canada, 20¢ elsewhere.
Guidance Centre, Univ. of Toronto
371 Bloor St. W., Toronto 5, Ontario

This is one of a series of "monographs" presenting a definition of the occupation, importance and nature of the work, working conditions, qualifications, preparation, opportunities for advancement, earnings, getting started, advantages and disadvantages, and related occupations.

ADVERTISING SALESPEOPLE:
(D.O.T. No.: 1-87.26)

MAGIC IN HER VOICE. *P. Panzer.* 1953.

184 pages—$2.95.
Julian Messner, Inc.
8 West 40th St., New York 18, N. Y.

Incorporated into the romance theme of this career novel is information about the heroine's job as a newspaper advertising salesgirl. The book includes material on the nature of the work, qualifications for the job, and methods of advancement. *(For teen-age girls)*

MARKET RESEARCH PERSONNEL:
(D.O.T. No.: 0-36.11)

CAREERS IN RESEARCH. 1952.

6 pages—10¢.
Glamour Magazine
420 Lexington Ave., New York 17, N.Y.

Included in this "fact sheet" are the qualifications and training for non-technical research jobs, demand for new workers, places of employment, nature of the jobs, and earnings. *(For female readers)*

JOBS IN MARKET RESEARCH. *Mademoiselle's College and Careers Dept.* Revised 1955.

5 pages—25¢.
Alumnae Advisory Center, Inc.
541 Madison Ave., New York 22, N. Y.

The importance of this work to society, miscellaneous job opportunities, qualifications, places of employment, educational preparation, salaries, and methods of advancement are contained in this reprint. *(For female college students)*

OPPORTUNITIES IN MARKET RESEARCH. *J. H. Platten.* 1951.

112 pages—$1.00.
Vocational Guidance Manuals, Inc.
1011 East Tremont Ave., New York 60, N. Y.

This "manual" describes the market research field and analyzes the different types of jobs in this field. It includes information about preparation for employment, getting the job, and advancement in the field. It also contains a list of colleges offering training in market research.

PATSY'S MEXICAN ADVENTURE. *E. E. Grumbine*. 1953.

245 pages—$2.50.
Dodd, Mead and Co., Inc.
432 Fourth Ave., New York 16, N. Y.

Another career novel, this book weaves information about the nature of the work and problems of consumer research into the fictional tale. *(For teen-age girls)*

PUBLIC RELATIONS PERSONNEL:
(D.O.T. No.: 0-06.97)

CAREERS IN PUBLIC RELATIONS. *D. Frifield*. 1955.

8 pages—25¢.
B'nai B'rith Vocational Service Bureau
1129 Vermont Ave., N. W., Washington 5, D. C.

This booklet presents the history and importance of the field, and describes the nature of the work, employment outlook, qualifications and preparation, how to get started, earnings, and advancement opportunities.

JEAN READE IN PUBLIC RELATIONS. *P. Mandigo,* 1954.

248 pages—$2.50.
Dodd, Mead and Co., Inc.
432 Fourth Ave., New York 16, N. Y.

This career novel includes information on the nature of the work in this field as it relates the heroine's adventures as an employee of a public relations firm. *(For teenage girls)*

OPPORTUNITIES IN PUBLIC RELATIONS. *S. Henkin,* 1951.

112 pages—$1.00.
Vocational Guidance Manuals, Inc.
1011 East Tremont Ave., New York 60, N. Y.

This comprehensive manual presents a description of the field and its several areas and specializations. It describes public relations and publicity work, educational preparation, personal qualifications, opportunities for success, how to get started, advantages and disadvantages, and a list of colleges offering public relations courses.

PUBLIC RELATIONS. *Mademoiselle's College and Careers Dept.* 1956.

5 pages—25¢.
Alumnae Advisory Center, Inc.
541 Madison Ave., New York 22, N. Y.

The nature of public relations work is described here. It also includes its drawbacks and compensations, opportunities for women, experience and qualifications for the work, and a typical day in the life of a public relations woman. *(For female college students)*

MISCELLANEOUS:

ADVERTISING AGENCY JOBS. 1955.
  6 pages—10¢.
  Glamour Magazine
  420 Lexington Ave., New York 17,
  N. Y.

This "fact sheet" surveys the qualifications and training of value in advertising. It describes beginning jobs, and the opportunities in the copy, art, research, radio and television, media, and production departments. *(For female readers)*

THE ADVERTISING BUSINESS. *A. D. Conkey.* 1951.
  29 pages—25¢.
  Adcraft Club of Detroit
  2237 Book Tower, Detroit 26, Mich.

An analysis of the place of advertising in our economy is followed by the employment opportunities in this field. It includes typical places of employment, procedures for starting out in advertising, qualifications, preparation, earnings, and how to apply for the job.

ADVERTISING JOBS. *Mademoiselle's College and Careers Dept.* Revised 1955.
  5 pages—25¢.
  Alumnae Advisory Center, Inc.
  541 Madison Ave., New York 22, N. Y.

The results of a Jobs and Futures Panel survey on how to get into advertising, this magazine reprint presents the nature of the work, salaries, opportunities for women, and how to get started in research, media, production, copy and account work. *(For female college students)*

ADVERTISING MEN. 1955.
  4 pages—35¢; special to students, 25¢.
  Chronicle Guidance Publications
  Moravia, N. Y.

One of a series of "occupational briefs," this pamphlet discusses the nature of advertising work, working conditions, wages, qualifications and training requirements for employment, how to enter the field, advancement, places of employment, and outlook.

For additional information, write to:

THE ADVERTISING FEDERATION OF AMERICA
330 West 42nd St., New York 36, N. Y.

AMERICAN ASSOCIATION OF ADVERTISING AGENCIES
420 Lexington Ave., New York 17, N. Y.

PUBLIC RELATIONS SOCIETY OF AMERICA
2 West 46th St., New York 36, N. Y.

AGRICULTURE

BEEKEEPERS:
(D.O.T. No.: 3-07.70)

BEEKEEPER. Revised 1956.

4 pages—15¢ in Canada, 20¢ elsewhere.
Guidance Centre, Univ. of Toronto
371 Bloor St. W., Toronto 5, Ontario

This "monograph" defines the job, its history and importance, working conditions, qualifications and preparation, employment and advancement, remuneration, advantages and disadvantages, how to get started, and related occupations.

COWBOYS:
(D.O.T. No.: 3-17.20)

GENE RHODES, COWBOY. *B. F. Day.* 1954.

192 pages—$2.95.
Julian Messner, Inc.
8 West 40th St., New York 18, N. Y.

An action-packed biography of Eugene Manlove Rhodes, this book narrates the vocational adventures of this fast-riding cowboy who for some thirty years rode in the New Mexico territory. (*For teen-age boys*)

FARMERS:
(D.O.T. Nos.:3-01 through 3-09)

FRUIT GROWER. 1955.

4 pages—15¢ in Canada, 20¢ elsewhere.
Guidance Centre, Univ. of Toronto
371 Bloor St. W., Toronto 5, Ontario

This "monograph" describes the nature of the work and its importance to society, working conditions, personal requirements and preparation, earnings, how to get started, and related occupations.

GENERAL FARMER. 1955.

4 pages—35¢; special to students, 25¢.
Chronicle Guidance Publications
Moravia, N. Y.

Reviewed in this "occupational brief" are definitions of the occupation, duties, working conditions, earnings, personal requirements, training, outlook, places of employment, getting started, and related jobs.

GENERAL FARMER. Revised 1955.

4 pages—15¢ in Canada, 20¢ elsewhere.
Guidance Centre, Univ. of Toronto
371 Bloor St. W., Toronto 5, Ontario

Another of this Centre's "monographs," it presents information on the nature of the farmer's work, qualifications, training, getting started, advancement, earnings, related occupations, and advantages and disadvantages.

POULTRY FARMER. *H. A. Robinson.* 1955.

6 pages—50¢; special to students, 25¢.
Personnel Services, Inc.
Main St., Peapack, N. J.

One of the series of "occupational abstracts," this pamphlet summarizes the nature of the work, supply of farmers, prospects, qualifications, educational requirements, related occupations, earnings, and advantages and disadvantages.

POULTRYMAN. Revised 1954.

4 pages—15¢ in Canada, 20¢ elsewhere.
Guidance Centre, Univ. of Toronto
371 Bloor St. W., Toronto 5, Ontario

This "monograph" defines the job, and includes information on requirements, methods of entrance, advancement in this field, related occupations, and earnings.

SHOULD YOU BE A FARMER? *R. I. Throckmorton.* 1955.

8 pages—free.
New York Life Insurance Co.
51 Madison Ave., New York 10, N. Y.

This is one of a series of free authoritative career booklets. It illustrates the existence of an average farm family. It discusses the farmers' average incomes, farm values, attractive aspects of the work, personal requirements, and training.

TRUCK FARMER. 1955.

4 pages—15¢ in Canada, 20¢ elsewhere.
Guidance Centre, Univ. of Toronto
371 Bloor St. W., Toronto 5, Ontario

Definition and nature of the work, working conditions, qualifications, training, earnings, methods of advancement, getting started, and related occupations are presented in this "monograph."

FLORISTS:

(D.O.T. Nos.: 0-43.60; 0-72.41; 1-75.92)

FLORIST. Revised 1955.

4 pages—15¢ in Canada, 20¢ elsewhere.
Guidance Centre, Univ. of Toronto
371 Bloor St. W., Toronto 5, Ontario

This "monograph" describes the nature of the work, working conditions, qualifications and preparation for entrance, advancement, earnings, how to get started, advantages and disadvantages, and related occupations.

HORTICULTURISTS:

(D.O.T. No.: 0-35.05)

OPPORTUNITIES IN HORTICULTURE. *C. O. Brantley.* Revised 1953.

96 pages—$1.00.
Vocational Guidance Manuals, Inc.
1011 East Tremont Ave., New York 60, N. Y.

Another in this series of "manuals," it describes the growth and branches of horticulture, educational requirements, how to get started, earnings, advancement, varied opportunities, and a list of agricultural colleges.

NURSERYMEN:

(D.O.T. No.: 3-38.20)

NURSERYMAN. 1954.

4 pages—35¢; special to students, 25¢.
Chronicle Guidance Publications
Moravia, N. Y.

This "occupational brief" defines the job, and gives a history of the work. It describes working conditions, earnings, qualifications and preparation, advancement, outlook, opportunities for women in this field, typical places of employment, and methods of entry.

MISCELLANEOUS:

CAREERS IN TECHNICAL
AGRICULTURE. *G. E. Turner*. 1952.

8 pages—25¢.
B'nai B'rith Vocational Service Bureau
1129 Vermont Ave., N. W., Washington 5, D. C.

This booklet discusses the nature of the careers available in the areas of technical agriculture. The animal, food, plant, and soil branches of the field are presented.

OCCUPATIONAL GOALS FOR COL-
LEGE STUDENTS. PART II: AGRI-
CULTURE AND RELATED SCI-
ENCES. Edited by *M. Hammond*. 1954.

145 pages—$1.50.
Ohio State University Press
Columbus 10, Ohio

Here is a comprehensive presentation of the many varied opportunities in agriculture and related fields. It highlights the nature of the work, qualifications, preparation and future prospects in such areas as agricultural economics, agronomy, botany, dairy technology, entomology, genetics, horticulture, and nutrition.

(also see fields of CONSERVATION, and FOOD AND HOME ECONOMICS)

For additional information, write to:

AMERICAN SOCIETY OF AGRICULTURAL ENGINEERS
505 Pleasant St., St. Joseph, Mich.

AMERICAN SOCIETY OF AGRONOMY
2702 Monroe St., Madison 5, Wisc.

U. S. DEPT. OF AGRICULTURE
Washington 25, D. C.

ARCHITECTURE

ARCHITECTS:

(D.O.T. No.: 0-03.10)

ARCHITECT. 1953.

4 pages—35¢; special to students, 25¢.
Chronicle Guidance Publications
Moravia, N. Y.

Another in the series of "occupational briefs," this pamphlet defines the job and describes the working conditions, qualifications, educational preparation, salaries, how to obtain employment, outlook, and licensing.

ARCHITECT. Revised 1955.

4 pages—15¢ in Canada, 20¢ elsewhere.
Guidance Centre, Univ. of Toronto
371 Bloor St. W., Toronto 5, Ontario

This "monograph" includes information on the importance of the architect to society, nature of the work, working conditions, qualifications, preparation, earnings, how to get started, and advantages and disadvantages.

ARCHITECT. *J. M. Shelley.* 1956.

32 pages—$1.00.
Research Publishing Co., Inc.
P. O. Box 245, Boston 1, Mass.

Definition of the occupation, its history, and importance to society. Trends, salaries, advantages and disadvantages, education and training, working conditions, how to secure employment, and related occupations are presented in this pamphlet.

ARCHITECTURE. 1952.

9 pages—10¢.
Glamour Magazine
420 Lexington Ave., New York 17, N. Y.

This "fact sheet," prepared by the Job Dept. of *Glamour,* describes the nature of the architect's work, qualifications and training, apprenticeship, fees, and licensing. It also lists the schools which are members of the Association of Collegiate Schools of architecture. *(For female readers)*

SHOULD YOU BE AN ARCHITECT?
P. Belluschi. 1956.

8 pages—free.
New York Life Insurance Co.
51 Madison Ave., New York 10, N. Y.

This attractive, authoritative booklet, one of a series published as a public service, discusses the gratifications of the architect's work, supply and demand, work performed, qualifications, and preparation.

MISCELLANEOUS:

OCCUPATIONAL GOALS FOR COLLEGE STUDENTS. PART I: ARCHITECTURE, ENGINEERING, AND THE PHYSICAL SCIENCES. Edited by *M. Hammond.* 1951.

96 pages—75¢.

Ohio State University Press
Columbus 10, Ohio

Here is a comprehensive presentation of basic information for those who aspire to careers in these fields. Coverage is given to such matters as the nature of the work, qualifications, future prospects, educational requirements, and opportunities available. *(For college students)*

OPPORTUNITIES IN ARCHITECTURE. *Wm. Thorpe.* 1951.

112 pages—$1.00.
Vocational Guidance Manuals, Inc.
1011 East Tremont Ave., New York
   60, N. Y.

A typical day in an architect's office is described in this "manual." Also included are facts about getting started in the field, personal attributes necessary, earnings, where to study architecture, and related fields of work.

(also see field of ENGINEERING)

For additional information, write to:

AMERICAN INSTITUTE OF ARCHITECTS
1735 New York Ave., N. W., Washington 6, D. C.

ART

CARTOONISTS:
(D.O.T. No.: 0-04.41)

CARTOONIST. 1955.

4 pages—35¢; special to students, 25¢.
Chronicle Guidance Publications
Moravia, N. Y.

This "occupational brief" defines the job, its history, working conditions, earnings, qualifications and preparation, outlook, opportunities for women, places of employment, how to get started, and related jobs.

CARTOONIST. *S. Splaver.* 1956.

6 pages—50¢; special to students, 25¢.
Personnel Services, Inc.
Main St., Peapack, N. J.

Summarized in this "occupational abstract" are the history and nature of the work, qualifications, preparation, entrance and advancement, supply and demand, opportunities for servicemen, earnings, and advantages and disadvantages.

COMMERCIAL ARTISTS:
(D.O.T. Nos.: 0-44.; 0-46.)

COMMERCIAL ART. 1955.

7 pages—10¢.
Glamour Magazine
420 Lexington Ave., New York 17, N. Y.

Describes the nature of the work of the commercial artist, qualifications, preparation, entering the field, sources of employment, and opportunities. *(For female readers)*

COMMERCIAL ART. *V. F. Group.* 1951.

6 pages—50¢; special to students, 25¢.
Personnel Services, Inc.
Main St., Peapack, N. J.

Another in the series of authoritative "occupational abstracts," the pamphlet summarizes the nature of the work, outlook, qualifications, preparation, entrance and advancement, earnings, supply and distribution of workers, and advantages and disadvantages.

COMMERCIAL ARTIST. Revised 1956.

4 pages—15¢ in Canada, 20¢ elsewhere.
Guidance Centre, Univ. of Toronto
371 Bloor St. W., Toronto 5, Ontario

This "monograph" includes a job definition, history of the work, working conditions, qualifications and preparation, employment and advancement, remuneration, advantages and disadvantages, and related occupations.

ILLUSTRATING COMMERCIAL ARTIST. Revised 1956.

4 pages—35¢; special to students, 25¢.
Chronicle Guidance Publications
Moravia, N. Y.

One of a series of "occupational briefs," the pamphlet includes the nature of the work, qualifications, educational preparation, working conditions, opportunities, earnings, outlook, where employed, and methods of entry.

MISCELLANEOUS:

A PALETTE FOR INGRID. *L. Hobart.* 1956.

192 pages—$2.95.
Julian Messner, Inc.
8 West 40th St., New York 18, N. Y.
Another in the series of "romances for young moderns," this entertaining tale includes valuable occupational information for those aspiring to art careers. *(For teen-age girls)*

THE ARTIST IN THE
PUBLISHING TRADES. 1952.

4 pages—free to high school principals and guidance officers.
Simmons College
300 The Fenway, Boston 15, Mass.

The role of art in publishing, preparation for the work, qualifications, earnings, and opportunities are contained in this folder.

CAREERS IN COMMERCIAL ART.
J. I. Biegeleisen. Revised 1952.

255 pages—$4.00.
E. P. Dutton and Co., Inc.
300 Fourth Ave., New York 10, N. Y.
This well-illustrated book is a comprehensive presentation of the varied opportunities in this field among which are caricaturing, cartooning, covers of books, motion pictures, sign painting, stage settings and window displays.

For additional information, write to:

ARTISTS EQUITY ASSOCIATION
625 Madison Ave., New York 22, N. Y.

NATIONAL CARTOONISTS SOCIETY
140 West 57th St., New York 19, N. Y.

SOCIETY OF ILLUSTRATORS
128 East 63rd St., New York 21, N. Y.

AUTOMOBILE INDUSTRY

AUTOMOBILE MECHANICS:
(D.O.T. No.: 5-81.010)

AUTOMOBILE MECHANIC. 1953.

4 pages—35¢; special to students, 25¢.
Chronicle Guidance Publications
Moravia, N. Y.

Another of the "occupational briefs" in this series, this pamphlet defines the job, the nature of the work performed, working conditions, wages, personal and training requirements, outlook, how to gain employment, and related jobs.

AUTOMOBILE MECHANIC. Revised 1954.

4 pages—15¢ in Canada, 20¢ elsewhere.
Guidance Centre, Univ. of Toronto
371 Bloor St. W., Toronto 5, Ontario

This "monograph" prepared by the Centre highlights the history of the occupation, describes the nature of the work, working conditions, qualifications, preparation, advancement opportunities, earnings, advantages and disadvantages, and methods of obtaining employment.

AUTOMOBILE AND TRUCK MECHANICS. Revised 1954.

33 pages—25¢.
Michigan Employment Security Comm.
7310 Woodward Ave., Detroit 2, Mich.

This "occupational guide" discusses the development of the automotive industry, nature of the work of these mechanics, educational and physical requirements, working conditions, hazards of work, unions, and advantages and disadvantages . . . earnings and job prospects in Michigan are indicated.

AUTOMOBILE-BODY REPAIRING OCCUPATIONS. 1951.

24 pages—25¢.
Michigan Employment Security Comm.
7310 Woodward Ave., Detroit 2, Mich.

Here are facts on the importance of these occupations to society, descriptions of the jobs, future prospects, working conditions, remuneration, advancement, and union organizations.

AUTOMOBILE-BODY REPAIRMAN. 1954.

4 pages—35¢; special to students, 25¢.
Chronicle Guidance Publications
Moravia, N. Y.

This "brief" contains information on the nature of the work performed, working conditions, earnings, personal qualifications, training required, outlook, places of employment, and methods of getting the job.

AUTOMOBILE SALESMEN:
(D.O.T. Nos.: 1-75.)

AUTOMOBILE SALESMAN. 1956.

4 pages—35¢; special to students, 25¢.
Chronicle Guidance Publications
Moravia, N. Y.

This "occupational brief" describes the nature of the work performed, its history, job requirements, working conditions, wages, personal and training requirements, outlook, places of employment, how to enter this occupation, and related jobs.

KEYS TO CAREERS IN THE RETAIL AUTOMOTIVE BUSINESS. 1955.

36 pages—free.
General Motors Corp.

Service Section, Detroit 2, Mich.

This pamphlet gives job opportunities in retail automotive servicing and selling, and describes the nature of the work, qualifications, working conditions, earnings, and what to do to get started.

SERVICE STATION ATTENDANTS:
(D.O.T. No.: 7-60.500)

SERVICE-STATION ATTENDANT. 1953.

4 pages—35¢; special to students, 25¢.
Chronicle Guidance Publications
Moravia, N. Y.

Another of the "occupational briefs" in this series, this pamphlet reviews the history of the occupation, nature of the work, working conditions, wages, personal and training requirements, future prospects, opportunities for women, methods of entering the field, and related jobs.

SERVICE STATION ATTENDANT. 1956.

4 pages—15¢ in Canada, 20¢ elsewhere.
Guidance Centre, Univ. of Toronto
371 Bloor St. W., Toronto 5, Ontario

This "monograph" defines the job, describes working conditions, qualifications and preparation needed, advancement, earnings, advantages and disadvantages, how to get started, and related occupations.

MISCELLANEOUS:

EMPLOYMENT OUTLOOK IN THE AUTOMOBILE INDUSTRY. BULLETIN NO. 1138. *Bureau of Labor Statistics, U. S. Dept. of Labor.* 1953.

33 pages—25¢.
Supt. of Documents, Govt. Printing Office
Washington 25, D. C.

The outlook in several areas of this industry is reviewed. The nature of the work, qualifications, preparation, working conditions, and supply and demand are presented for numerous automotive occupations.

For additional information, write to:

AUTOMOBILE MANUFACTURERS ASSOCIATION
320 New Center Bldg., Detroit 2, Mich.

AVIATION

AIRPLANE HOSTESSES:
(D.O.T. No.: 2-25.37)

AIR LINE STEWARDESS. Revised 1956.

    4 pages—15¢ in Canada, 20¢ elsewhere.
Guidance Centre, Univ. of Toronto
371 Bloor St. W., Toronto 5, Ontario
This "monograph" defines the job, its history and importance, nature of the work, working conditions, qualifications and preparation necessary for entry and success, opportunities for advancement, remuneration, advantages and disadvantages, how to get started, and related occupations.

AIRLINE STEWARDESS AND AIRLINE RESERVATIONIST. 1955.

    4 pages—10¢.
Glamour Magazine
420 Lexington Ave., New York 17, N. Y.
In this "fact sheet" is information on the personal and physical requirements of the job, duties of the work, training, earnings, and how to apply for both of these occupations. Included also are the names and addresses of fourteen airlines. *(For female readers)*

AIRPLANE HOSTESS. 1953.

    4 pages—35¢; special to students, 25¢.
Chronicle Guidance Publications
Moravia, N. Y.

This "occupational brief" defines the occupation, outlines working conditions, requirements, training, advantages and disadvantages, advancement, how to enter the field, future prospects, and related jobs.

CHART: AIRLINE HOSTESS REQUIREMENTS. *Mademoiselle's College and Careers Dept.* Revised 1956.

    4 pages—25¢.
Alumnae Advisory Center, Inc.
541 Madison Ave., New York 22, N. Y.
This pamphlet lists personal qualifications, preparation, on-the-job training, earnings, work assignments, and where to apply for positions as airline hostesses for eleven airlines and the supplemental (non-schedule) airlines. *(For female readers)*

SKYGIRL: A CAREER HANDBOOK FOR THE AIRLINE STEWARDESS. *M. F. Murray.* 1951.

    256 pages—$3.00.
Duell, Sloan and Pearce, Inc.
124 East 30th St., New York 16, N. Y.
In a delightfully informative manner, this book describes the history of aviation, qualifications for the job, preparation, how to obtain employment, nature of the work, working conditions, advancement opportunities, and related jobs. Many excellent photographs are included.

AIRPLANE MECHANICS:

(D.O.T. No.: 5-80.120)

AIRCRAFT MECHANIC. Revised 1954.

4 pages—15¢ in Canada, 20¢ elsewhere.

Guidance Centre, Univ. of Toronto
371 Bloor St. W., Toronto 5, Ontario

This "monograph" stresses the importance of this work to society, describes the nature of the work performed, personal qualifications, training requirements, job advancement, earnings, advantages and disadvantages, and related occupations.

AIRCRAFT MECHANICS. Revised 1954.

24 pages—25¢.

Michigan Employment Security Comm.
7310 Woodward Ave., Detroit 2, Mich.

One of this Commission's "occupational guides," this pamphlet contains information on the history of the occupation, nature of the work, requirements, job prospects, working conditions, hazards on the job, earnings, training, and disadvantages and advantages.

AIRPLANE NAVIGATORS:

(D.O.T. No.: 0-41.60)

NAVIGATOR. 1953.

4 pages—35¢; special to students, 25¢.
Chronicle Guidance Publications
Moravia, N. Y.

This "occupational brief" defines the job, working conditions, wages, personal and training requirements, employment outlook, and related jobs.

AIRPLANE PILOTS:

(D.O.T. No.: 0-41.10)

AIR LINE PILOT. Revised 1953.

4 pages—15¢ in Canada, 20¢ elsewhere.

Guidance Centre, Univ. of Toronto
371 Bloor St. W., Toronto 5, Ontario

Contained in this "monograph" are a definition of the occupation, qualifications and preparation, working conditions, earnings, advantages and disadvantages, and how to get started.

AIR LINE PILOT. *H. A. Robinson.* 1954.

6 pages—50¢; special to students, 25¢.

Personnel Services, Inc.
Main St., Peapack, N. J.

This "occupational abstract" summarizes the nature of the work, future prospects, licensing, qualifications, preparation, entrance and advancement, earnings, advantages and disadvantages, and related occupations.

CHARTER PILOT. *J. Hambleton.* 1953.

216 pages—$3.00.

Longmans, Green and Co.
55 Fifth Ave., New York 3, N. Y.

This is an entertaining and informative career novel. *(For teen-age boys)*

COMMERCIAL AIRPLANE PILOT.
1952.

    4 pages—35¢; special to students, 25¢.
Chronicle Guidance Publications
Moravia, N. Y.

In this "occupational brief" information is included on the history and nature of the work, working conditions, personal and educational requirements, opportunities for training, job trends, where employed, licensing, and related jobs.

MISCELLANEOUS:

AVIATION FROM THE GROUND UP.
J. J. Floherty. Revised 1956.

    192 pages—$2.75.
J. B. Lippincott Co.
227 So. 6th St., Philadelphia 5, Pa.

This career book offers much valuable information concerning present-day aviation and the activities of persons employed in varied phases of the field. *(For teen-agers)*

EMPLOYMENT OUTLOOK FOR AIR TRANSPORTATION. BULLETIN NO. 1128. *Bureau of Labor Statistics, U. S. Dept. of Labor.* 1953.

    24 pages—20¢.
Supt. of Documents, Govt. Printing Office
Washington 25, D. C.

Summarizations of the future prospects in such occupations as airplane hostess, airplane mechanic, airplane pilot, airport traffic controller, dispatcher, flight engineer, flight steward, radio operator and traffic agent are offered here. Information is included on the nature of the work, qualifications, working conditions and earnings.

THE STARS AT NOON. *J. Cochran.*
1954.

    274 pages—$4.50.
Little, Brown and Co.
34 Beacon St., Boston 6, Mass.

Young people will enjoy reading this inspiring autobiography of a famous aviatrix as she relates her many adventures. *(For teen-age girls)*

THE STORY OF AMELIA EARHART.
A. deLeeuw. 1955.

    181 pages—$1.50.
Grosset and Dunlap, Inc.
1107 Broadway, New York 10, N. Y.

The exploits of one of the most famous women in aviation, the late Miss Earhart, provide engrossing reading plus worthwhile occupational information for those who aspire to aviation careers. *(For teen-age girls)*

WINGS IN YOUR FUTURE. *L. Schneider and M. Ames.* 1955.

    151 pages—$2.75.
Harcourt, Brace and Co.
383 Madison Ave., New York 17, N. Y.

The potentials and opportunities which the field of aviation has to offer to young people are presented in this book. *(For teen-agers)*

(also see fields of TRANSPORTATION AND TRAVEL)

For additional information, write to:

AIR TRANSPORT ASSOCIATION OF AMERICA
1107—16th St., N. W., Washington, D. C.

CIVIL AERONAUTICS ADMINISTRATION
U. S. Dept. of Commerce
Washington 25, D. C.

INSTITUTE OF THE AERONAUTICAL SCIENCES, INC.
2 East 64th St., New York 21, N. Y.

BANKING AND FINANCE

BANK MANAGERS AND TELLERS:
(D.O.T. Nos.: 0-97.; 0-98.; 1-65.)

BANK MANAGER. Revised 1953.

4 pages—15¢ in Canada, 20¢ elsewhere.

Guidance Centre, Univ. of Toronto

371 Bloor St. W., Toronto 5, Ontario

This "monograph," contains a job definition, shows the importance of bank work, duties, working conditions, qualifications, preparation, advancement, earnings, advantages and disadvantages, and how to get started.

BANK TELLER. 1954.

4 pages—35¢; special to students, 25¢.

Chronicle Guidance Publications

Moravia, N. Y.

This "occupational brief" defines the job, describes working conditions, salaries, personal and educational requirements, future prospects, opportunities for women, and methods of obtaining employment.

BANK TELLER. 1955.

4 pages—15¢ in Canada, 20¢ elsewhere.

Guidance Centre, Univ. of Toronto

371 Bloor St. W., Toronto 5, Ontario

This "monograph" defines the job, describes working conditions, personal qualifications, preparation, how to get started, earnings, and advantages and disadvantages.

BANK TELLER. *S. Splaver.* 1956.

6 pages—50¢; special to students, 25¢.

Personnel Services, Inc.

Main St., Peapack, N. J.

Summarized in this occupational abstract are the history and nature of the work, qualifications, preparation, entrance and advancement, supply and demand, opportunities for women, earnings, and advantages and disadvantages.

BANKING. 1955.

3 pages—10¢.

Glamour Magazine

420 Lexington Ave., New York 17, N. Y.

Another of this magazine's "fact sheets," it points out the job opportunities in the field, qualifications and educational background, where to apply for jobs, advantages and compensations, and banking associations. *(For female readers)*

SHOULD YOU BE A BANKER? *F. F. Florence.* 1955.

8 pages—free.

New York Life Insurance Co.

51 Madison Ave., New York 10, N. Y.

This public service booklet sets forth the growth and development of banking, opportunities in the field, women's place in banking, earnings and other benefits, attractive features of the work, training, and qualifications for employment.

ECONOMISTS:
(D.O.T. No.: 0-36.11)

ECONOMISTS—EDUCATIONAL
REQUIREMENTS FOR EMPLOY-
MENT OF. V.A. PAMPHLET 7-8.4.
*Veterans Administration in cooperation
with Bureau of Labor Statistics, U. S.*
Dept. of Labor. 1955.

    11 pages—15¢.
    *Supt. of Documents, Govt. Printing
      Office*
Washington 25, D. C.

This pamphlet is part of a series prepared
for the Veterans Administration's vocational rehabilitation program. It includes
the nature of the work and education
necessary for varied types of employment
in the field. *(For counselors)*

STOCK AND BOND BROKERS:
(D.O.T. No.: 1-06.87)

BOND TRADER. 1955.

    4 pages—15¢ in Canada, 20¢ else-
    where.
    Guidance Centre, Univ. of Toronto
    371 Bloor St. W., Toronto 5, Ontario

This is another of the Centre's "monographs." It defines the job and describes
qualifications, training, advancement, earnings, working conditions, advantages and
disadvantages, and how to get started.

STOCK BROKERAGE BUSINESS.
E. M. Fowler. 1955.

    31 pages—$1.00.
    Bellman Publishing Co.
    P. O. Box 172, Cambridge 38, Mass.

This pamphlet contains information on
job opportunities in the field. It describes

the role played by the broker and his relation to society, and outlines the preparation for employment, advancement possibilities, salaries, and future for women in
the field.

WOMAN STOCK BROKER. *Mademoiselle's College and Careers Dept.* 1955.

    3 pages—25¢.
    Alumnae Advisory Center, Inc.
    541 Madison Ave., New York 22, N. Y.

This magazine reprint describes the work
activities of one of the few female stock
brokers. It outlines working conditions,
preparation for the work, earnings, and
opportunities for women. *(For female college students)*

MISCELLANEOUS:

CAREERS IN THE CONSUMER
FINANCE FIELD. 1953.

  8 pages—25¢.
  B'nai B'rith Vocational Service Bureau
  1129 Vermont Ave., N. W., Washington 5, D. C.

This booklet belongs to the Bureau's career series and describes the varied jobs in the field, nature of the work, personal qualifications, training, opportunities for advancement, earnings, and advantages and disadvantages.

EMPLOYMENT OUTLOOK IN
BANKING OCCUPATIONS.
BULLETIN NO. 1156. *Bureau of Labor Statistics, U. S. Dept. of Labor.* 1954.

  42 pages—30¢.
  Supt. of Documents, Govt. Printing Office
  Washington 25, D. C.

In this comprehensive pamphlet is information on the development and function of modern banking, opportunities in the field, nature of the work, qualifications for entering the field, working conditions, trends, and earnings.

MONEY JOBS. *Mademoiselle's Jobs and Futures Dept.* 1953.

  4 pages—25¢.
  Alumnae Advisory Center, Inc.
  541 Madison Ave., New York 22, N. Y.

This magazine reprint discusses the opportunities in banking, accounting, investment, coinage, and credit. *(For female readers)*

OPPORTUNITIES IN FINANCE.
S. Shulsky. 1951.

  112 pages—$1.00.
  Vocational Guidance Manuals, Inc.
  1011 East Tremont Ave., New York 60, N. Y.

This "manual" presents a comprehensive analysis of the opportunities in such fields as banking, brokerage, investment banking and investment counseling. It lists qualifications and preparation needed for jobs in finance, earnings, and tells how to obtain employment. It also contains information on related fields.

For additional information, write to:

AMERICAN BANKERS ASSOCIATION
12 East 36th St., New York 16, N. Y.

INVESTMENT BANKERS ASSOCIATION OF AMERICA
33 So. Clark St., Chicago 3, Ill.

THE NEW YORK STOCK EXCHANGE
11 Wall St., New York 5, N. Y.

BARBERING AND BEAUTY CULTURE

BARBERS:
(D.O.T. No.: 2-32.01)

BARBER. 1953.

4 pages—35¢; special to students, 25¢.
Chronicle Guidance Publications
Moravia, N. Y.

This "occupational brief" contains a job definition, describes working conditions, wages, personal qualifications, training requirements, future prospects. It tells how to enter the occupation and how to obtain a license.

BARBER. Revised 1954.

4 pages—15¢ in Canada, 20¢ elsewhere.
Guidance Centre, Univ. of Toronto
371 Bloor St. W., Toronto 5, Ontario

This "monograph" includes a history of the profession, its importance to society, the nature of the work, and lists qualifications, preparation, advancement opportunities, earnings.

BARBER. Revised 1954.

16 pages—25¢.
Michigan Employment Security Comm.
7310 Woodward Ave., Detroit 2, Mich.

This "occupational guide" presents the employment opportunities for barbers in the state of Michigan. However, the information on the nature of the work, qualifications, training, earnings, working conditions, and advantages and disadvantages is applicable throughout the country.

BEAUTY OPERATORS:
(D.O.T. No.: 2-32.15)

BEAUTY OPERATOR. 1952.

4 pages—35¢; special to students, 25¢.
Chronicle Guidance Publications
Moravia, N. Y.

Described in this "occupational brief" are the work performed, working conditions, personal qualifications necessary for success, training, wages, opportunities for promotion, where employed, outlook, and related jobs.

BEAUTY OPERATOR. Reprinted 1954.

24 pages—25¢.
Michigan Employment Security Comm.
7310 Woodward Ave., Detroit 2, Mich.

This occupational guide includes information about the nature of the work and the jobs performed in the field, supply and demand, training, licensing, earnings, working conditions, qualifications for entering field, and advantages and disadvantages.

ELECTROLOGISTS:

(D.O.T. No.: 2-32.23)

ELECTROLOGIST. 1953.

3 pages—35¢; special to students, 25¢.
Chronicle Guidance Publications
Moravia, N. Y.

This "occupational brief" describes the nature of the work performed, wages, qualifications, training requirements, training opportunities, outlook, method of entry, and licensing.

ELECTROLOGIST. *L. Shuman.* 1955.

32 pages—$1.00.
Research Publishing Co., Inc.
P. O. Box 245, Boston 1, Mass.

Included in this little pamphlet are the history of electrolysis, nature of the work of the electrologist, earnings, qualifications, trends, advantages and disadvantages, working conditions, and related occupations.

HAIRDRESSERS:

(D.O.T. No.: 2-32.11)

HAIRDRESSER. Revised 1954.

4 pages—15¢ in Canada, 20¢ elsewhere.
Guidance Centre, Univ. of Toronto
371 Bloor St. W., Toronto 5, Ontario

This "monograph" sets forth the history of hairdressing, describes the nature of the work, working conditions, qualifications and preparation, earnings, how to obtain the job, and lists related jobs.

MISCELLANEOUS:

EMPLOYMENT OPPORTUNITIES FOR WOMEN IN BEAUTY SERVICE. BULLETIN NO. 260. *Women's Bureau, U. S. Dept. of Labor.* 1956.

51 pages—25¢.
Supt. of Documents, Govt. Printing Office
Washington 25, D. C.

This pamphlet analyzes the opportunities available in the field. It contains information on advancement, preparation for beauty occupations, licensing, earnings, organizations for beauticians, personal qualifications, "pros and cons" of beau-

tician's job, and examples of cosmetology training courses.

OPPORTUNITIES IN BEAUTY CULTURE. *F. E. Wall.* 1952.

112 pages—$1.00.
Vocational Guidance Manuals, Inc.
1011 East Tremont Ave., New York 60, N. Y.

Here is another of the authoritative "manuals" in the series. It discusses the positions in branches of the field, future prospects, requirements for success, earnings, and beauty culture organizations.

For additional information, write to:

BEAUTY CAREER COUNCIL
949 Broadway, New York 10, N. Y.

BUSINESS ADMINISTRATION

ADMINISTRATIVE PERSONNEL:

(D.O.T. Nos.: 0-91.; 0-97.; 0-98.)

JUNIOR EXECUTIVE. 1954.

4 pages—35¢; special to students, 25¢.
Chronicle Guidance Publications
Moravia, N. Y.

This "occupational brief" includes a job definition, discusses working conditions, earnings, personal and training requirements, employment outlook, and methods of entry.

JUNIOR EXECUTIVE. *V. F. Group.* 1952.

6 pages—50¢; special to students, 25¢.
Personnel Services, Inc.
Main St., Peapack, N. J.

Here is another "occupational abstract" which highlights the nature of the work, future prospects, qualifications, preparation for employment, earnings, and entrance and advancement.

PURCHASING AGENT. *V. F. Group.* 1954.

6 pages—50¢; special to students, 25¢.

Personnel Services, Inc.
Main St., Peapack, N. J.

Summarized in this "occupational abstract" are the nature of the work, future prospects, qualifications and preparation necessary for success, entrance and advancement, earnings, and distribution of workers.

YOUR OPPORTUNITIES IN MANAGEMENT. Revised 1954.

29 pages—free.
National Association of Manufacturers
2 East 48th St., New York 17, N. Y.

This public service pamphlet tells what management is and how it grew, opportunities in the field for men and women, preparation, personal qualities necessary for success, and nature of the work of varied management personnel.

MISCELLANEOUS:

A BUSINESS IN PETS. *N. M. Dean.* 1956.

192 pages—$2.95.
Julian Messner, Inc.
8 West 40th St., New York 18, N. Y.

Worthwhile information about the management of a pet shop and the care and training of pets is incorporated into the romance theme of this career novel. *(For teen-age girls)*

THE CORDAGE BUSINESS.
Wm. A. Scherff. 1951.

32 pages—$1.00.
Research Publishing Co., Inc.
P. O. Box 245, Boston 1, Mass.

The author takes the reader on a tour through a plant showing the processes which are involved in the manufacture of cord and analyzes the opportunities in this business. The Plymouth Cordage Co.,

Plymouth, Mass., offers free copies to schools and libraries.

ESTABLISHING AND OPERATING YOUR OWN BUSINESS. DOMESTIC SERIES NO. 22. *Small Business Division, U. S. Dept. of Commerce.* Reprinted 1954.

42 pages—35¢.
Supt. of Documents, Govt. Printing Office
Washington 25, D. C.

A most valuable pamphlet for all who eventually want to own their own businesses. It presents basic information on chances of success, what business to choose, buying a going business, establishing a new business, operating the business, keeping up-to-date, and a check list for establishing a business.

HOUSE OF HOLLY. *M. M. Freer.* 1954.

183 pages—$2.95.
Julian Messner, Inc.
8 West 40th St., New York 18, N. Y.

Another of Messner's series of "romances for young moderns," this career novel includes information on the nature of the work and getting started in the mail-order business. *(For teen-age girls)*

SHOULD YOU GO INTO BUSINESS FOR YOURSELF? *M. Sontheimer.* 1955.

8 pages—free.
New York Life Insurance Co.
51 Madison Ave., New York 10, N. Y.

This attractive public service booklet offers illustrations of successful small businesses and discusses personality factors essential for business success, capital requirements, opportunities for embarking upon one's own business, and women in business.

WHAT IT TAKES TO OPERATE YOUR OWN BUSINESS. 1952.

6 pages—10¢.
Glamour Magazine
420 Lexington Ave., New York 17, N. Y.

This magazine reprint highlights the importance of managerial know-how, capital, and personality, and illustrates with examples of six women who operate their own businesses. *(For female readers)*

(also see fields of MERCHANDISING AND RETAILING)

For additional information, write to:

AMERICAN MANAGEMENT ASSOCIATION
330 West 42nd St., New York 18, N. Y.

U. S. DEPT. OF COMMERCE, OFFICE OF SMALL BUSINESS
Washington 25, D. C.

CLERICAL AND SECRETARIAL WORK

CLERKS—TYPISTS:

(D.O.T. Nos.: 1-01. through 1-49.)

CLERK-TYPIST. *H. A. Robinson*. 1955.

6 pages—50¢; special to students, 25¢.
Personnel Services, Inc.
Main St., Peapack, N. J.

This "occupational abstract" summarizes the history of clerical work, duties, future prospects, qualifications, preparation, opportunities for service-women, methods of entering the field, advancement, earnings, and advantages and disadvantages.

GENERAL OFFICE CLERK. Revised 1956.

4 pages—35¢; special to students, 25¢.
Chronicle Guidance Publications
Moravia, N. Y.

This "occupational brief" contains a history of the occupation, and discusses duties, working conditions, earnings, personal and training requirements, opportunities for advancement, outlook, opportunities for men, where employed, methods of entry, and related jobs.

OFFICE BOY—OFFICE GIRL. 1954.

4 pages—35¢; special to students, 25¢.
Chronicle Guidance Publications
Moravia, N. Y.

Reviewed in this "brief" are the kinds of activities performed, personal and training requirements, working conditions, earnings, opportunities for promotion, outlook, where employed, methods of entry, and related jobs.

STOCK CLERK. 1955.

4 pages—35¢; special to students, 25¢.
Chronicle Guidance Publications
Moravia, N. Y.

This "occupational brief" includes a job definition and history of the work. It discusses working conditions, earnings, personal and training requirements, advancement, prospects, and how to get started.

TYPING OCCUPATIONS. Revised 1956.

20 pages—25¢.
Michigan Employment Security Comm.
7310 Woodward Ave., Detroit 2, Mich.

Presented in this "occupational guide" are the history of the typewriter, nature of the work of typists, working conditions, places of employment, prospects, earnings, qualifications, and disadvantages and advantages.

TYPIST. 1955.

4 pages—35¢; special to students, 25¢.
Chronicle Guidance Publications
Moravia, N. Y.

This "occupational brief" describes duties, entering a typing job, advancement, personal qualifications, preparation, earnings, working conditions, typical places of employment, and related jobs.

RECEPTIONISTS:

(D.O.T. No.: 1-18.43)

RECEPTIONIST. 1955.

4 pages—35¢; special to students, 25¢.
Chronicle Guidance Publications
Moravia, N. Y.

Included in this "occupational brief" are job definition, nature of the work, working conditions, earnings, training requirements, advancement, methods of obtaining employment, and future prospects.

RECEPTIONIST. *S. Splaver.* 1954.

6 pages—50¢; special to students, 25¢.
Personnel Services, Inc.
Main St., Peapack, N. J.

Abstracted here are the nature of the work, qualifications, preparation, entrance and advancement, supply and demand of receptionists, opportunities for servicemen, earnings, and advantages and disadvantages.

SECRETARIES AND STENOGRAPHERS:

(D.O.T. Nos.: 1-33.; 1-37.00 through 1-37.29)

LEGAL SECRETARY. 1954.

5 pages—10¢.
Glamour Magazine
420 Lexington Ave., New York 17, N. Y.

This "fact sheet" discusses qualifications, methods of entering the field, duties, training, typical places of employment, and salaries. *(For female readers)*

MALE SECRETARY. 1956.

4 pages—35¢; special to students, 25¢.
Chronicle Guidance Publications
Moravia, N. Y.

Included in this "occupational brief" are job definition, working conditions, wages, personal and training requirements, advancement, outlook, places of employment, methods of entry, and related jobs.

MEDICAL SECRETARY. 1954.

4 pages—10¢.
Glamour Magazine
420 Lexington Ave., New York 17, N. Y.

This "fact sheet" contains information on the qualifications and educational requirements for success in the field, nature of the work, sources of employment, and a list of books and trade directories. *(For female readers)*

PUBLIC STENOGRAPHER, SHORTHAND REPORTER, AND NOTARY PUBLIC. 1951.

4 pages—10¢.
Glamour Magazine
420 Lexington Ave., New York 17, N. Y.

This "fact sheet" describes the qualifications, duties, preparation for the work, and earnings in these three occupations. *(For female readers)*

SECRETARY. Revised 1956.

4 pages—35¢; special to students, 25¢.
Chronicle Guidance Publications
Moravia, N. Y.

This "occupational brief" presents the nature of the secretary's work, working conditions, earnings, personal and training requirements, opportunities for men, and job prospects.

SECRETARY. 1954.

> 4 pages—15¢ in Canada, 20¢ elsewhere.
>
> *Guidance Centre, Univ. of Toronto*
> 371 Bloor St. W., Toronto 5, Ontario

This "monograph" defines the job, it discusses the importance of the work, duties, working conditions, qualifications, preparation, advancement opportunities, how to enter the field, earnings, and advantages and disadvantages.

THE SECRETARY. 1955.

> 4 pages—free to high school principals and guidance officers.
>
> *Simmons College*
> 300 The Fenway, Boston 15, Mass.

This folder discusses the nature of the work, personal qualifications and training necessary for a secretarial career, and opportunities for advancement.

STENOGRAPHER. 1954.

> 4 pages—35¢; special to students, 25¢.
> *Chronicle Guidance Publications*
> Moravia, N. Y.

This "occupational brief" includes a history of the occupation, work performed, working conditions, salaries, personal qualifications, training for the work, places of employment, getting the job, future prospects, opportunities for men, and related jobs.

STENOGRAPHER. Revised 1954.

> 4 pages—15¢ in Canada, 20¢ elsewhere.
>
> *Guidance Centre, Univ. of Toronto*
> 371 Bloor St. W., Toronto 5, Ontario

Described in this "monograph" are the importance and nature of the stenographer's work, working conditions, qualifications and preparation, earnings, advancement opportunities, how to get started, and the advantages and disadvantages.

STENOGRAPHIC OCCUPATIONS.
Revised 1955.

> 24 pages—25¢.
> *Michigan Employment Security Comm.*
> 7310 Woodward Ave., Detroit 2, Mich.

A comprehensive presentation of the opportunities in this field, this booklet discusses the history of these job activities, nature of the work, physical and personal qualifications, educational requirements, how to get started in this field, earnings, and advantages and disadvantages.

MISCELLANEOUS:

CAN I BE AN OFFICE WORKER?
1956.

> 32 pages—free.
> *General Motors Corp.*
> Dept. of Public Relations, Detroit 2, Mich.

This attractive pamphlet discusses the history of the field, what office workers do, the various categories of office workers, and what it takes to become an office worker.

CAREERS IN OFFICE MANAGEMENT. 1956.

> 12 pages—25¢.
> *B'nai B'rith Vocational Service Bureau*
> 1129 Vermont Ave., N. W., Washington 5, D. C.

This booklet discusses the development of the field of office management, employment opportunities, duties of office manager, personal qualifications, preparation, entry and beginning jobs, advancement, working conditions, and earnings.

OFFICE-MACHINE OPERATORS.
1954.

    4 pages—35¢; special to students, 25¢.
Chronicle Guidance Publications
Moravia, N. Y.

This "occupational brief" contains a job definition, describes working conditions, earnings, personal qualifications, training, typical places of employment, methods of entering this field, and future prospects.

For additional information, write to:

NATIONAL OFFICE MANAGEMENT ASSOCIATION
1900 Old York Rd., Abington, Pa.

NATIONAL SECRETARIES ASSOCIATION
222 West 11th St., Kansas City 5, Mo.

CLOTHING AND FASHION

CLEANERS AND DYERS:
(D.O.T. Nos.: 6-27.122; 5-57.410)

CAREER AS DRY CLEANER AND SPOTTER. 1952.

    6 pages—25¢.
    B'nai B'rith Vocational Service Bureau
    1129 Vermont Ave., N.W., Washington 5, D. C.

Included in this booklet are the duties of cleaners and spotters, preparation, qualifications, working conditions, entering the field, and future prospects.

SKILLED JOBS IN THE GARMENT DRY CLEANING INDUSTRY. 1953.

    4 pages—35¢; special to students, 25¢.
    Chronicle Guidance Publications
    Moravia, N. Y.

This "occupational brief" describes the varieties of dry cleaning establishments, history, functions of the dry cleaner, dyer and spotter, working conditions, qualifications, earnings, obtaining employment, and outlook.

DESIGNERS:
(D.O.T. No.: 0-46.01)

BUTTONS AND BEAUX. *L. Gallagher and L. Wyndham.* 1953.

    276 pages—$2.50.
    Dodd, Mead and Co., Inc.
    432 Fourth Ave., New York 16, N. Y.

This career novel tells the tale of a young fashion designer, the nature of her work, opportunities in the field, and the attractive aspects of her career. *(For teen-age girls)*

CLOTHES DESIGNER. Revised 1956.

    4 pages—15¢ in Canada, 20¢ elsewhere.
    Guidance Centre, Univ. of Toronto
    371 Bloor St. W., Toronto 5, Ontario

This "monograph" contains a job definition, and describes working conditions, qualifications and preparation, advancement, remuneration, advantages and disadvantages, how to get started, and related occupations.

DESIGNERS—CLOTHING. 1952.

    4 pages—35¢; special to students, 25¢.
    Chronicle Guidance Publications
    Moravia, N. Y.

Presented in this "occupational brief" is information on the nature of the work performed, history, working conditions, wages, personal and training requirements, methods of entering the field, and future prospects.

FASHION DESIGN. *M. N. Lillard.* 1955.

    18 pages—$1.00
    Bellman Publishing Co.
    P. O. Box 172, Cambridge 38, Mass.

The history and development of the fashion industry, training and education, personal qualifications, nature of the work of the fashion designer, related fashion careers, employment opportunities, earnings, advancement, advantages and disadvantages, and future prospects are discussed in this phamphlet.

FASHION DESIGNER. *S. Splaver*. Revised 1956.

   6 pages—50¢; special to students, 25¢.
   Personnel Services, Inc.
   Main St., Peapack, N. J.

This "occupational abstract" summarizes the history of designing, nature of the work, qualifications, preparation, entrance and advancement in this field, earnings, and advantages and disadvantages.

FASHION DESIGNING. 1955

   3 pages—10¢.
   Glamour Magazine.
   420 Lexington Ave., New York 17, N. Y.

This "fact sheet" highlights qualifications for fashion work, education and special training, getting started, and the fashion centers. *(For female readers)*

NO PATTERN FOR LOVE. *B Williams.* 1951.

   178 pages—$2.95.
   Julian Messner, Inc.
   8 West 40th St., New York 18, N. Y.

The heroine in this career novel is attending a fashion design school. Occupational information on the nature of the work, preparation, and entrance into the fashion designing field are incorporated into this entertaining book. *(For teen-age girls)*

YOUNG FACES IN FASHION.
B. Williams. 1956.

   192 pages—$2.75.
   J. B. Lippincott Co.
   227 So. 6th St., Philadelphia 5, Pa.

The nature of the work of eight top designers provides educational and entertaining reading for would-be designers. *(For junior and senior high school students)*

DRESSMAKERS:
(D.O.T. No.: 4-25.030)

DRESSMAKING OCCUPATIONS. Revised 1954.

   20 pages—25¢.
   Michigan Employment Security Comm.
   7310 Woodward Ave., Detroit 2 Mich.

Another "occupational guide" prepared by the Commission, it discusses the history and nature of the work in these occupations, working conditions, qualifications and training necessary for employment, earnings, and advantages and disadvantages.

FURRIERS:
(D.O.T. No.: 4-21.010)

FURRIER. 1956.

   4 pages—15¢ in Canada, 20¢ elsewhere.
   Guidance Centre, Univ. of Toronto
   371 Bloor St. W., Toronto 5, Ontario

This "monograph" includes a job definition and history of the work performed, and discusses working conditions, qualifications and preparation, advantages and disadvantages, how to get started, and related occupations.

TAILORS:

(D.O.T. Nos.: 4-26.101; 4-26.201)

TAILOR. Revised 1956.

4 pages—35¢; special to students, 25¢.
Chronicle Guidance Publications
Moravia, N. Y.

This "occupational brief" reviews the functions of tailors, working conditions, wages, personal qualifications, training requirements, opportunities for promotion, outlook, opportunities for women, where employed, and methods of entry.

TAILOR. Revised 1952.

4 pages—15¢ in Canada, 20¢ elsewhere.
Guidance Centre, Univ. of Toronto
371 Bloor St. W., Toronto 5, Ontario

This "monograph" defines the job, and discusses working conditions, qualifications and preparation, advancement, remuneration, advantages and disadvantages, how to get started, and related occupations.

TAILOR. *S. Splaver.* 1952.

6 pages—50¢; special to students, 25¢.
Personnel Services, Inc.
Main St., Peapack, N. J.

This "occupational abstract" describes the nature of the tailor's work, qualifications, preparation, entrance and advancement, earnings, and supply and demand.

MISCELLANEOUS:

CAREERS IN MEN'S CLOTHING INDUSTRY. Revised 1956.

8 pages—25¢.
B'nai B'rith Vocational Service Bureau
1129 Vermont Ave., N. W., Washington 5, D. C.

This booklet presents the outlook, nature of the job opportunities, working conditions, earnings, and how to get started in this field.

CAREERS IN THE WORLD OF FASHION. *F. S. Curtis.* 1952.

268 pages—$3.50.
Whiteside, Inc.
425 Fourth Ave., New York 16, N. Y.

Numerous opportunities in the fashion field are discussed with illustrations from the lives of noted fashion-world successes.

EMPLOYMENT OUTLOOK IN MEN'S TAILORED CLOTHING INDUSTRY.

BULLETIN NO. 1010. *Bureau of Labor Statistics, U. S. Dept. of Labor.* 1951.

32 pages—25¢.
Supt. of Documents, Govt. Printing Office
Washington 25, D. C.

This is one of the pamphlets in the employment outlook series. It comprehensively analyzes the employment opportunities in the industry and describes such jobs as those of the cutter, designer, patternmaker, presser and tailor.

FASHION JOBS. 1956.

9 pages—10¢.
Glamour Magazine
420 Lexington Ave., New York 17, N. Y.

This "fact sheet" discusses opportunities in the following categories of the fashion world: fashion art, retailing, styling and fashion coordination, advertising and publicity, and fashion editorial. *(For female readers)*

FASHION SPECIALISTS. *Mademoiselle's Jobs and Futures Dept.* 1952.

3 pages—25¢.
Alumnae Advisory Center, Inc.
541 Madison Ave., New York 22, N. Y.

The nature of the work of fashion coordinators and their special abilities are discussed here. *(For female readers)*

THE JOB PATTERN IN THE PATTERN BUSINESS. 1953.

4 pages—10¢.
Glamour Magazine
420 Lexington Ave., New York 17, N. Y.

This reprint briefly highlights the nature of the work of the many persons involved in the production of a pattern from the initial idea to the finished product. *(For female readers)*

JOBS IN DRESS FABRICS. *Mademoiselle's College and Careers Dept.* Revised 1956.

6 pages—25¢.
Alumnae Advisory Center, Inc.
541 Madison Ave., New York 22, N. Y.

Opportunities available in wool, cotton, rayon and silk houses are discussed in this magazine reprint. It also lists the schools of textile design and textile technology. *(For female readers)*

KIT CORELLI, TV STYLIST. *E. A. Nash.* 1955.

182 pages—$2.95.
Julian Messner, Inc.
8 West 40th St., New York 18, N. Y.

One of their "romances for young moderns," this career novel relates the occu-

pational adventures of the heroine as a fashion stylist in the television field. *(For teen-age girls)*

LUCKY MISS SPAULDING. *E. A. Nash.* 1952.

182 pages—$2.95.
Julian Messner, Inc.
8 West 40th St., New York 18, N. Y.

In this career novel, the heroine is in the field of fashion retailing. Into the romance theme is woven information about the nature of the work, qualifications for success, and advancement opportunities. *(For teen-age girls)*

MAGAZINE FASHION JOBS. *Mademoiselle's College and Careers Dept.* Revised 1956.

6 pages—25¢.
Alumnae Advisory Center, Inc.
541 Madison Ave., New York 22, N. Y.

The functions of a fashion editor, training, qualifications, the nature of the work of other members of a magazine fashion department, and some pointers on how to get started are included in this reprint. *(For female readers)*

OPPORTUNITIES IN FASHION. *A. Vreeland.* 1951.

112 pages—$1.00.
Vocational Guidance Manuals, Inc.
1011 East Tremont Ave., New York 60, N. Y.

This authoritative manual presents a comprehensive analysis of the opportunities in the fashion and related fields. Nature of the work, personal qualifications, educational preparation, earnings and future prospects are discussed. It also lists schools and colleges offering training in fashion designing and illustration.

For additional information, write to:

53 AMALGAMATED CLOTHING WORKERS OF AMERICA
15 Union Square, New York 3, N. Y.

54 FASHION GROUP, INC.
9 Rockefeller Plaza, New York 20, N. Y.

55 INTERNATIONAL LADIES GARMENT WORKERS UNION
1710 Broadway, New York 19, N. Y.

56 NATIONAL INSTITUTE OF CLEANING AND DYEING
Silver Springs, Md.

COMMUNICATIONS AND ELECTRONICS

ELECTRONIC ENGINEERS:
(D.O.T. No.: 0-17.01)

SHOULD YOU BE AN ELECTRONIC ENGINEER? *M. J. Kelly.* 1955.

8 pages—free.
New York Life Insurance Co.
51 Madison Ave., New York 10, N. Y.

This public service career booklet describes the opportunities in the field, nature of the work performed, demand and supply of electronic engineers, advancement, salaries and other rewards, drawbacks, qualifications, college training, and opportunities for women.

RADIO ANNOUNCERS:
(D.O.T. No.: 0-69.21)

A MIKE FOR MARION. *J. Dennis.* 1952.

200 pages—$3.00.
Longmans, Green and Co.
55 Fifth Ave., New York 3, N. Y.

This career novel centers about the occupation of the radio announcer. It provides the readers with information on the nature of the work performed in the field. *(For teen-agers)*

RADIO ANNOUNCER. 1953.

4 pages—35¢; special to students, 25¢.
Chronicle Guidance Publications
Moravia, N. Y.

This "occupational brief" reviews the history of the occupation, nature of activities on the job, wages, working conditions, preparation, qualifications, opportunities for women, how to obtain employment, outlook, and related jobs.

RADIO AND TELEVISION OPERATORS:
(D.O.T. No.: 0-63.30)

RADIO AND TV OPERATORS. 1953.

4 pages—35¢; special to students, 25¢.
Chronicle Guidance Publications
Moravia, N. Y.

This "occupational brief" defines the jobs, discusses wages, personal qualifications, preparation, requirements for amateur and commercial licenses, future prospects, and opportunities for women.

TECHNICIANS:

(D.O.T. Nos.: 0-48. through 0-50.)

CAREER AS ELECTRONICS
TECHNICIAN. *M. A. Rutzick.* 1955.

8 pages—25¢.
B'nai B'rith Vocational Service Bureau
1129 Vermont Ave., N. W., Washington 5, D. C.

This booklet describes the importance of the field, duties of the technician, job prospects, working conditions, earnings, and typical places of employment.

ELECTRONIC TECHNICIAN. *H. A. Robinson.* 1956.

6 pages—50¢; special to students, 25¢.
Personnel Services, Inc.
Main St., Peapack, N. J.

This "occupational abstract" summarizes the development of the occupation, nature of the work, future prospects, opportunities for servicemen, qualifications, preparation, entrance and advancement, earnings, number and distribution, advantages and disadvantages, and related occupations.

EMPLOYMENT OUTLOOK FOR
TECHNICIANS. BULLETIN NO. 1131.
Bureau of Labor Statistics, U. S. Dept. of Labor. 1953.

29 pages—25¢.
Supt. of Documents, Govt. Printing Office
Washington 25, D. C.

Miscellaneous positions for technicians are presented here, including opportunities and future prospects, nature of the work, places of employment, preparation, and salaries.

RADIO AND TELEVISION
TECHNICIAN. Revised 1955.

4 pages—15¢ in Canada, 20¢ elsewhere.
Guidance Centre, Univ. of Toronto
371 Bloor St. W., Toronto 5, Ontario

This "monograph" shows the importance of the occupation, describes the work performed, qualifications and training requirements, entrance into this field, advancement opportunities, working conditions, and advantages and disadvantages.

TELEPHONE TECHNICIAN. Revised 1954.

4 pages—15¢ in Canada, 20¢ elsewhere.
Guidance Centre, Univ. of Toronto
371 Bloor St. W., Toronto 5, Ontario

This "monograph" contains the history and importance of the occupation, duties, working conditions, advancement opportunities, qualifications and preparation, earnings, and how to get the job.

TELEPHONE OPERATORS:

(D.O.T. Nos.: 1-42.)

TELEPHONE OPERATOR. Revised
1956.

4 pages—35¢; special to students, 25¢.
Chronicle Guidance Publications
Moravia, N. Y.

This "occupational brief" reviews the duties, working conditions, wages, qualifications and training, employment prospects, getting the job, and related jobs.

TELEPHONE OPERATOR. Revised 1954.

    4 pages—15¢ in Canada, 20¢ elsewhere.
    Guidance Centre, Univ. of Toronto
    371 Bloor St. W., Toronto 5, Ontario

Included in this "monograph" are job definition, importance of the work to society, duties, working conditions, qualifications and preparation, earnings, how to get started, and advantages and disadvantages.

TELEPHONE OPERATOR. *H. A. Robinson.* 1954.

    6 pages—50¢; special to students, 25¢.
    Personnel Services, Inc.
    Main St., Peapack, N. J.

Summarized in this "occupational abstract" are the nature of the work, future prospects, qualifications, preparation, entrance and advancement, earnings, and advantages and disadvantages.

TELEPHONE OPPORTUNITIES FOR WOMEN. 1955.

    24 pages—free to school counselors.
    New York Telephone Co.
    101 Willoughby St., Brooklyn 1, N. Y. C.

Included here are the nature of the opportunities, duties, working conditions, advancement, qualifications, preparation, and salaries. *(For counselors)*

TELEVISION PERSONNEL:
(D.O.T. Nos.: 0-02.; 0-17.; 0-66.; 0-69.)

LYNN DECKER, TV APPRENTICE. *D. L. McFadden.* 1953.

    256 pages—$2.50.
    Dodd, Mead and Co., Inc.
    432 Fourth Ave., New York 16, N. Y.

This career novel traces the vocational growth of the heroine from television apprentice to the production of her own show. Worthwhile information is contained on the opportunities in this field, how to get started, and nature of the work. *(For teen-age girls)*

OPPORTUNITIES IN TELEVISION. *J. Ranson and R. Pack.* 1951.

    128 pages—$1.00.
    Vocational Guidance Manuals, Inc.
    1011 East Tremont Ave., New York 60, N. Y.

This manual presents the outlook in the field, the nature of the job opportunities in television acting, writing, directing, engineering, production, sales and promotion, research, programming, special events, news announcing, and installation and repair.

TELEVISION, NEW JOB HORIZON. 1952.

    6 pages—10¢.
    Glamour Magazine
    420 Lexington Ave., New York 17, N. Y.

This reprint highlights a wide variety of job opportunities in the field, and presents a "career dictionary" defining numerous television jobs. *(For female readers)*

TELEVISION STORY. *J. J. Floherty.* Revised 1956.

    160 pages—$3.00.
    J. B. Lippincott Co.
    227 So. 6th St., Philadelphia 5, Pa.

This book narrates the growth and development of the television industry. It contains valuable information on the nature of the work of those who are behind and in front of the camera. *(For teen-agers)*

YOUR PLACE IN TV. *E. B. Broderick.* 1954.

　142 pages—$2.75.

D. McKay Co., Inc.
116 So. 7th St., Philadelphia 6, Pa.
The nature of the job opportunities in this field and the qualifications required for these jobs are presented here. *(For teen-agers)*

MISCELLANEOUS:

CAREERS FOR RADIO ARTISTS. 1952.

　8 pages—25¢.
　B'nai B'rith Vocational Service Bureau
　1129 Vermont Ave., N. W., Washington 5, D. C.

Among the "artists" discussed in this booklet are the actor, announcer, singer, and sound-effects man. Nature of the work, job opportunities, and future prospects are included.

EMPLOYMENT OUTLOOK IN ELECTRONICS MANUFACTURING. BULLETIN NO. 1072. *Bureau of Labor Statistics, U. S. Dept of Labor.* 1952.

　30 pages—25¢.
　Supt. of Documents, Govt. Printing Office
　Washington 25, D. C.

This pamphlet describes the nature of the work and outlook in the industry, working conditions, wages, obtaining employment, promotional opportunities, and training requirements.

EMPLOYMENT OUTLOOK IN SKILLED ELECTRICAL AND ELECTRONIC OCCUPATIONS. V. A. PAMPHLET 7-9. *Veterans Administration in cooperation with U. S. Dept of Labor.* 1955.

　49 pages—40¢.
　Supt. of Documents, Govt. Printing Office
　Washington 25, D. C.

Prepared for use in the Veterans Administration vocational rehabilitation and education program, this pamphlet discusses the nature of the work, qualifications and training, working conditions, earnings, and outlook in varied electrical and electronic occupations. *(For counselors)*

MEN AGAINST DISTANCE. *J. J. Floherty.* 1954.

　160 pages—$2.85.
　J. B. Lippincott Co.
　227 So. 6th St., Philadelphia 5, Pa.

This book tells of the wonders of the world of communications and traces its progress from tom-toms to television. The nature of the work of the people who helped toward this progress is detailed. *(For teen-agers)*

RADIO-TV, NOT NEW YORK.
Mademoiselle's Jobs and Futures Dept. 1953.

　5 pages—25¢.
　Alumnae Advisory Center, Inc.
　541 Madison Ave., New York 22, N. Y.

Here is a discussion of the various job opportunities in the radio-tv field outside of New York; case histories of girls who have succeeded are included. *(For female readers)*

(also see fields of ENGINEERING, and PERFORMANCE)

For additional information, write to:

AMERICAN FEDERATION OF TELEVISION AND RADIO ARTISTS
15 West 44th St., New York 18, N. Y.

AMERICAN TELEPHONE AND TELEGRAPH CO.
195 Broadway, New York 7, N. Y.

45

CONSERVATION

DEEP SEA DIVERS:
(D.O.T. No.: 5-89.011)

DEEP DOWN UNDER. *J. J. Floherty.* 1953.

146 pages—$2.85.

J. B. Lippincott Co.

227 So. 6th St., Philadelphia 5, Pa.

Nature of the work and conditions under which the work is performed are highlighted in the diving experiences described in this engrossing book. *(For teen-age boys)*

DIVER. 1955.

4 pages—15¢ in Canada, 20¢ elsewhere.

Guidance Centre, Univ. of Toronto

371 Bloor St. W., Toronto 5, Ontario

This "monograph" includes a job definition, describes importance of work to society, functions, physical and personal requirements, training, getting started in this field, earnings, and advantages and disadvantages.

DOWN TO THE SHIPS IN THE SEA. *H. Grossett.* 1954.

256 pages—$3.75.

J. B. Lippincott Co.

227 So. 6th St., Philadelphia 5, Pa.

The author's experiences as a deep sea diver provide delightful reading. Included here is occupational information on the nature of the diver's work, hazards, working conditions, and gratifications. *(For teen-age boys)*

TO HIDDEN DEPTHS. *P. Tailliez.* 1954.

188 pages—$5.00.

E. P. Dutton and Co., Inc.

300 Fourth Ave., New York 10, N. Y.

This illustrated book consists of the diving experiences of a French naval captain, the nature of the work, the hazards involved, the equipment needed for diving, and a history of deep sea diving.

FISHERMEN:
(D.O.T. Nos.: 3-87.)

FISHERMAN. 1954.

4 pages—15¢ in Canada, 20¢ elsewhere.

Guidance Centre, Univ. of Toronto

371 Bloor St. W., Toronto 5, Ontario

This "monograph" defines the job, discusses working conditions, qualifications and preparation necessary to enter this occupation, advancement opportunities, earnings, getting started, advantages and disadvantages, and related jobs.

FORESTERS AND RANGERS:

(D.O.T. Nos.: 0-35.)

AVALANCHE PATOL. *M. M. Atwater.*
1951.
    247 pages—$2.50.
    Random House
    457 Madison Ave., New York 22,
        N. Y.
This adventure of a U.S. Forest Service
snow ranger gives information on the nature of the work, its hazards, and gratifications. *(For teen-age boys)*

CAREERS IN FORESTRY. *U. S. Dept.
of Agriculture.* Revised 1955.
    22 pages—15¢.
    *Supt. of Documents, Govt. Printing
        Office*
    Washington 25, D. C.
The many opportunities in the field, nature of the work performed, professional
training, requisites for success, jobs for
women, and the future of forestry are
detailed in this pamphlet.

FOREST RANGER. *J. J. Floherty.*
1956.
    143 pages—$2.75.
    J. B. Lippincott Co.
    227 So. 6th St., Philadelphia 5, Pa.
This entertaining and informative career
book, employs a readable anecdotal technique to tell of the work of the men in the
United States Forest Service and of the
opportunities in the field of forestry. *(For
teen-agers)*

FOREST RANGER (ONTARIO).
1956.
    4 pages—15¢ in Canada, 20¢ else-
        where.
    Guidance Centre, Univ. of Toronto
    371 Bloor St. W., Toronto 5, Ontario
This "monograph" presents the history
and importance of forestry work in On-

tario, Canada; it discusses working conditions, qualifications and preparation,
advancement, earnings, advantages and
disadvantages, and tells how to get started.

FORESTER. 1954.
    4 pages—35¢; special to students, 25¢.
    Chronicle Guidance Publications
    Moravia, N. Y.
This "occupational brief" shows the importance of the forester's work, his duties,
working conditions, earnings, requirements for getting started in this field,
places of employment, and related jobs.

FORESTER. Revised 1956.
    4 pages—15¢ in Canada, 20¢ else-
        where.
    Guidance Centre, Univ. of Toronto
    371 Bloor St. W., Toronto 5, Ontario
This "monograph" discusses the history of
forestry, nature of the work, qualifications
and training necessary for entrance into
this field, advancement, earnings, working conditions, and advantages and disadvantages.

FORESTER. *S. Splaver.* 1953.
    6 pages—50¢; special to students, 25¢.
    Personnel Services, Inc.
    Main St., Peapack, N. J.
Summarized in this "occupational abstract" are the nature of the work, qualifications, preparation, entrance and advancement, earnings, opportunities for
servicemen, and advantages and disadvantages.

FORESTRY AND ITS CAREER
OPPORTUNITIES. *H. L. Shirley.* 1952.
    492 pages—$6.50.
    McGraw-Hill Book Co., Inc.
    330 West 42nd St., New York 36,
        N. Y.

A comprehensive presentation of the development and importance of this field is contained in this book, including the job opportunities, qualifications, and preparation for the work.

FORESTS AND MEN. *W. B. Greeley.* 1951.

> 255 pages—$3.00.
> *Doubleday and Co., Inc.*
> Garden City, N. Y.

Fifty years of progress in American forestry and the nature of the work of forestry personnel are presented here.

JEFF WHITE, YOUNG TRAPPER. *L. Dietz.* 1951.

> 191 pages—$2.50.

Little, Brown and Co., Inc.
34 Beacon St., Boston 6, Mass.

An engrossing career novel, it incorporates occupational information about the jobs of the trapper and game warden into an adventure tale. *(For teen-age boys)*

PARK RANGER. 1955.

> 4 pages—35¢; special to students, 25¢.
> *Chronicle Guidance Publications*
> Moravia, N. Y.

This "occupational brief" reviews the history of the occupation, nature of the work, qualifications, educational requirements, methods of entering this occupation, advancement, outlook, earnings, and typical places of employment.

SOIL CONSERVATIONISTS:

(D.O.T. Nos.: 0-35.)

A SOIL SCIENCE CAREER FOR YOU IN SOIL CONSERVATION SERVICE. *U. S. Dept. of Agriculture.* 1956.

> 8 pages—5¢.
> *Supt. of Documents, Govt. Printing Office*
> Washington 25, D. C.

This pamphlet discusses the duties of the soil conservationists, the need for soil scientists, and how to obtain employment.

AN ENGINEERING CAREER FOR YOU IN SOIL CONSERVATION SERVICE. *U. S. Dept. of Agriculture.* 1956.

> 12 pages—10¢.
> *Supt. of Documents, Govt. Printing Office*
> Washington 25, D. C.

The opportunities available in the Soil Conservation Service, nature of the work performed, and the varied conservationist positions are discussed here.

CAREERS IN SOIL CONSERVATION SERVICE. *U. S. Dept. of Agriculture.* 1956.

> 12 pages—5¢.
> *Supt. of Documents, Govt. Printing Office*
> Washington 25, D. C.

Presented in this pamphlet are the duties and qualifications needed for employment in the Soil Conservation Service of the Department of Agriculture.

MISCELLANEOUS:

FROM TREES TO PAPER. *H. B. Lent.* 1952.

149 pages—$2.75.
Macmillan Co., Inc.
60 Fifth Ave., New York 11, N. Y.

Written for youngsters, this book tells of the men and the work processes which go into the manufacture of paper, starting with trees from the Canadian woods and ending with newsprint. *(For ten- to thirteen-year-olds)*

NATURE'S GUARDIANS: YOUR CAREER IN CONSERVATION. *H. E. Neal.* 1956.

192 pages—$3.50.
Julian Messner, Inc.
8 West 40th St., New York 18, N. Y.

A most thorough presentation of the job opportunities available to young people with the interests and talents for careers in the field of conservation. Qualifications, educational requirements, working conditions, places of employment, and salaries are among the topics discussed. There are lists of schools and colleges offering training in this field. *(For teen-agers)*

SKILLED OCCUPATIONS IN THE PRODUCTION OF LUMBER PRODUCTS. 1953.

4 pages—35¢; special to students, 25¢.
Chronicle Guidance Publications
Moravia, N. Y.

This "occupational brief" describes the nature of the work performed in these occupations, working conditions, wages, personal and training requirements, places of employment, getting started on the jobs, and related jobs.

THE TREE EXPERT. *F. A. Bartlett.* 1956.

32 pages—$1.00.
Research Publishing Co., Inc.
P. O. Box 245, Boston 1, Mass.

A brief history of the tree expert profession, contribution to society, supply and demand, trends, what it takes to be a tree expert, educational requirements, salaries, working conditions, advantages and disadvantages, and related occupations are contained in this little pamphlet.

(also see field of AGRICULTURE)

For additional information, write to:

AMERICAN FOREST PRODUCTS INDUSTRIES, INC.
1319—18th St., N. W., Washington 6, D. C.

SOCIETY OF AMERICAN FORESTERS
825 Mills Bldg., Washington 6, D. C.

U. S. DEPT. OF INTERIOR
Washington 25, D. C.

CONSTRUCTION AND REAL ESTATE

BRICKLAYERS AND MASONS:
(D.O.T. Nos.: 5-24.010; 5-24.210)

BRICKLAYER. Revised 1956.

4 pages—35¢; special to students, 25¢.
Chronicle Guidance Publications
Moravia, N. Y.

This "occupational brief" contains the history of bricklaying, nature of work performed, working conditions, personal qualifications and training for success, earnings, advantages and disadvantages, opportunities for promotion, outlook, where employed, and related jobs.

BRICKLAYER. Revised 1955.

4 pages—15¢ in Canada, 20¢ elsewhere.
Guidance Centre, Univ. of Toronto
371 Bloor St. W., Toronto 5, Ontario

Included in this "monograph" are nature of the work performed, working conditions, qualifications and preparation for the work, advancement, how to get started, and related jobs.

BRICKLAYERS. *H. L. McCandless.*
1953.

16 pages—25¢.
Michigan Employment Security Comm.
7310 Woodward Ave., Detroit 2, Mich.

This "occupational guide" presents the outlook for bricklayers, nature of the work, physical and personal qualifications, training for this work, methods of obtaining employment, earnings, job hazards, and typical places of employment.

STONEMASON. *V. F. Group.* 1956.

6 pages—50¢; special to students, 25¢.
Personnel Services, Inc.
Main St., Peapack, N. J.

This "occupational abstract" presents the history of the occupation, nature of the work, future prospects, qualifications, preparation, entrance and advancement, earnings, and advantages and disadvantages.

CARPENTERS:
(D.O.T. Nos.: 5-25.)

CARPENTER. 1954.

4 pages—35¢; special to students, 25¢.
Chronicle Guidance Publications
Moravia, N. Y.

This "occupational brief" discusses the work performed by carpenters, working conditions, wages, requirements and preparation, places of employment, outlook, and related jobs.

CARPENTER. 1955.

4 pages—15¢ in Canada, 20¢ elsewhere.
Guidance Centre, Univ. of Toronto
371 Bloor St. W., Toronto 5, Ontario

This "monograph" discusses the importance of the occupation, nature of the work, working conditions, qualifications and preparation, how to get started, and advancement opportunities.

CONTRACTORS:

(D.O.T. No.: 0-99.21)

CAREER AS ELECTRICAL CON-
TRACTOR. *M. A. Rutzick*. 1954.

> 8 pages—25¢.
> *B'nai B'rith Vocational Service Bureau*
> 1129 Vermont Ave., N.W., Washing-
> ton 5, D. C.

Here information is found on the nature
of the work, preparation and qualifications for success, earnings, capital needed
for getting started, unions, and advantages and disadvantages.

CAREER AS PAINTING CONTRAC-
TOR. *M. A. Rutzick*. 1954.

> 8 pages—25¢.
> *B'nai B'rith Vocational Service Bureau*
> 1129 Vermont Ave., N.W., Washing-
> ton 5, D. C.

This booklet contains information on how
to get started in the business, qualifications for success, number of persons in
this field, earnings, outlook, and advantages and disadvantages.

CAREER AS PLASTERING CON-
TRACTOR. 1955.

> 8 pages—25¢.
> *B'nai B'rith Vocational Service Bureau*
> 1129 Vermont Ave., N.W., Washing-
> ton 5, D. C.

This pamphlet presents the future outlook
in the field, nature of the work, qualifications, apprenticeship, entering into and
building this business, and earnings.

CAREER AS REFRIGERATION AND
AIR CONDITIONING CONTRACTOR.
M. A. Rutzick. 1954.

> 8 pages—25¢.
> *B'nai B'rith Vocational Service Bureau*
> 1129 Vermont Ave., N.W., Washing-
> ton 5, D. C.

In this booklet information is included on
the nature of the work, future prospects,
qualifications and training, getting this
business started, earnings, and advantages
and disadvantages.

CAREERS IN HOME IMPROVEMENT
CONTRACTING. *M. A. Rutzick*. 1955.

> 8 pages—25¢.
> *B'nai B'rith Vocational Service Bureau*
> 1129 Vermont Ave., N.W., Washing-
> ton 5, D. C.

This booklet presents future prospects in
the field, nature of services performed,
qualifications and training, how to get
started in this business, earnings, and advantages and disadvantages.

CAREERS IN PLUMBING AND
HEATING CONTRACTING. *M. A.
Rutzick*. 1954.

> 8 pages—25¢.
> *B'nai B'rith Vocational Service Bureau*
> 1129 Vermont Ave., N.W., Washing-
> ton 5, D. C.

This booklet contains apprenticeship information and training requirements for
conducting this type of business, qualifications, earnings, and opportunities available.

ELEVATOR OPERATORS:
(D.O.T. Nos.: 2-95.20; 2-95.30)

ELEVATOR OPERATOR. 1954.

    4 pages—35¢; special to students, 25¢.
Chronicle Guidance Publications
Moravia, N. Y.

This "occupational brief" describes the nature of the work, working conditions, earnings, personal requirements, opportunities for promotion, places of employment, and future prospects.

ELECTRICIANS:
(D.O.T. Nos.: 4-97.)

CONSTRUCTION ELECTRICIAN. 1952.

    4 pages—35¢; special to students, 25¢.
Chronicle Guidance Publications
Moravia, N. Y.

This "occupational brief" includes a job definition, discusses working conditions, wages, personal and training requirements, how to enter the field, advantages and disadvantages, and future prospects.

ELECTRICIAN. Revised 1954.

    4 pages—15¢ in Canada, 20¢ elsewhere.
Guidance Centre, Univ. of Toronto
371 Bloor St. W., Toronto 5, Ontario

This "monograph" discusses the history of this occupation, nature of the work performed, working conditions, qualifications and preparation, getting started in this field, earnings, and related jobs.

OPPORTUNITIES IN ELECTRICAL TRADES. *J. S. Hyman.* 1953.

    96 pages—$1.00.
Vocational Guidance Manuals, Inc.
1011 East Tremont Ave., New York 60, N. Y.

This comprehensive "manual" describes the scope of the field, the opportunities in civilian employment and in the U. S. Armed Forces. Nature of the work in varied jobs in this field, preparation necessary, getting started, working conditions, and earnings are included.

PAINTERS AND PAPERHANGERS:
(D.O.T. Nos.: 5-27.010; 5-28.100)

PAINTER. Revised 1955.

    4 pages—15¢ in Canada, 20¢ elsewhere.
Guidance Centre, Univ. of Toronto
371 Bloor St. W., Toronto 5, Ontario

Included in this "monograph" are the history of this occupation, nature of the work, working conditions, qualifications, preparation, how to enter the field, earnings, advancement opportunities, advantages and disadvantages, and related occupations.

PAINTER. *V. F. Group.* 1953.

    6 pages—50¢; special to students, 25¢.
Personnel Services, Inc.
Main St., Peapack, N. J.

This "occupational abstract" summarizes the nature of the work performed, qualifications, preparation, entrance and advancement, earnings, and advantages and disadvantages.

PAINTER, CONSTRUCTION. 1952.

4 pages—35¢; special to students, 25¢.
Chronicle Guidance Publications
Moravia, N. Y.

This "occupational brief" reviews the history of painting, work performed, working conditions, wages, personal and training requirements, opportunities for promotion, outlook, advantages and disadvantages, and related jobs.

PAINTERS. 1955.

16 pages—25¢.

Michigan Employment Security Comm.
7310 Woodward Ave., Detroit 2, Mich.

History and nature of the work, future prospects, personal qualifications, educational requirements, methods of entry, advancement, working conditions, and advantages and disadvantages are presented herein.

PAPERHANGER. 1954.

4 pages—35¢; special to students, 25¢.
Chronicle Guidance Publications
Moravia, N. Y.

Included in this "occupational brief" is information about the nature of the work, working conditions, earnings, personal qualifications, preparation, places of employment, future prospects, unions, and related jobs.

PLASTERERS:
(D.O.T. No.: 5-29.100)

PLASTERER. 1953.

4 pages—35¢; special to students, 25¢.
Chronicle Guidance Publications
Moravia, N. Y.

This "occupational brief" discusses the importance of the occupation, nature of the work performed, working conditions, earnings, personal requirements, preparation, advancement opportunities, typical places of employment, prospects, and related jobs.

PLASTERER. 1956.

4 pages—15¢ in Canada, 20¢ elsewhere.
Guidance Centre, Univ. of Toronto
371 Bloor St. W., Toronto 5, Ontario

This "monograph" discusses the history and nature of the work, working conditions, qualifications, preparation, advancement, advantages and disadvantages, how to get started, and related occupations.

PLASTERERS. 1954.

20 pages—25¢.
Michigan Employment Security Comm.
7310 Woodward Ave., Detroit 2, Mich.

This pamphlet reviews the history of the occupation, nature of the work, future prospects, qualifications and preparation necessary for obtaining employment, working conditions, earnings, and advantages and disadvantages.

PLUMBERS:
(D.O.T. No.: 5-30.210)

PLUMBER. 1953.

    4 pages—35¢; special to students, 25¢.
Chronicle Guidance Publications
Moravia, N. Y.

This "occupational brief" summarizes the functions of the plumber, working conditions, wages, personal and training requirements, typical places of employment, obtaining employment, future prospects, and related jobs.

PLUMBER. Revised 1953.

    4 pages—15¢ in Canada, 20¢ elsewhere.
Guidance Centre, Univ. of Toronto
371 Bloor St. W., Toronto 5, Ontario
Presented in this "monograph" is information on the nature of the work, qualifi-

cations and preparation necessary for success, advancement opportunities, earnings, advantages and disadvantages, and how to enter this field.

PLUMBING OCCUPATIONS. Revised 1953.

    20 pages—25¢.
Michigan Employment Security Comm.
7310 Woodward Ave., Detroit 2, Mich.

This "occupational guide" discusses the importance of these occupations, nature of the work, opportunities available, working conditions, entering into these occupations, and advantages and disadvantages. Earnings are given for workers in Michigan, but most of the material is pertinent to all of the states.

REAL ESTATE SALESPEOPLE:
(D.O.T. No.: 1-63.10)

CAREERS IN REAL ESTATE. Revised 1956.

    8 pages—25¢.
B'nai B'rith Vocational Service Bureau
1129 Vermont Ave., N.W., Washington 5, D. C.

Included in this booklet is information on the outlook in this field, duties, preparation, qualifications for entry, getting started, advancement, earnings, and opportunities for women.

REAL ESTATE AGENT. 1953.

    4 pages—15¢ in Canada, 20¢ elsewhere.
Guidance Centre, Univ. of Toronto
371 Bloor St. W., Toronto 5, Ontario

This "monograph" describes the nature of the work of the agent, working conditions, qualifications for employment, preparation, advancement opportunities, earnings,

advantages and disadvantages, how to get started, and related occupations.

REAL ESTATE SALESMAN. 1953.

    4 pages—35¢; special to students, 25¢.
Chronicle Guidance Publications
Moravia, N. Y.

Reviewed in this "occupational brief" are such topics as history, duties, working conditions, earnings, personal requirements, preparation, opportunities for women, methods of entry, places of employment, prospects, and related jobs.

SALLY'S REAL ESTATE VENTURE.
E. and M. Johnson. 1954.

    190 pages—$2.95.
Julian Messner, Inc.
8 West 40th St., New York 18, N. Y.

This entertaining career novel includes information about the nature of the work, training, working conditions, and advantages and disadvantages of the real estate agent's job. *(For teen-age girls)*

TILE SETTERS:

(D.O.T. No.: 5-24.410)

TILE SETTER. *S. Splaver*. 1954.

6 pages—50¢; special to students, 25¢.
Personnel Services, Inc.
Main St., Peapack, N. J.

This "occupational abstract" reviews the history of tile setting, nature of the work, qualifications, preparation, entrance and advancement, supply and demand, and advantages and disadvantages.

MISCELLANEOUS:

CAREERS AS BRICKLAYER AND SHEET METAL WORKER. Revised 1954.

8 pages—25¢.
B'nai B'rith Vocational Service Bureau
1129 Vermont Ave., N.W., Washington 5, D. C.

Included in this booklet is information on the future prospects in these occupations, nature of the work performed, qualifications and preparation necessary for success, wages, and advantages and disadvantages.

CAREERS AS CARPENTER AND PAINTER. Revised 1954.

8 pages—25¢.
B'nai B'rith Vocational Service Bureau
1129 Vermont Ave., N.W., Washington 5, D. C.

This booklet presents the outlook in these occupations, nature of the work of the carpenter and painter, preparation for this work, qualifications, and earnings.

CAREERS AS ELECTRICIAN AND PLUMBER. Revised 1954.

8 pages—25¢.

B'nai B'rith Vocational Service Bureau
1129 Vermont Ave., N.W., Washington 5, D. C.

This occupational booklet discusses the job prospects for electricians and plumbers, nature of their work, preparation and qualifications, wages, and advantages and disadvantages.

CAREERS AS PLASTERER AND CEMENT FINISHER. Revised 1954.

8 pages—25¢.
B'nai B'rith Vocational Service Bureau
1129 Vermont Ave., N.W., Washington 5, D. C.

Here another Bureau booklet presents the employment outlook for plasterers and cement finishers, work performed by them, qualifications and preparation, advantages and disadvantages, and earnings.

CAREERS IN PROPERTY MANAGEMENT. *R. Shosteck*. 1954.

8 pages—25¢.
B'nai B'rith Vocational Service Bureau
1129 Vermont Ave., N.W., Washington 5, D. C.

The outlook in this field, nature of the work performed, personal qualifications, preparation for employment, how to get started, earnings, and advancement opportunities are presented here.

LINEMAN (LIGHT, HEAT, AND POWER). 1955.

4 pages—35¢; special to students, 25¢.
Chronicle Guidance Publications
Moravia, N. Y.

This "occupational brief" includes job definition, nature of the work, working conditions, wages, personal and training requirements, opportunities for promotion, outlook, methods of entry, and related jobs.

STEAM FITTERS AND PIPE FITTERS. Revised 1954.

16 pages—25¢.
Michigan Employment Security Comm.
7310 Woodward Ave., Detroit 2, Mich.

This "occupational guide" highlights the nature of the work of steam fitters and pipe fitters, outlook in these occupations, physical and personal requirements, preparation for this work, methods of gaining employment, earnings, and typical places of employment.

For additional information, write to:

APPRENTICESHIP COMMITTEE OF THE
ASSOCIATED GENERAL CONTRACTORS
1227 Munsey Bldg.,
Washington 4, D. C.

BRICKLAYERS, MASONS AND PLASTERERS
INTERNATIONAL UNION OF AMERICA
815 Fifteenth St., N. W.,
Washington 5, D. C.

UNITED BROTHERHOOD OF CARPENTERS AND
JOINERS OF AMERICA
Carpenters Building,
Indianapolis 4, Ind.

DENTISTRY

DENTAL ASSISTANTS:
(D.O.T. No.: 1-32.10)

CAREER AS DENTAL ASSISTANT.
Revised 1956.

8 pages—25¢.
B'nai B'rith Vocational Service Bureau
1129 Vermont Ave., N.W., Washington 5, D. C.

Presented in this booklet is information on the nature of the work, prospects, qualifications, training, entering the field, advancement, earnings, working conditions, and advantages and disadvantages.

DENTAL ASSISTANT—DENTAL
HYGIENIST. 1955.

4 pages—10¢.
Glamour Magazine
420 Lexington Ave., New York 17, N. Y.

This "fact sheet" discusses the opportunities in these occupations, nature of the work, earnings, training and qualifications required, sources of employment, and professional associations. *(For female readers)*

DENTIST'S ASSISTANT. Revised 1954.

4 pages—15¢ in Canada, 20¢ elsewhere.
Guidance Centre, Univ. of Toronto
371 Bloor St. W., Toronto 5, Ontario

This "monograph" contains the history of the occupation, work performed, working conditions, qualifications and preparation, earnings, how to get started, and related occupations.

DENTAL HYGIENISTS:
(D.O.T. No.: 0-50.07)

CAREER AS A DENTAL HYGIENIST.
1956.

8 pages—25¢.
B'nai B'rith Vocational Service Bureau
1129 Vermont Ave., N.W., Washington 5, D. C.

The nature of the work of the dental hygienist, training, state licensing, personal qualifications, entry and advancement, salaries, working conditions, and advantages and disadvantages are presented here.

DENTAL HYGIENIST. 1952.

4 pages—35¢; special to students, 25¢.

Chronicle Guidance Publications
Moravia, N. Y.

This "occupational brief" reviews the history and nature of the work of the hygienist, income, working conditions, qualifications, training requirements, future prospects, where employed, methods of entry, and licensing.

SMART YOUNG WOMEN ARE
CHOOSING DENTAL HYGIENE AS
A CAREER. *R. A. Miller*. 1953.

66 pages—$1.50.
Fairleigh Dickinson College Press
Rutherford, N. J.

In this comprehensive presentation, duties of the dental hygienist, getting started in the field, advancement opportunities, qualifications, training, licensing, salaries, and future prospects are discussed.

DENTAL TECHNICIANS:

(D.O.T. No.: 0-50.06)

DENTAL TECHNICIAN. 1953.

4 pages—35¢; special to students, 25¢. *Chronicle Guidance Publications* Moravia, N. Y.

This "occupational brief" discusses the nature of the work performed, working conditions, personal and training requirements, where employed, methods of entering field, related jobs, job prospects, and advantages and disadvantages.

DENTAL TECHNICIANS. Reprinted 1954.

16 pages—25¢. *Michigan Employment Security Comm.* 7310 Woodward Ave., Detroit 2, Mich.

This "occupational guide" analyzes the history of the occupation, job definition, nature of the work, personal qualifications, working conditions, apprenticeships, and earnings.

DENTISTS:

(D.O.T. No.: 0-13.10)

DENTIST. 1953.

4 pages—35¢; special to students, 25¢. *Chronicle Guidance Publications* Moravia, N. Y.

This "occupational brief" discusses the nature of the work, working conditions, earnings, personal and training requirements, advantages and disadvantages, places of employment, future prospects, licensing, and related jobs.

DENTIST. Revised 1954.

4 pages—15¢ in Canada, 20¢ elsewhere. *Guidance Centre, Univ. of Toronto* 371 Bloor St. W., Toronto 5, Ontario

This "monograph" contains the history and importance to society of this profession, work performed, working conditions, qualifications and training required for entering field, earnings, and advantages and disadvantages.

DENTIST. Reprinted 1955.

23 pages—25¢. *Michigan Employment Security Comm.* 7310 Woodward Ave., Detroit 2, Mich.

Described in this "occupational guide" are the nature of the work, personal qualifications, educational requirements, methods of entering the field, advancement, earnings, typical places of employment, and related occupations.

DENTISTRY. *L. M. Miner.* 1955.

19 pages—$1.00. *Bellman Publishing Co.* P. O. Box 172, Cambridge 38, Mass.

This pamphlet includes history, nature of dentistry, demand and supply, distribution of dentists, licensure, list of dental schools, requirements for admission to dental schools, earnings, specialization, and qualifications for success. It also includes brief information on the dental hygienist.

SHOULD YOU BE A DENTIST?
P. E. Blackerby, Jr. 1955.
 8 pages—free.
 New York Life Insurance Co.
 51 Madison Ave., New York 10, N. Y.

This attractive public service booklet presents the rewards and growth of the dental field, nature of the work, earnings, supply and demand, qualifications, training costs, women as dentists, working conditions, and prospects.

(also see fields of MEDICAL AND HEALTH SERVICES)

For additional information, write to:

AMERICAN DENTAL ASSISTANTS ASSOCIATION
410 First National Bank Bldg., La Porte, Ind.

AMERICAN DENTAL ASSOCIATION
222 East Superior St., Chicago 11, Ill.

AMERICAN DENTAL HYGIENISTS ASSOCIATION
1735 Eye St., N. W., Washington 6, D. C.

EDUCATION

AUDIO-VISUAL AIDS PERSONNEL:
(D.O.T. Nos.: 0-30.; 0-31.; 0-32.; 0-36.)

AUDIO-VISUAL JOBS. *Mademoiselle's Jobs and Futures Dept.* 1952.
    5 pages—25¢.
    Alumnae Advisory Center, Inc.
    541 Madison Ave., New York 22, N. Y.

The opportunities in this new field and the future which lies ahead for specialists in audio-visual aids are presented in this magazine reprint. *(For female readers)*

STUDENT PERSONNEL WORKERS:
(D.O.T. Nos.: 0-11.; 0-32.; 0-36.; 0-39.)

JOB ANALYSIS OF EDUCATIONAL PERSONNEL WORKERS. 1951.
    22 pages—20¢.
    National Vocational Guidance Assoc.
    1534 "O" St., N. W., Washington 5, D. C.

This pamphlet describes the nature of the work, qualifications and preparation for varied student personnel jobs, such as that of the counselor, dean, director of guidance, director of placement, director of religious activities, director of student affairs, and personal counselor.

TEACHERS, ADULT EDUCATION:
(D.O.T. Nos.: 0-32.)

ADULT EDUCATION. *R. A. Luke.* 1955.
    19 pages—$1.00.
    Bellman Publishing Co.
    P. O. Box 172, Cambridge 38, Mass.
Contained in this pamphlet are the history

and description of the field, training and education required for professional careers in adult education, employment opportunities, remuneration, advancement, advantages and disadvantages, and outlook for the future.

TEACHERS, COLLEGE:
(D.O.T. No.: 0-11.50)

CAREERS IN COLLEGE TEACHING. D. Frifield. 1954.
    12 pages—25¢.

B'nai B'rith Vocational Service Bureau
1129 Vermont Ave., N.W., Washington 5, D. C.

Future prospects, personal qualifications, educational requirements, nature of the work, advancement, how to enter the field, salaries, and gratifications of the work are discussed here.

COLLEGE TEACHER. *V. F. Group.* 1956.

6 pages—50¢; special to students, 25¢.
Personnel Services, Inc.
Main St., Peapack, N. J.

This "occupational abstract" summarizes the history and nature of the work, future prospects, qualifications, preparation, en-trance and advancement, earnings, and advantages and disadvantages.

COLLEGE TEACHING. *Mademoiselle's Jobs and Futures Dept.* 1951.

6 pages—25¢.
Alumnae Advisory Center, Inc.
541 Madison Ave., New York 22, N. Y.

The opportunities in this field, advantages and disadvantages, educational prepara-tion, application for first job, advance-ment, earnings, and research grants are discussed in this magazine reprint. *(For female college students)*

TEACHERS, ELEMENTARY SCHOOL:
(D.O.T. No.: 0-30.11)

ELEMENTARY SCHOOL TEACHER. *S. Splaver.* 1953.

6 pages—50¢; special to students, 25¢.
Personnel Services, Inc.
Main St., Peapack, N. J.

This authoritative "occupational abstract" reviews the history and nature of the work, qualifications, preparation, entrance and advancement, earnings, and advan-tages and disadvantages.

TEACHERS, NURSERY SCHOOL:
(D.O.T. No.: 0-30.02)

KAREN'S NURSERY SCHOOL PROJECT. *B. K. Harris.* 1955.

189 pages—$2.95.
Julian Messner, Inc.
8 West 40th St., New York 18, N. Y.

The heroine of this career novel is an assistant in a nursery school. It is an enter-taining book which includes information on the nature of the work of the nursery school teacher, qualifications and prepara-tion for the position, and working condi-tions. *(For teen-age girls)*

NURSERY-SCHOOL TEACHER. 1954.

3 pages—15¢ in Canada, 20¢ elsewhere.
Guidance Centre, Univ. of Toronto
371 Bloor St. W., Toronto 5, Ontario

This "monograph" describes the history and nature of the work, working condi-tions, qualifications and preparation, ad-vancement opportunities, advantages and disadvantages, how to get started, and re-lated occupations.

TEACHERS, SECONDARY SCHOOL:
(D.O.T. No.: 0-31.01)

SECONDARY SCHOOL TEACHER.
S. Splaver. 1954.

> 6 pages—50¢; special to students, 25¢.
> *Personnel Services, Inc.*
> Main St., Peapack, N. J.

Summarized in this "occupational abstract" are the nature of the work, qualifications, preparation, certification, entrance and advancement, geographic distribution of high school teachers, opportunities for servicemen, supply and demand, earnings, and advantages and disadvantages.

THE YOUNG AMERICAN HIGH
SCHOOL TEACHER. *Mademoiselle's College and Careers Dept.* 1955.

> 6 pages—25¢.
> *Alumnae Advisory Center, Inc.*
> 541 Madison Ave., New York 22, N. Y.

Case histories of a big city public school teacher, a private school teacher and a small-town teacher are presented to illustrate the nature of their work and the different problems which they encounter as a result of their individual surroundings. *(For female college students)*

TEACHERS, SPECIALIZED:
(D.O.T. No.: 0-32.01)

TEACHERS OF CHILDREN WHO
ARE BLIND. BULLETIN NO. 10.
Office of Education, U. S. Dept. of Health, Education, and Welfare. 1956.

> 109 pages—40¢.
> *Supt. of Documents, Govt. Printing Office*
> Washington 25, D. C.

This is a report based on findings from a study on the qualifications and preparation of teachers of exceptional children and includes the special competencies needed by teachers of blind children, preparation for such teaching, and professional background for teacher candidates most likely to succeed.

TEACHERS OF CHILDREN WHO
ARE PARTIALLY SEEING. BULLETIN NO. 4. *Office of Education, U. S. Dept. of Health, Education, and Welfare.* 1955.

> 71 pages—30¢.
> *Supt. of Documents, Govt. Printing Office*
> Washington 25, D. C.

This report analyzes the training, personal qualities, and professional preparation needed by such specialized teachers. It is of value to teachers and administrators in this area and to schools and colleges offering training for these specialized teachers.

TEACHERS, VOCATIONAL:
(D.O.T. No.: 0-32.30)

THE HOME ECONOMICS TEACHER.
1956.

> 4 pages—free to high school principals
> and guidance officers.
> *Simmons College*
> 300 The Fenway, Boston 15, Mass.

This folder indicates what this teacher
does, the rewards of home economics
teaching, beginners' positions, personal
qualifications, and high school and college
preparation for this work.

VOCATIONAL TRAINING
TEACHER. *V. F. Group.* Revised 1956.

> 6 pages—50¢; special to students, 25¢.
> *Personnel Services, Inc.*
> Main St., Peapack, N. J.

This "occupational abstract" reviews the
nature of the work, future prospects, qualifications, preparation, entrance and advancement, earnings, and advantages and
disadvantages.

MISCELLANEOUS:

CAREERS IN TEACHING. *R. Wolozin.*
1955.

> 8 pages—25¢.
> *B'nai B'rith Vocational Service Bureau*
> 1129 Vermont Ave., N.W., Washing-
> ton 5, D. C.

This booklet discusses future prospects in
the field of teaching, its importance to society, places of employment, nature of the
work, qualifications and preparation, how
to enter the field, earnings, and advantages
and disadvantages.

CAREERS ON THE CAMPUS. 1955.

> 13 pages—10¢.
> *Glamour Magazine*
> 420 Lexington Ave., New York 17,
> N. Y.

This "fact sheet" describes the nature of
the opportunities available (business administrative jobs, student personnel jobs,
academic administrative jobs, classroom
and laboratory jobs, library and museum
jobs, public relations jobs, press jobs,
campus radio jobs), how to apply for a
college job, qualifications, and associations. *(For female readers)*

JOBS IN TEACHING. *Mademoiselle's
College and Careers Dept.* Revised 1955.

> 4 pages—25¢.
> *Alumnae Advisory Center, Inc.*
> 541 Madison Ave., New York 22, N. Y.

This magazine reprint stresses the advantages of a teaching career, opportunities,
nature of the work, and earnings. *(For
female college students)*

OPPORTUNITIES IN TEACHING.
B. Fine. 1952.

> 112 pages—$1.00.
> *Vocational Guidance Manuals, Inc.*
> 1011 East Tremont Ave., New York
> 60, N. Y.

Future prospects in this field, personal
qualifications for teaching, different levels
of teaching, methods of entry, earnings,
advancement, advantages and disadvantages, and related fields are presented in
this "manual."

SHOULD YOUR CHILD BE A
TEACHER? *Wm. F. Russell.* 1955.

> 8 pages—free.
> *New York Life Insurance Co.*
> 51 Madison Ave., New York 10, N. Y.

This public service career booklet presents the rewards of teaching, opportunities, training and fees, financial prospects, supply and demand, and qualifications for a teaching career.

TEACHER. 1954.

4 pages—35¢; special to students, 25¢.
Chronicle Guidance Publications
Moravia, N. Y.

Reviewed in this "occupational brief" are the history of education, work performed by the teacher (kindergarten, elementary, secondary school, and specialized), working conditions, earnings, personal and training requirements, advancement, outlook, where employed, and certification.

TEACHER. Revised 1956.

4 pages—15¢ in Canada, 20¢ elsewhere.
Guidance Centre, Univ. of Toronto
371 Bloor St. W., Toronto 5, Ontario

This "monograph" describes the history, importance, and nature of the work, working conditions, qualifications and preparation, advancement, advantages and disadvantages, how to get started, and related occupations.

THE TEACHER AND HIS WORK.
G. Gould and G. A. Yoakam. Reprinted 1954.

402 pages—$4.50.
Ronald Press Co.
15 East 26th St., New York 10, N. Y.

The nature of the teacher's job, qualifications necessary for the successful teacher, educational preparation for the work, and how to get started in the field are discussed.

TEACHERS. 1956.

24 pages—25¢.
Michigan Employment Security Comm.
7310 Woodward Ave., Detroit 2, Mich.

This "occupational guide" presents the history of teaching, nature of the work on different levels of teaching, working conditions, location of jobs, employment outlook, earnings, qualifications for entry, and advantages and disadvantages.

TEACHING AS A CAREER. *U. S. Dept. of Health, Education, and Welfare.* 1955.

20 pages—15¢.
Supt. of Documents, Govt. Printing Office
Washington 25, D. C.

Discussed herein are the importance of teaching, what a teacher does, duties of various teachers and administrators, certification requirements, preparing for teaching, getting employment, advancement, salaries, and qualifications for entrance into the profession.

TEACHING IN EUROPE. *Mademoiselle's College and Careers Dept.* 1955.

5 pages—25¢.
Alumnae Advisory Center, Inc.
541 Madison Ave., New York 22, N. Y.

The opportunities offered by the Fulbright exchange program and the armed services for civilian teachers to teach overseas are detailed in this magazine reprint. Working and living conditions, qualifications, earnings, and where to make application for such positions are included. *(For female college students)*

TEACHING IS AN ATTRACTIVE CAREER. *U. S. Dept. of Health, Education, and Welfare.* 1955.

4 pages—5¢.
Supt. of Documents, Govt. Printing Office
Washington 25, D. C.

This leaflet tells of the opportunities available in the elementary and secondary schools, the duties of these teachers, and requirements for obtaining such positions.

YOUR CAREER IN TEACHING. Revised 1955.

29 pages—free.

National Assoc. of Manufacturers

2 East 48th St., New York 17, N. Y. This public service pamphlet describes the varied opportunities in the field of education, nature of the work in the different positions, supply and demand, opportunities available, personal qualifications needed for success, getting started, training, and outlook.

For additional information, write to:

NATIONAL EDUCATION ASSOCIATION
1201 Sixteenth St., N. W., Washington 6, D. C.

ENGINEERING

AERONAUTICAL ENGINEERS:
(D.O.T. No.: 0-19.03)

SHOULD YOU BE AN AERONAUTICAL ENGINEER? *I. Sikorsky*. 1955.
8 pages—free.
New York Life Insurance Co.
51 Madison Ave., New York 10, N. Y.

This booklet describes the qualifications for success, opportunities, development of this field, nature of the work, training requirements, salaries, and outlook.

CHEMICAL ENGINEERS:
(D.O.T. No.: 0-15.01)

CHEMICAL ENGINEER. 1955.
4 pages—15¢ in Canada, 20¢ elsewhere.
Guidance Centre, Univ. of Toronto
371 Bloor St. W., Toronto 5, Ontario

Described in this "monograph" are the history of chemical engineering and its importance to society, duties, qualifications, preparation, entrance and advancement in this field, earnings, related occupations, and advantages and disadvantages.

CHEMICAL ENGINEER. *H. A. Robinson*. 1951.
6 pages—50¢; special to students, 25¢.
Personnel Services, Inc.
Main St., Peapack, N. J.

This "occupational abstract" summarizes the nature of the work, opportunities, qualifications, preparation, entrance and advancement, earnings, related occupations, and outlook.

CIVIL ENGINEERS:
(D.O.T. No.: 0-16.01)

CIVIL ENGINEER. *H. A. Robinson*. Revised 1956.
6 pages—50¢; special to students, 25¢.
Personnel Services, Inc.
Main St., Peapack, N. J.

This "occupational abstract" reviews the nature of the work performed, qualifications and preparation, entrance and advancement in this field, earnings, outlook, and advantages and disadvantages.

DRAFTSMEN:

(D.O.T. Nos.: 0-48.)

CAREERS IN CARTOGRAPHY. 1952.
4 pages—25¢.
B'nai B'rith Vocational Service Bureau
1129 Vermont Ave., N. W., Washington 5, D. C.

Included here are the outlook for map makers, the nature of jobs in this field, places of employment, and examinations required for employment with government agencies.

DRAFTSMAN. 1952.
4 pages—35¢; special to students, 25¢.
Chronicle Guidance Publications
Moravia, N. Y.

This "occupational brief" presents the nature of the work, specialized areas of the field, working conditions, personal and training requirements, future prospects, where employed, and methods of entry.

DRAFTSMAN. *H. A. Robinson.* 1951.
6 pages—50¢; special to students, 25¢.
Personnel Services, Inc.
Main St., Peapack, N. J.

Summarized in this "occupational abstract" are the nature of the work, qualifications, preparation, entrance and advancement, distribution of draftsmen, earnings, prospects, and advantages and disadvantages.

MACHINE DAFTSMAN. Revised 1953.
4 pages—15¢ in Canada, 20¢ elsewhere.
Guidance Centre, Univ. of Toronto
371 Bloor St. W., Toronto 5, Ontario

This "monograph" contains information on the history of this occupation, duties, qualifications, preparation, remuneration, working conditions, advancement opportunities, getting started, and related occupations.

ELECTRICAL ENGINEERS:

(D.O.T. No.: 0-17.01)

ELECTRICAL ENGINEER. *H. A. Robinson.* 1954.
6 pages—50¢; special to students, 25¢.
Personnel Services, Inc.
Main St., Peapack, N. J.

This "occupational abstract" reviews the nature of the work of the electrical engineer, opportunities for servicemen, qualifications, preparation, methods of entry into this field, earnings, number and distribution of such engineers, advantages and disadvantages, and related occupations.

OPPORTUNITIES IN ELECTRICAL ENGINEERING. *S. P. Shackleton.* 1953.
128 pages—$1.00.
Vocational Guidance Manuals, Inc.
1011 East Tremont Ave., New York 60, N. Y.

This manual describes the several branches of this field, qualifications, training requirements, licensing, getting started, advancement, future prospects, related jobs, and a list of colleges offering undergraduate training.

INDUSTRIAL DESIGNERS:
(D.O.T. No.: 0-46.88)

CAREER AS INDUSTRIAL
DESIGNER. 1954.

8 pages—25¢.
B'nai B'rith Vocational Service Bureau
1129 Vermont Ave., N. W., Washington 5, D.C.

Described here are the nature of the work, future prospects, jobs for beginners, qualifications, training, earnings, and advantages and disadvantages.

INDUSTRIAL DESIGNER. 1956.

4 pages—35¢; special to students, 25¢.
Chronicle Guidance Publications
Moravia, N. Y.

This "occupational brief" discusses the work performed, working conditions, wages, personal and training requirements, opportunities for promotion, outlook, and opportunities for women.

INDUSTRIAL DESIGNER. 1956.

4 pages—15¢ in Canada, 20¢ elsewhere.
Guidance Centre, Univ. of Toronto
371 Bloor St. W., Toronto 5, Ontario

This "monograph" discusses the history and importance of the profession, nature of the work, working conditions, qualifications and preparation necessary for entry and success, employment and advancement, remuneration, advantages and disadvantages, how to get started, and related occupations.

MECHANICAL ENGINEERS:
(D.O.T. No.: 0-19.01)

MECHANICAL ENGINEER. *H. A. Robinson.* 1953.

6 pages—50¢; special to students, 25¢.
Personnel Services, Inc.
Main St., Peapack, N. J.

This "occupational abstract" reviews the nature of the work, qualifications, preparation, number and distribution of mechanical engineers, earnings, methods of entering the field, outlook, and advantages and disadvantages.

PACKAGING ENGINEERS:
(D.O.T. No.: 0-68.60)

PACKAGING ENGINEER. *V. F. Group.* 1954.

6 pages—50¢; special to students, 25¢.
Personnel Services, Inc.
Main St., Peapack, N. J.

Discussed in this "occupational abstract" are the history of this work, duties, future prospects, qualifications, preparation, entrance and advancement, earnings, and advantages and disadvantages.

SANITARY ENGINEERS:

(D.O.T. No.: 0-16.01)

CAREER AS SANITARIAN. 1953.

4 pages—25¢.
B'nai B'rith Vocational Service Bureau
1129 Vermont Ave., N. W., Washington 5, D. C.

Discussed herein is information on the nature of the work performed, training for entrance and success in this field, future prospects, and job opportunities.

HEALTH ABROAD—AN OPPORTUNITY FOR SANITARY ENGINEERS.

U. S. Dept. of Health, Education, and Welfare in cooperation with U. S. Foreign Operations Administration. 1954.

16 pages—20¢.
Supt. of Documents, Govt. Printing Office
Washington 25, D. C.

The major problems faced by American sanitary engineers overseas, the nature of their work, appointments and assignments in this program, salaries, and where to apply are presented in this pamphlet.

SURVEYORS:

(D.O.T. No.: 0-64.10)

SURVEYOR. Revised 1956.

4 pages—15¢ in Canada, 20¢ elsewhere.
Guidance Centre, Univ. of Toronto
371 Bloor St. W., Toronto 5, Ontario

This "monograph" contains a definition of the occupation, describes working conditions, qualifications and preparation needed, advancement opportunities, how to get started, earnings, and advantages and disadvantages.

TIME STUDY MEN:

(D.O.T. No.: 0-18.01)

TIME STUDY MAN. *V. F. Group.* 1953.

6 pages—50¢; special to students, 25¢.
Personnel Services, Inc.
Main St., Peapack, N. J.

This "occupational abstract" summarizes the nature of the work, opportunities for servicemen, qualifications and preparation, entrance and advancement, earnings, supply of workers, advantages and disadvantages, and opportunities for women.

MISCELLANEOUS:

AN ENGINEERING CAREER FOR YOUR SCHOOL-AGE CHILD. *J. S. Lampe.* 1956.

15 pages—free.
General Motors Corp.
Dept. of Public Relations, Detroit 2, Mich.

This public service pamphlet offers information about today's shortage of trained engineers and scientists, the advantages of an engineering career, the variety of opportunities available, the bright future ahead in this field, typical requirements for admission to engineering college, and financing the college education. *(For parents)*

CAN I BE AN ENGINEER? LET'S FIND OUT. 1952.

24 pages—free.
General Motors Corp.
Dept. of Public Relations, Detroit 2, Mich.

This attractive public service pamphlet analyzes the opportunities in the branches of engineering, the requirements for admission to engineering schools, and the typical freshman program. *(For young people)*

CAREER AS ENGINEER. 1952.

12 pages—25¢.
B'nai B'rith Vocational Service Bureau
1129 Vermont Ave., N. W., Washington 5, D.C.

The development of the field of engineering, nature of the work, specialized branches, qualifications, entrance and advancement, salaries, and future prospects are discussed in this booklet.

ENGINEER, PROFESSIONAL. Revised 1956.

4 pages—15¢ in Canada, 20¢ elsewhere.

Guidance Centre, Univ. of Toronto
371 Bloor St. W., Toronto 5, Ontario

This "monograph" presents a history and nature of the work, describes working conditions, qualifications and preparation needed, advancement, remuneration, advantages and disadvantages, how to get started, and related occupations.

ENGINEERING AS A CAREER. *R. J. Smith.* 1956.

365 pages—$4.75.
McGraw-Hill Book Co., Inc.
330 West 42nd St., New York 36, N. Y.

A textbook for the orientation of beginners in engineering curricula, this book presents the role of the engineer, nature of the engineering profession, training, and the courses of study which lie ahead for the prospective engineer. *(For engineering students)*

OCCUPATIONAL GOALS FOR COLLEGE STUDENTS. PART I: ARCHITECTURE, ENGINEERING, AND THE PHYSICAL SCIENCES. edited by *M. Hammond.* 1951.

96 pages—75¢.
Ohio State University Press
Columbus 10, Ohio

Included in this book are the opportunities in engineering, the nature of the different work assignments, preparation and qualifications for employment, and future prospects.

PROFESSIONAL ENGINEERING—EMPLOYMENT OPPORTUNITIES FOR WOMEN. BULLETIN NO. 254. *Women's Bureau, U. S. Dept. of Labor.* 1954.

38 pages—20¢.
Supt. of Documents, Govt. Printing Office
Washington 25, D. C.

This pamphlet discusses engineering manpower and prospects for women, traditional attitudes, women's mechanical aptitude, training opportunities, number of women professional engineers, and fields of specialization for women.

SHOULD YOU BE AN ENGINEER?
T. K. Glennan. 1957.
　8 pages—free.
New York Life Insurance Co.
51 Madison Ave., New York 10, N. Y.

"To be an engineer," this public service career pamphlet says, "means to practice any one of over 150 specialties in modern technology." The broadness of engineering training, and opportunities for well-paid creative activity and responsible leadership are stressed. The author also describes salaries, aptitudes, and demand for women engineers.

(also see fields of COMMUNICATIONS AND ELECTRONICS, CONSERVATION, MINING AND METALLURGY, and SCIENCE)

For additional information, write to:

ENGINEERING MANPOWER COMMISSION
OF THE ENGINEERS JOINT COUNCIL
29 West 39th St.
New York 18, N. Y.

FOOD AND HOME ECONOMICS

BAKERS:
(D.O.T. No.: 4-01.100)

BAKER. Revised 1956.

> 4 pages—35¢; special to students, 25¢.
> *Chronicle Guidance Publications*
> Moravia, N. Y.

This "occupational brief" discusses the duties of the baker, working conditions, wages, personal and training requirements, opportunities for advancement, future prospects, opportunities for women, and related jobs.

BAKER. Revised 1955.

> 4 pages—15¢ in Canada, 20¢ elsewhere.
> *Guidance Centre, Univ. of Toronto*
> 371 Bloor St. W., Toronto 5, Ontario

Included in this "monograph" are the history and importance of this work, duties, working conditions, qualifications and preparation, earnings, advancement opportunities, and material on how to get started, and related occupations.

BAKER. *H. A. Robinson.* 1953.

> 6 pages—50¢; special to students, 25¢.
> *Personnel Services, Inc.*
> Main St., Peapack, N. J.

This "occupational abstract" reviews the nature of the work, future prospects, opportunities for servicemen, opportunities for women, qualifications, preparation, entrance and advancement, earnings, and advantages and disadvantages.

BUTCHERS:
(D.O.T. No.: 5-58.100)

BUTCHER—MEAT CUTTER. 1954.

> 4 pages—35¢; special to students, 25¢.
> *Chronicle Guidance Publications*
> Moravia, N. Y.

Described in this "occupational brief" are the history and nature of the work, working conditions, earnings, qualifications and training requirements, advancement opportunities, places of employment, methods of entry, and future prospects.

CHEFS–COOKS:
(D.O.T. Nos.: 2-05.; 2-26.)

CHEF. *S. Splaver.* 1955.

> 6 pages—50¢; special to students, 25¢.
> *Personnel Services, Inc.*
> Main St., Peapack, N. J.

This "occupational abstract" summarizes the nature of the work, qualifications, preparation, entrance and advancement, supply and demand, opportunities for servicemen, earnings, and advantages and disadvantages.

CHEF—COOK. 1953.

4 pages—35¢; special to students, 25¢.
Chronicle Guidance Publications
Moravia, N. Y.

This "occupational brief" defines the job, describes work performed by the cook and the chef, working conditions, earnings, preparation, opportunities for promotion, advantages and disadvantages, opportunities for women, and methods of entering these occupations.

COOK OR CHEF. Revised 1955.

3 pages—15¢ in Canada, 20¢ elsewhere.
Guidance Centre, Univ. of Toronto
371 Bloor St. W., Toronto 5, Ontario

This "monograph" presents the history and importance of this work, nature of the work performed, working conditions, qualifications and preparation, earnings, advantages and disadvantages, getting started, and related occupations.

DIETICIANS:
(D.O.T. No.: 0-39.93)

DIETITIAN. 1954.

4 pages—35¢; special to students, 25¢.
Chronicle Guidance Publications
Moravia, N. Y.

This "occupational brief" describes the nature of the work, working conditions, earnings, qualifications, training opportunities, advancement, methods of entering this field, typical places of employment, and outlook.

DIETITIAN. Revised 1956.

4 pages—15¢ in Canada, 20¢ elsewhere.
Guidance Centre, Univ. of Toronto
371 Bloor St. W., Toronto 5, Ontario

Described in this "monograph" are the nature of the work, working conditions, qualifications and preparation, getting started, advancement opportunities, related occupations, and advantages and disadvantages.

THE DIETITIAN. 1953.

4 pages—free to high school principals and guidance officers.
Simmons College
300 The Fenway, Boston 15, Mass.

One of the folders in this college's vocational guidance series, it discusses the nature of the dietitian's work, typical places of employment, qualifications for the work, earnings, and preparation.

HOME ECONOMISTS:
(D.O.T. Nos.: 0-12.35; 0-12.36)

HOME ECONOMICS. 1955.

7 pages—10¢.
Glamour Magazine
420 Lexington Ave., New York 17, N. Y.

This "fact sheet" describes the opportunities available to college graduates who have majored in home economics, nature of the work, and places of employment.
(For female readers)

HOME ECONOMIST. 1955.

4 pages—35¢; special to students, 25¢.
Chronicle Guidance Publications
Moravia, N. Y.

This "occupational brief" discusses the nature of the work, working conditions, personal and training requirements, earnings, outlook, opportunities for men, typical places of employment, entrance into the field, and related jobs.

HOME ECONOMIST. Revised 1954.

4 pages—15¢ in Canada, 20¢ elsewhere.
Guidance Centre, Univ. of Toronto
371 Bloor St. W., Toronto 5, Ontario

This "monograph" contains a job definition, describes working conditions, qualifications, preparation, advancement opportunities, how to get started, earnings, and advantages and disadvantages.

SHOULD YOU BE A HOME ECONOMIST? *C. T. Dennis.* 1955.

12 pages—free.
New York Life Insurance Co.
51 Madison Ave., New York 10, N. Y.

This attractive career booklet describes the scope of home economics, typical places of employment, personal rewards, training, opportunities in this field, cost of training, financial rewards, qualifications for success, and future prospects.

WAITERS:

(D.O.T. Nos.: 2-27.)

WAITER—WAITRESS. Revised 1956.

4 pages—35¢; special to students, 25¢.
Chronicle Guidance Publications
Moravia, N. Y.

The nature of the work, wages, qualifications for success, training requirements, future prospects, where employed, and methods of entry are reviewed in this "occupational brief."

WAITER OR WAITRESS. 1956.

4 pages—15¢ in Canada, 20¢ elsewhere.
Guidance Centre, Univ. of Toronto
371 Bloor St. W., Toronto 5, Ontario

This "monograph" discusses the history and nature of the work, working conditions, qualifications and preparation needed, advancement, remuneration, advantages and disadvantages, how to get started, and related occupations.

MISCELLANEOUS:

CAREER AS FOOD TECHNOLOGIST.
L. Spritzer. 1954.

8 pages—25¢.
B'nai B'rith Vocational Service Bureau
1129 Vermont Ave., N. W., Washington 5, D. C.

This booklet contains information on the outlook in the field, nature of the work performed, qualifications, educational requirements, advancement opportunities, remuneration, and advantages and disadvantages.

CAREERS IN FOOD PREPARING. *R. Shosteck*. 1953.

8 pages—25¢.
B'nai B'rith Vocational Service Bureau
1129 Vermont Ave., N. W., Washington 5, D. C.

Described in this booklet are the opportunities for employment in this field, typical places of employment, preparation, nature of the work, qualifications, wages, entrance, advancement opportunities, and future prospects.

THE CHOCOLATE INDUSTRY. *D. C. Mitchell*. 1951.

47 pages—$1.00.
Bellman Publishing Co.
P. O. Box 172, Cambridge 38, Mass.

This pamphlet analyzes the history and growth of this industry, nature of the jobs and qualifications for them, opportunities for employment, training, earnings, advantages and disadvantages, and future prospects.

THE DAIRY INDUSTRY. *H. F. Judkins*. 1955.

17 pages—$1.00.
Bellman Publishing Co.
P. O. Box 172, Cambridge 38, Mass.

Another of the vocational pamphlets in this series, it discusses the development of this industry, varied job opportunities, qualifications for success, opportunities for advancement, earnings, advantages and disadvantages, and outlook.

GAY ENTERPRISES. *M. M. Freer*. 1952.

176 pages—$2.95.
Julian Messner, Inc.
8 West 40th St., New York 18, N. Y.

This career novel provides information on the starting of one's own business in the realm of cooking and baking and the nature of the activities involved in such a business. *(For teen-age girls)*

THE MEAT PACKING INDUSTRY. *E. L. Heckler*. 1954.

23 pages—$1.00.
Bellman Publishing Co.
P. O. Box 172, Cambridge 38, Mass.

Presented here are the history of this industry, job opportunities available, earnings, chances for advancement, preparation for this work, advantages and disadvantages, and opportunities for women.

THE OUTLOOK FOR WOMEN AS FOOD-SERVICE MANAGERS AND SUPERVISORS. *Women's Bureau, U. S. Dept. of Labor*. 1952.

54 pages—20¢.
Supt. of Documents, Govt. Printing Office
Washington 25, D. C.

The future prospects for food service personnel in commercial eating places, industrial cafeterias and college residence halls are detailed here. Also included are the demand and supply for such workers, earnings, training, working conditions, advancement opportunities, and some suggestions on entering the field.

For additional information, write to:

AMERICAN DIETETIC ASSOCIATION
620 No. Michigan Ave., Chicago 11, Ill.

AMERICAN HOME ECONOMICS ASSOCIATION
1600 Twentieth St., N. W., Washington 9, D. C.

NATIONAL DAIRY COUNCIL
111 No. Canal St., Chicago 6, Ill.

NATIONAL RESTAURANT ASSOCIATION
8 So. Michigan Ave., Chicago 3, Ill.

HOBBY, PART-TIME, AND SUMMER WORK

HOME WORKERS:

WAYS TO MAKE MONEY AT HOME. 1952.

> 2 pages—10¢.
> *Glamour Magazine*
> 420 Lexington Ave., New York 17, N. Y.

This "fact sheet" offers suggestions under the following headings: if you like to gift-wrap packages, if your hobby is handicrafts, if you like to cook, if you can type, and if you can draw.

PART-TIME WORKERS:

BABYSITTER'S HANDBOOK. LIFE ADJUSTMENT BOOKLET. *J. Flander.* 1952.

> 48 pages—40¢.
> *Science Research Associates*
> 57 West Grand Ave., Chicago 10, Ill.

This pamphlet, prepared for baby-sitters, presents the qualifications for this type of work, duties, care of infants and children, and wages. *(For teen-agers)*

CAMPUS JOBS. 1952.

> 13 pages—10¢.
> *Glamour Magazine*
> 420 Lexington Ave., New York 17, N. Y.

This "fact sheet" discusses numerous opportunities for part-time employment under the following categories: clerical jobs, sales and concessions jobs, service jobs, and creative jobs. It includes qualifications, nature of the work, and places of employment. *(For female readers)*

PART-TIME WORK: HOW TO PREPARE FOR IT. *Mademoiselle's Jobs and Futures Dept.* 1954.

> 4 pages—25¢.
> *Alumnae Advisory Center, Inc.*
> 541 Madison Ave., New York 22, N. Y.

Future mothers are offered tips on planning for eventual part-time employment which they may wish to combine with running a home. *(For female college students)*

WORKING FOR COLLEGE EXPENSES. *Mademoiselle's Jobs and Futures Dept.* 1952.

> 5 pages—25¢.
> *Alumnae Advisory Center, Inc.*
> 541 Madison Ave., New York 22, N. Y.

Varied part-time job opportunities which may defray college expenses are discussed here. *(For female college students)*

SUMMER WORKERS:

STERLING GUIDE TO SUMMER JOBS. Revised 1956.

128 pages—$2.50.
Sterling Publishing Co., Inc.
215 East 37th St., New York 16, N. Y.

This "guide" aims to inform young people of the numerous opportunities available to them for summer employment and includes many unusual occupations. *(For college students)*

SUMMER JOB NOTES. *Mademoiselle's College and Careers Dept.* 1955.

4 pages—25¢.
Alumnae Advisory Center, Inc.
541 Madison Ave., New York 22, N. Y.

This magazine reprint offers some advice on where to seek summer employment, the nature of the opportunities, and earnings. *(For female college students)*

SUMMER JOB PROSPECTUS. 1956.

9 pages—10¢.
Glamour Magazine
420 Lexington Ave., New York 17, N. Y.

This "fact sheet" highlights how, where, and when to get a summer job, the nature of such job opportunities, and addresses to contact for summer jobs. *(For female readers)*

SUMMER JOBS FOR TEEN-AGERS. 1956.

4 pages—35¢; special to students, 25¢.
Chronicle Guidance Publications
Moravia, N. Y.

Included in this "occupational brief" are reasons for working summers, choosing your summer job, when to look for a summer job, what summer jobs are available, earnings, laws governing employment of minors, and how to locate and enter summer jobs.

YOUR VACATION JOB AND YOUR CAREER. 1952.

8 pages—25¢.
B'nai B'rith Vocational Service Bureau
1129 Vermont Ave., N. W., Washington 5, D. C.

This booklet discusses the values of summer work experiences and the nature of the summer job opportunities for prospective entrants into the fields of physical sciences, engineering, health, dentistry, nursing, veterinary medicine, forestry, agriculture, teaching, accountancy, home economics, law, library service, social work, economics, psychology, personnel work, newspaper work, public relations, and landscape architecture. *(For counselors and students)*

MISCELLANEOUS:

NUMISMATICS. *L. M. Reagan.* 1955.
16 pages—$1.00.
Bellman Publishing Co.
P. O. Box 172, Cambridge 38, Mass.

This pamphlet deals with the professional aspects of coin collecting, the nature of the work of the curator and the coin dealer, the coin collectors as customers, part-time dealers, and coin speculators.

(also see fields of PHYSICAL EDUCATION AND RECREATION)

78

HOTEL ADMINISTRATION

HOTEL MANAGERS:
(D.O.T. Nos.: 0-71.)

HOTEL MANAGER. *S. Splaver*. Revised 1955.

6 pages—50¢; special to students, 25¢.
Personnel Services, Inc.
Main St. Peapack, N. J.

This "occupational abstract" summarizes the nature of the work, qualifications, preparation, entrance and advancement, number and varieties of hotels, supply and demand of managers, earnings, and advantages and disadvantages.

ROOM CLERKS:
(D.O.T. No.: 1-07.60)

ROOM CLERK. 1953.

4 pages—35¢; special to students, 25¢.
Chronicle Guidance Publications
Moravia, N. Y.

This "occupational brief" reviews the history and nature of the work performed, preparation, qualifications, working conditions, getting started, outlook, and related jobs.

ROOM CLERK. 1956.

4 pages—15¢ in Canada, 20¢ elsewhere.
Guidance Centre, Univ. of Toronto
371 Bloor St. W., Toronto 5, Ontario

This "monograph" describes the history and nature of the work, working conditions, qualifications and preparation needed, advancement, remuneration, advantages and disadvantages, how to get started, and related occupations.

MISCELLANEOUS:

HOTEL WORK. 1954.

7 pages—10¢.
Glamour Magazine
420 Lexington Ave., New York 17, N. Y.

This "fact sheet" discusses the nature of hotels and motels, general qualifications and training for work in this field, salaries, advantages and disadvantages, major departments in large hotels, locations of hotels, and trade associations.
(For female readers)

OPPORTUNITIES IN THE HOTEL INDUSTRY. *S. Henkin*. Revised 1953.

96 pages—$1.00.
Vocational Guidance Manuals, Inc.
1011 East Tremont Ave., New York 60, N. Y.

This comprehensive "manual" discusses the many job opportunities in varied hotel departments, the types of hotels, the future of the industry, remuneration, personal requirements, educational preparation, how to start out, future prospects, and a list of schools and colleges offering hotel training.

WELCOME TO DUNECREST. *F. L. Williams.* 1955.
    189 pages—$2.95.

Julian Messner, Inc.
8 West 40th St., New York 18, N. Y.
This entertaining career novel has included some information on the administration of hotels, nature of the work, job opportunities in hotels, and preparation for such work. (*For teen-age girls*)

For additional information, write to:

AMERICAN HOTEL ASSOCIATION
221 West 57th St., New York 19, N. Y.

AMERICAN MOTEL ASSOCIATION
75 No. Maple Ave., Ridgewood, N. J.

INSURANCE

ACTUARIES:
(D.O.T. No.: 0-36.55)

ACTUARIES—EDUCATIONAL RE-QUIREMENTS FOR EMPLOYMENT OF. V.A. PAMPHLET 7-8.1. *Veterans Administration in cooperation with Bureau of Labor Statistics, U. S. Dept. of Labor.* 1955.

> 14 pages—15¢.
> *Supt. of Documents, Govt. Printing Office*
> Washington 25, D. C.

This is one of a series of pamphlets prepared for use in the Veterans Administration rehabilitation program and includes the nature of the work, places of employment, qualifications, and educational requirements. *(For counselors)*

ACTUARY. Revised 1953.

> 4 pages—15¢ in Canada, 20¢ elsewhere.

Guidance Centre, Univ. of Toronto
371 Bloor St. W., Toronto 5, Ontario

Included in this "monograph" are the history of this profession, nature of the work, working conditions, qualifications and training needed, advancement opportunities, methods of entry, earnings, and related occupations.

ACTUARY. *C. W. Jordan.* 1954.

> 36 pages—$1.00.
> *Research Publishing Co., Inc.*
> P. O. Box 245, Boston 1, Mass.

This little pamphlet discusses the history of actuarial work, duties of actuaries, personal qualifications, preparation, opportunities for advancement, entering this profession, working conditions, earnings, supply and demand, and future prospects.

AGENTS:
(D.O.T. Nos.: 1-57.)

CAREERS IN INSURANCE SELLING. 1953.

> 8 pages—25¢.
> *B'nai B'rith Vocational Service Bureau*
> 1129 Vermont Ave., N. W., Washington 5, D. C.

Contained herein are the growth and development of this industry, future prospects, nature of the work, qualifications, preparation, getting started as an agent, working conditions, remuncration, and advantages and disadvantages.

LIFE INSURANCE AGENT. Revised 1953.

> 4 pages—15¢ in Canada, 20¢ elsewhere.
> *Guidance Centre, Univ. of Toronto*
> 371 Bloor St. W., Toronto 5, Ontario

This "monograph" discusses the history and nature of the work, working conditions, qualifications and preparation needed for entry and success, advancement opportunities, earnings, getting started, and related occupations.

MISCELLANEOUS:

INSURANCE. 1953.

11 pages—10¢.

Glamour Magazine

420 Lexington Ave., New York 17, N. Y.

This "fact sheet" describes the seven branches of the insurance field, advantages of employment in this field, education and opportunity for advancement, and nature of the work in several job opportunities among which are the agent, broker, claims examiner, actuary, underwriter, and investor.

INVITATION TO YOUTH: CAREERS IN LIFE INSURANCE. 1954.

32 pages—free.

Institute of Life Insurance

488 Madison Ave., New York 22, N. Y.

The history of this field, its importance to society, varied job opportunities, nature of the work, qualifications, preparation, how to get started, and advantages are included in this attractive pamphlet.

LIFE INSURANCE. *M. F. Stone*. 1955.

32 pages—$1.00.

Bellman Publishing Co.

P. O. Box 172, Cambridge 38, Mass.

Another in this series of "vocational and professional monographs," this pamphlet presents the history of insurance, how life insurance companies work, job opportunities in these companies, qualifications, earnings, working conditions, how to get a life insurance job, and future prospects.

For additional information, write to:

INSTITUTE OF LIFE INSURANCE
488 Madison Ave., New York 22, N. Y.

INSURANCE SOCIETY OF NEW YORK
225 Broadway, New York 7, N. Y.

SOCIETY OF ACTUARIES
208 So. LaSalle St., Chicago 4, Ill.

INTERIOR DECORATION

INTERIOR DECORATOR:
(D.O.T. No.: 0-43.40)

CAREER AS INTERIOR DECORATOR. Revised 1955.

> 8 pages—25¢.
> *B'nai B'rith Vocational Service Bureau*
> 1129 Vermont Ave., N. W., Washington 5, D. C.

Discussed here are the nature of the work of the interior decorator, qualifications and educational training for this field, beginning jobs, incomes, advantages and disadvantages, and future prospects.

INTERIOR DECORATION. 1955.

> 7 pages—10¢.
> *Glamour Magazine*
> 420 Lexington Ave., New York 17, N. Y.

This "fact sheet" highlights the qualifications and training for success, beginning jobs, advantages and disadvantages, outlook, and magazines and trade journals in this field. *(For female readers)*

INTERIOR DECORATION. *S. Splaver*. 1956.

> 6 pages—50¢; special to students, 25¢.
> *Personnel Services, Inc.*
> Main St., Peapack, N. J.

This "occupational abstract" summarizes the growth of the field, nature of the work, qualifications, preparation, entrance and advancement, supply and demand, earnings, and advantages and disadvantages.

INTERIOR DECORATOR. 1953.

> 4 pages—35¢; special to students, 25¢.
> *Chronicle Guidance Publications*
> Moravia, N. Y.

Reviewed in this "occupational brief" are the history and nature of the work performed, working conditions, wages, personal and training requirements, methods of entering this field, places of employment, related jobs, and outlook.

INTERIOR DECORATOR. Revised 1954.

> 4 pages—15¢ in Canada, 20¢ elsewhere.
> *Guidance Centre, Univ. of Toronto*
> 371 Bloor St. W., Toronto 5, Ontario

This "monograph" outlines the history and importance of this work, and describes the duties, working conditions, qualifications and preparation, advancement opportunities, advantages and disadvantages, methods of entering this field, and related occupations.

MISCELLANEOUS:

OPPORTUNITIES IN INTERIOR DECORATION. *S. Conn.* 1951.
106 pages—$1.00.
Vocational Guidance Manuals, Inc.
1011 East Tremont Ave., New York 60, N. Y.

This manual presents a historical survey of the field, prospects, financial returns, educational requirements, how to get started, personal qualifications, related fields, and a list of schools and colleges offering courses in interior decoration.

For additional information, write to:

AMERICAN INSTITUTE OF DECORATORS
41 East 57th St., New York 22, N. Y.

JEWELRY AND WATCHMAKING

GEMOLOGISTS:
(D.O.T. No.: 4-71.220)

GEMOLOGIST. *P. H. Juergens.* 1954.
  32 pages—$1.00.
  Research Publishing Co., Inc.
  P. O. Box 245, Boston 1, Mass.
The history of gemology, nature of the work performed, outlook in this field, importance to society, personal qualifications and training for this work, earnings, typical places of employment, and how to enter this field are presented in this little pamphlet.

JEWELERS:
(D.O.T. Nos.: 4-71.)

JEWELER. *H. A. Robinson.* Revised 1956.
  6 pages—50¢; special to students, 25¢.
  Personnel Services, Inc.
  Main St., Peapack, N. J.
This "occupational abstract" summarizes the nature of the work, future prospects, qualifications, preparation, entrance and advancement, earnings, number of distribution, advantages and disadvantages, and related occupations.

JEWELER. 1954.
  4 pages—15¢ in Canada, 20¢ elsewhere.
  Guidance Centre, Univ. of Toronto
  371 Bloor St. W., Toronto 5, Ontario
This "monograph" highlights the history and importance of the work, duties of the jeweler, working conditions, qualifications and educational preparation, earnings, getting started, and advantages and disadvantages.

WATCHMAKERS:
(D.O.T. No.: 4-71.510)

WATCH AND CLOCK REPAIRMEN. Reprinted 1955.
  20 pages—25¢.
  Michigan Employment Security Comm.
  7310 Woodward Ave., Detroit 2, Mich.
Here is a comprehensive presentation of the history and importance of this occupation, nature of the work performed, physical and personal qualifications, training requirements, licensing, getting started in this work, apprenticeships, employment regularity, and typical places of employment.

WATCHMAKER. Revised 1952.
  4 pages—15¢ in Canada, 20¢ elsewhere.
  Guidance Centre, Univ. of Toronto
  371 Bloor St. W., Toronto 5, Ontario

This "monograph" discusses the history and importance, nature of the work, qualifications and preparation needed, advancement, remuneration, advantages and disadvantages, how to get started, and related occupations.

WATCH REPAIRMAN. *H. A. Robinson.* Revised 1956.

6 pages—50¢; special to students, 25¢.
Personnel Services, Inc.
Main St., Peapack, N. J.

Summarized in this "occupational abstract" are future prospects, nature of the work, qualifications, preparation, licensing, women in the field, entrance and advancement, earnings, number and distribution, and advantages and disadvantages.

MISCELLANEOUS:

JEWELER AND WATCHMAKER. 1953.

4 pages—35¢; special to students, 25¢.
Chronicle Guidance Publications
Moravia, N. Y.

This "occupational brief" reviews the nature of the work performed, working conditions, wages, personal and training requirements, future prospects, typical places of employment, getting started, and related jobs.

THE JEWELRY INDUSTRY. *G. R. Frankovich.* 1955.

26 pages—$1.00.
Bellman Publishing Co.
P. O. Box 172, Cambridge 38, Mass.

Included in this pamphlet are the history of the industry, the modern jewelry industry in the United States, job opportunities, working and earning conditions, how to get a jewelry job, getting ahead in this industry, advantages and disadvantages, and the jewelry future.

For additional information, write to:

HOROLOGICAL INSTITUTE OF AMERICA
P. O. Box 4355, Washington 12, D. C.

LAW

LAWYERS:

(D.O.T. Nos.: 0-22.)

CAREERS IN LAW. *R. Shosteck.* 1954.
12 pages—25¢.
B'nai B'rith Vocational Service Bureau
1129 Vermont Ave., N. W., Washington 5, D. C.
This booklet discusses the nature of legal work, women in this profession, training requirements, qualifications, licensing, getting started, earnings, working conditions, and advantages and disadvantages.

LAW. 1955.
3 pages—10¢.
Glamour Magazine
420 Lexington Ave., New York 17, N. Y.
This "fact sheet" presents the opportunities for women lawyers, qualifications and training, and a suggested reading list. *(For female readers)*

LAWYER. 1954.
4 pages—35¢; special to students, 25¢.
Chronicle Guidance Publications
Moravia, N. Y.
This "occupational brief" reviews the history and nature of the work performed, working conditions, earnings, personal and training requirements, advancement, opportunities for women, typical places of employment, licensing, and future prospects.

LAWYER. Revised 1954.
4 pages—15¢ in Canada, 20¢ elsewhere.
Guidance Centre, Univ. of Toronto
371 Bloor St. W., Toronto 5, Ontario
This "monograph" reviews the history and importance of this profession, the nature of the lawyer's work, working conditions, qualifications and preparation, advancement opportunities, earnings, getting started in this profession, and related occupations.

LINDA JORDAN, LAWYER. *J. L. Block.* 1953.
173 pages—$2.95.
Julian Messner, Inc.
8 West 40th St., New York 18, N. Y.
This career novel tells the tale of two law school students. Information on the preparation for admission into the profession and some of the gratifications of the work are interwoven into the romance theme. *(For teen-age girls)*

SHOULD YOU BE A LAWYER?
R. Pound. 1955.
8 pages—free.
New York Life Insurance Co.
51 Madison Ave., New York 10, N. Y.
This public service booklet highlights the importance of the legal profession, nature of the lawyer's work, supply and demand, educational requirements, personal qualifications, cost of preparation, and number of women lawyers.

SO YOU WANT TO BE A LAWYER!
K. Redden. 1953.
139 pages—$2.50.
Bobbs-Merrill Co., Inc.
730 No. Meridian St., Indianapolis 7, Ind.
This book describes the nature of lawyers' activities, what it takes to be a lawyer, preparation for the legal profession, how to enter the profession, number and distribution of lawyers, opportunities for women lawyers, earnings, and future prospects in this field.

MISCELLANEOUS:

CAREER PLANNING IN THE LAW. K. Redden. 1953.

  206 pages—$3.00.
  Bobbs-Merrill Co., Inc.
  730 No. Meridian St., Indianapolis 7, Ind.

The different types of legal practices, specialization in this field, and opportunities in government agencies are presented in this book. *(For law students and young law school graduates)*

For additional information, write to:

AMERICAN BAR ASSOCIATION
1140 No. Dearborn St., Chicago 10, Ill.

LIBRARY WORK

LIBRARIANS:

(D.O.T. Nos.: 0-23.)

CAREERS IN LIBRARY WORK.
R. Wolozin. 1955.

    8 pages—25¢.
B'nai B'rith Vocational Service Bureau
1129 Vermont Ave., N. W., Washington 5, D. C.

This booklet discusses the nature of library work, future prospects, personal and educational requirements, costs of specialized training, methods of entering this field, earnings, and advantages and disadvantages.

EDUCATION FOR THE PROFESSIONAL LIBRARIAN. 1956.

    4 pages—free to high school principals and guidance officers.
Simmons College
300 The Fenway, Boston 15, Mass.

This folder states the functions of a library, what a librarian does, opportunities for librarians, supply and demand, salaries, and educational programs for librarianship.

LIBRARIAN. 1954.

    4 pages—35¢; special to students, 25¢.
Chronicle Guidance Publications
Moravia, N. Y.

This "occupational brief" reviews the history and nature of the work performed, working conditions, personal and training requirements, chances for promotion, future prospects, typical places of employment, methods of entering the field, and licensing.

LIBRARIAN. Revised 1955.

    4 pages—15¢ in Canada, 20¢ elsewhere.

Guidance Centre, Univ. of Toronto
371 Bloor St. W., Toronto 5, Ontario

Included in this "monograph" are the history and importance of the work, nature of the work, qualifications and training, entrance and advancement, working conditions, earnings, related occupations, and advantages and disadvantages.

LIBRARIANS. 1951.

    43 pages—25¢.
Michigan Employment Security Comm.
7310 Woodward Ave., Detroit 2, Mich.

This comprehensive pamphlet describes the history of the profession, nature of the work performed, earnings, working conditions, personal and educational requirements for entrance and success in this field, advantages and disadvantages, chances for advancement, and future prospects.

LIBRARY WORK. 1955.

    3 pages—10¢.
Glamour Magazine
420 Lexington Ave., New York 17, N. Y.

This "fact sheet" discusses the differences between today's librarian and the librarian of the past, professional training requirements, supply and demand, methods of entering the field, salaries, opportunities for advancement, and advantages. *(For female readers)*

LIBRARY WORK WITH TEEN-AGERS. *Mademoiselle's College and Careers Dept.* 1955.

    6 pages—25¢.

Alumnae Advisory Center, Inc.
541 Madison Ave., New York 22, N. Y.
The activities of a young people's librarian are described in this magazine reprint. Also briefly stated are the opportunities in this field, educational preparation, salaries, and places of employment. *(For female college students)*

"MISS LIBRARY LADY." *A. Pfaender.* 1954.

184 pages—$2.95.
Julian Messner, Inc.
8 West 40th St., New York 18, N. Y.
Valuable occupational information is incorporated into this career novel. It describes the nature of the work of the librarian, opportunities for young people in this field, working conditions, preparation, methods of getting started, and advantages and disadvantages. *(For teen-age girls)*

SHOULD YOU BE A LIBRARIAN?
Edward G. Freehafer. 1957.

8 pages—free.
New York Life Insurance Co.
51 Madison Ave., New York 10, N. Y.
This public service pamphlet begins with a history of librarianship in communities, schools, and industry. The author describes the duties of a modern librarian—selecting and cataloging books, administration, community service, and story-telling—and also training required, earnings, aptitudes, and specialties for men and women.

SPECIAL LIBRARIAN. 1955.

4 pages—35¢; special to students, 25¢.
Chronicle Guidance Publications
Moravia, N. Y.

This "occupational brief" reviews the librarian's importance to society, nature of the work, future prospects, opportunities for men, qualifications and training needed for entrance, working conditions, earnings, typical places of employment, and fields of specialization.

MISCELLANEOUS:

THE LIBRARY PROFESSION. *R. S. Leonard and M. P. Hazen.* 1955.

20 pages—$1.00.
Bellman Publishing Co.
P. O. Box 172, Cambridge 38, Mass.
Included in this pamphlet are the qualifications for the prospective librarian, opportunities and varied library careers, professional requirements, preparation for entering the field, salaries, and the future of libraries.

OPPORTUNITIES IN LIBRARY CAREERS. *R. E. Kingery.* 1952.

112 pages—$1.00.
Vocational Guidance Manuals, Inc.
1011 East Tremont Ave., New York 60, N. Y.
This authoritative "manual" describes the librarian's duties, qualifications and educational preparation necessary for success in this field, how to get started, nature of library careers, and outlook.

For additional information, write to:

AMERICAN LIBRARY ASSOCIATION
50 East Huron St., Chicago 11, Ill.

SPECIAL LIBRARIES ASSOCIATION
31 East 10th St., New York 3, N. Y.

MECHANICS

APPRENTICES:

(D.O.T. Nos.: 7-93. through 7-99.)

APPRENTICES. 1953.

4 pages—35¢; special to students, 25¢.
Chronicle Guidance Publications
Moravia, N. Y.

This "occupational brief" includes a job definition; it discusses common misconceptions, the need for apprenticeship, preparation and qualifications, apprenticeable trades, getting started, a typical apprenticeship program, and advantages of an apprenticeship.

CAREERS THROUGH APPRENTICE-SHIPS. 1954.

4 pages—25¢.
B'nai B'rith Vocational Service Bureau
1129 Vermont Ave., N. W., Washington 5, D. C.

This booklet discusses the outlook for apprentices, opportunities available, and the length of training necessary in a variety of apprenticeships.

DIESEL MECHANICS:

(D.O.T. No.: 5-83.931)

DIESEL MECHANIC. 1955.

4 pages—35¢; special to students, 25¢.
Chronicle Guidance Publications
Moravia, N. Y.

This "occupational brief" discusses the history of the diesel engine, work performed by the diesel mechanic, working conditions, wages, personal and training requirements, employment outlook, opportunities for women, where employed, and related jobs.

DIESEL MECHANIC. Revised 1955.

4 pages—15¢ in Canada, 20¢ elsewhere.
Guidance Centre, Univ. of Toronto
371 Bloor St. W., Toronto 5, Ontario

This "monograph" presents the history and nature of the work, working conditions, qualifications and preparation needed, advancement, remuneration, how to get started, and advantages and disadvantages.

HOUSEHOLD MECHANICS:

(D.O.T. Nos.: 5-83.041; 5-83.941)

ELECTRICAL-HOUSEHOLD-APPLIANCE SERVICEMAN. 1953.

4 pages—35¢; special to students, 25¢.
Chronicle Guidance Publications
Moravia, N. Y.

Reviewed in this "occupational brief" are the specializations, nature of the work, working conditions, earnings, personal and training requirements, future prospects, methods of entry, and related jobs.

REFRIGERATION MECHANIC. 1955.

    4 pages—35¢; special to students, 25¢.
Chronicle Guidance Publications
Moravia, N. Y.

This "occupational brief" contains infor-mation on the history and nature of the work performed, working conditions, wages, qualifications, training, typical places of employment, methods of entry, future prospects, and related jobs.

INSPECTORS:

(D.O.T. Nos.: 0-50.53; 7-76.)

INSPECTORS—SEMI-SKILLED AND UNSKILLED. 1952.

    4 pages—35¢; special to students, 25¢.
Chronicle Guidance Publications
Moravia, N. Y.

Reviewed herein are the nature of the work performed, typical places of employ-ment, working conditions, requirements for employment, methods of entry, and other types of inspectors.

MACHINE OPERATORS:

(D.O.T. Nos.: 6-27.; 6-33.)

SEMI-SKILLED MACHINE OPERATORS. 1953.

    4 pages—35¢; special to students, 25¢.
Chronicle Guidance Publications
Moravia, N. Y.

This "occupational brief" defines the job, discusses job opportunities, working con-ditions, wages, personal and training re-quirements, methods of gaining employ-ment, future prospects, and advantages and disadvantages.

SEWING-MACHINE OPERATORS. Reprinted 1954.

    20 pages—25¢.
Michigan Employment Security Comm.
7310 Woodward Ave., Detroit 2, Mich.

This "occupational guide" describes the history and nature of the work, physical and personal requirements, training, op-portunities for advancement, earnings, working conditions, and advantages and disadvantages.

MACHINISTS:

(D.O.T. No.: 4-75.010)

MACHINIST. 1953.

    6 pages—35¢; special to students, 25¢.
Chronicle Guidance Publications
Moravia, N. Y.

This "occupational brief" defines the job, the work performed, working conditions, wages, personal and training require-ments, physical demands, opportunities for promotion, where employed, job out-look, unionization, and related jobs.

MACHINIST. 1956.

4 pages—15¢ in Canada, 20¢ elsewhere.
Guidance Centre, Univ. of Toronto
371 Bloor St. W., Toronto 5, Ontario
Included in this "monograph" are the history and importance of the machinist's work, working conditions, qualifications and preparation needed, advancement opportunities, remuneration, advantages and disadvantages, how to get started, and related occupations.

METAL WORKERS:
(D.O.T. Nos.: 4-80.; 4-85.)

SHEET METAL WORKER. Revised 1953.

4 pages—15¢ in Canada, 20¢ elsewhere.
Guidance Centre, Univ. of Toronto
371 Bloor St. W., Toronto 5, Ontario
This "monograph" defines the job, the importance and nature of the work performed, qualifications and preparation, earnings, working conditions; it tells how to get started, and discusses advantages and disadvantages.

SHEET METAL WORKERS. 1956.

20 pages—25¢.
Michigan Employment Security Comm.
7310 Woodward Ave., Detroit 2, Mich.
This "occupational guide" discusses the history of metal working, nature of the work, places of employment, outlook, working conditions, earnings, qualifications for entry, and disadvantages and advantages.

WELDER. 1952.

4 pages—35¢; special to students, 25¢.
Chronicle Guidance Publications
Moravia, N. Y.
This "occupational brief" defines the job, describes the work performed, wages, working conditions, personal and training requirements, where to find employment, methods of entry, unionization, and licensing.

WELDER. Revised 1955.

4 pages—15¢ in Canada, 20¢ elsewhere.
Guidance Centre, Univ. of Toronto
371 Bloor St. W., Toronto 5, Ontario
This "monograph" reviews the history and importance of welding, it describes the nature of the work, working conditions, qualifications and preparation needed, advancement, remuneration, advantages and disadvantages, how to get started, and related occupations.

MILLWRIGHTS:
(D.O.T. No.: 5-78.100)

MILLWRIGHT. 1955.

4 pages—35¢; special to students, 25¢.
Chronicle Guidance Publications
Moravia, N. Y.
This "occupational brief" defines the job, the work performed, working conditions, wages, personal and training requirements, opportunities for promotion, where to find employment, methods of entry, unionization, and related jobs.

MOLDERS:
(D.O.T. Nos.: 4-66.; 4-76.; 6-66.; 6-82.; 6-98.)

MOLDER. 1956.

4 pages—35¢; special to students, 25¢.
Chronicle Guidance Publications
Moravia, N. Y.

This "occupational brief" contains a job definition, describes the history and nature of the work performed, working conditions, wages, personal and training requirements, training opportunities, where to find employment, methods of entry, and related jobs.

MOULDER. Revised 1953.

4 pages—15¢ in Canada, 20¢ elsewhere.
Guidance Centre, Univ. of Toronto
371 Bloor St. W., Toronto 5, Ontario

Included in this "monograph" are the history, importance, and nature of the work, working conditions, qualifications and preparation necessary for entry and success, advancement opportunities, remuneration, advantages and disadvantages, and how to get started.

OFFICE MACHINE SERVICEMEN:
(D.O.T. No.: 5-83.111)

CAREERS IN OFFICE MACHINERY REPAIR. *L. Ravin.* 1953.

8 pages—25¢.
B'nai B'rith Vocational Service Bureau
1129 Vermont Ave., N. W., Washington 5, D. C.

This booklet presents the varieties of office machine repair work, job prospects, typical places of employment, nature of the work, working conditions, remuneration, qualifications, training, and advantages and disadvantages.

OFFICE-MACHINE SERVICEMAN. 1954.

4 pages—35¢; special to students, 25¢.
Chronicle Guidance Publications
Moravia, N. Y.

This "occupational brief" contains a job definition, describes working conditions, wages, personal and training requirements, methods of entry, future prospects, where to find employment and related jobs.

OFFICE-MACHINE SERVICEMEN. Reprinted 1955.

20 pages—25¢.
Michigan Employment Security Comm.
7310 Woodward Ave., Detroit 2, Mich.

Included in this pamphlet are the history and nature of the work, outlook for employment, working conditions, wages, qualifications and training, obtaining employment, and opportunities for advancement.

OIL BURNER SERVICEMEN:
(D.O.T. No.: 5-83.024)

OIL BURNER SERVICE AND
INSTALLATION TECHNICIAN.
C. H. Burkhardt. 1956.

32 pages—$1.00.
Research Publishing Co., Inc.
P. O. Box 245, Boston 1, Mass.

This little pamphlet presents the history of the occupation, describes the nature of the work, its contributions to society, supply and demand, wages and benefits, personal qualifications, educational requirements, licenses required, promotional opportunities, methods of securing jobs, places of employment, and organizations in this field.

PATTERNMAKERS:
(D.O.T. Nos.: 4-27.; 4-61.; 5-17.)

PATTERNMAKER. 1953.

4 pages—35¢; special to students, 25¢.
Chronicle Guidance Publications
Moravia, N. Y.

This "occupational brief" discusses the history and nature of the work performed, working conditions, wages, personal and training requirements, where to find employment, methods of entering this occupation, and related jobs.

PATTERNMAKER. Revised 1954.

4 pages—15¢ in Canada, 20¢ elsewhere.
Guidance Centre, Univ. of Toronto
371 Bloor St. W., Toronto 5, Ontario

This "monograph" highlights the history, importance, and nature of the work, and describes working conditions, qualifications and preparation needed, opportunities for advancement, advantages and disadvantages, how to get started, and related occupations.

PATTERNMAKERS. Revised 1956.

16 pages—25¢.
Michigan Employment Security Comm.
7310 Woodward Ave., Detroit 2, Mich.

This "occupational guide" discusses the history of patternmaking, nature of the work, working conditions, location of jobs, employment outlook, earnings, qualifications, and disadvantages and advantages.

SHOE REPAIRMEN:
(D.O.T. No.: 4-60.100)

SHOE REPAIRMAN. 1954.

4 pages—35¢; special to students, 25¢.
Chronicle Guidance Publications
Moravia, N. Y.

This "occupational brief" discusses the nature of the work performed, working conditions, wages, personal and training requirements, methods of entry, where to find employment, and related jobs.

SHOE REPAIRMAN. Revised 1953.

4 pages—15¢ in Canada, 20¢ elsewhere.
Guidance Centre, Univ. of Toronto
371 Bloor St. W., Toronto 5, Ontario

This "monograph" presents the history and nature of the work, and discusses working conditions, qualifications and preparation needed, advancement, advantages and disadvantages, and how to get started in this occupation.

SHOE REPAIRMAN. Reprinted 1955.

24 pages—25¢.
Michigan Employment Security Comm.
7310 Woodward Ave., Detroit 2, Mich.

This "occupational guide" contains information about the history of the work, duties, location of jobs, employment prospects, working conditions, earnings, qualifications for entry, and advantages and disadvantages.

SHOE REPAIRMAN. *S. Splaver*. Revised 1956.

6 pages—50¢; special to students, 25¢.
Personnel Services, Inc.
Main St., Peapack, N. J.

Summarized in this "occupational abstract" are the nature of the work, qualifications, preparation, entrance and advancement, opportunities for servicemen, distribution, supply and demand, earnings, and advantages and disadvantages.

TOOL AND DIE MAKERS:
(D.O.T. No.: 4-76.040)

THE TOOL AND DIE INDUSTRY.
A. E. Rylander. 1955.

26 pages—$1.00.
Bellman Publishing Co.
P. O. Box 172, Cambridge 38, Mass.

This "vocational and professional monograph" contains the history and organization of the tool and die industry, discusses the importance and opportunities of the field, the professional and trade association, technical knowledge needed, and a typical apprenticeship course.

TOOL AND DIE MAKER. 1953.

4 pages—35¢; special to students, 25¢.
Chronicle Guidance Publications
Moravia, N. Y.

This "occupational brief" discusses the work performed, working conditions, wages, qualifications and preparation, advancement, specialization, future, where to find employment, and method of entry.

TOOL AND DIE MAKER. *H. A. Robinson.* 1956.

6 pages—50¢; special to students, 25¢.
Personnel Services, Inc.
Main St., Peapack, N. J.

This pamphlet reviews the nature of the work, future prospects, opportunities for servicemen, qualifications, preparation, entrance and advancement, earnings, number and distribution of tool and die makers, advantages and disadvantages, and related occupations.

TOOL MAKER. Revised 1955.

4 pages—15¢ in Canada, 20¢ elsewhere.
Guidance Centre, Univ. of Toronto
371 Bloor St. W., Toronto 5, Ontario

This "monograph" presents a job definition, and describes the qualifications necessary for entry and success in the field, preparation, remuneration, advantages and disadvantages, how to get started, and related occupations.

UPHOLSTERERS:

(D.O.T. No.: 4-35.720)

CAREER AS UPHOLSTERER. 1953.

8 pages—25¢.
B'nai B'rith Vocational Service Bureau
1129 Vermont Ave., N. W., Washington 5, D. C.

Included in this booklet are future prospects in the field, nature of the work, qualifications and preparation, working conditions, getting started, wages, and advantages and disadvantages.

MISCELLANEOUS:

CAN I BE A CRAFTSMAN? 1956.

21 pages—free.
General Motors Corp.
Dept. of Public Relations, Detroit 2, Mich.

This attractive public service pamphlet describes the importance of machines, explains what a craftsman is, nature of the work of different types of craftsmen, opportunities, qualifications, educational preparation, and a typical apprentice training schedule. *(For teen-agers)*

EMPLOYMENT OUTLOOK FOR MECHANICS AND REPAIRMEN. BULLETIN NO. 1129. *Bureau of Labor Statistics, U. S. Dept. of Labor.* 1953.

28 pages—20¢.
Supt. of Documents, Govt. Printing Office
Washington 25, D. C.

This pamphlet has reprinted information from the *Occupational Outlook Handbook.* It describes opportunities and prospects for miscellaneous mechanics and repairmen.

EMPLOYMENT OUTLOOK IN METALWORKING OCCUPATIONS. BULLETIN NO. 1130. *Bureau of Labor Statistics, U. S. Dept. of Labor.* 1953.

39 pages—30¢.
Supt. of Documents, Govt. Printing Office
Washington 25, D. C.

This pamphlet discusses machine shop occupations and future prospects, nature of the work, earnings, training, qualifications, and opportunities available.

OPPORTUNITIES IN MACHINE SHOP TRADES. *B. J. Stern.* 1953.

95 pages—$1.00.
Vocational Guidance Manuals, Inc.
1011 East Tremont Ave., New York 60, N. Y.

This "manual" discusses the history of the work, current needs and future outlook, requirements for success, how to become a machinist, getting started, varied machine shop occupations, and related fields.

THE PEN INDUSTRY. *D. Parker.* 1955.

16 pages—$1.00.
Bellman Publishing Co.
P. O. Box 172, Cambridge 38, Mass.

This "vocational and professional monograph" includes information on the history of the industry, production and distribution of pens, miscellaneous employment opportunities, earnings, advancement, educational requirements, and trends.

For additional information, write to:

BUREAU OF APPRENTICESHIP, U. S. DEPT. OF LABOR
Washington 25, D. C.

NATIONAL MACHINE TOOL BUILDERS ASSOCIATION
10525 Carnegie Ave., Cleveland 6, Ohio

NATIONAL METAL TRADES ASSOCIATION
122 So. Michigan Ave., Chicago 3, Ill.

NATIONAL TOOL AND DIE MANUFACTURERS ASSOCIATION
1412 Union Carbide Bldg., Cleveland 14, Ohio

MEDICAL AND HEALTH SERVICES

CHIROPODISTS:
(D.O.T. No.: 0-52.01)

CHIROPODIST. 1955.

4 pages—35¢; special to students, 25¢.
Chronicle Guidance Publications
Moravia, N. Y.

This "occupational brief" includes a job definition and history of the profession, it describes working conditions, wages, personal and training requirements, licensing, outlook, where to find employment, methods of entry, and opportunities for women.

CHIROPODIST. Revised 1953.

4 pages—15¢ in Canada, 20¢ elsewhere.
Guidance Centre, Univ. of Toronto
371 Bloor St. W., Toronto 5, Ontario

This "monograph" contains information on the importance of the occupation, nature of the work, working conditions, qualifications and preparation necessary for entry and success, earnings, how to get started, and related occupations.

CHIROPODIST. Reprinted 1955.

16 pages—25¢.

Michigan Employment Security Comm.
7310 Woodward Ave., Detroit 2, Mich.

This is another of the "occupational guides" in the series and it presents the history and nature of the work, number and distribution of chiropodists, personal qualifications, laws regulating this profession, training requirements, methods of entry, earnings, places of employment, and advantages and disadvantages.

CHIROPODY AS A CAREER. *W. E. Belleau.* Revised 1955.

27 pages—60¢.
Park Publishing House
4141 West Vliet St., Milwaukee 8, Wisc.

Included in this pamphlet are the history of chiropody, nature of the work and types of practice, training, qualifications, licensure, entering the field, conditions of work, a chiropodist's working day, income, opportunities, women in chiropody, geographical distribution of chiropodists, and professional organizations.

CHIROPRACTORS:
(D.O.T. No.: 0-39.90)

CHIROPRACTIC AS A CAREER. *W. E. Belleau.* 1953.

25 pages—60¢.
Park Publishing House
4141 West Vliet St., Milwaukee 8, Wisc.

This pamphlet discusses the nature of the work of the chiropractor, preparation and qualifications, licensure, getting started, employment outlook, earnings, opportunities for women, and advantages and disadvantages.

CHIROPRACTOR. Revised 1954.

 4 pages—15¢ in Canada, 20¢ elsewhere.
Guidance Centre, Univ. of Toronto
371 Bloor St. W., Toronto 5, Ontario
Discussed in this "monograph" are the
history, importance and nature of the
work, working conditions, qualifications
and preparation needed, advancement,
remuneration, advantages and disadvantages, how to get started, and related
occupations.

HOSPITAL ADMINISTRATORS:
(D.O.T. No.: 0-99.84)

CAREERS IN HOSPITAL ADMINIS-
TRATION. *R. Shosteck.* 1954.

 8 pages—25¢.
B'nai B'rith Vocational Service Bureau
1129 Vermont Ave., N. W., Washington 5, D. C.

Here is information on the development
of the field, nature of the work of the
administrator and assistant administrator,
qualifications and training, opportunities
for advancement, earnings, entering the
field, and opportunities for women.

HOSPITAL ADMINISTRATOR. 1955.

 4 pages—35¢; special to students, 25¢.
Chronicle Guidance Publications
Moravia, N. Y.

This "occupational brief" discusses the
history and nature of the work performed, working conditions, wages,
personal and training requirements, opportunities for women, where employed,
and methods of entry.

MEDICAL RECORD LIBRARIANS:
(D.O.T. No.: 0-23.25)

MEDICAL RECORD LIBRARIAN.
1955.

 4 pages—35¢; special to students, 25¢.
Chronicle Guidance Publications
Moravia, N. Y.

This "occupational brief" reviews the history and importance of the work, duties,
working conditions, earnings, personal
and training qualifications, registration,
advancement, where to find employment,
and related jobs.

MEDICAL RECORD LIBRARIAN. *S.
Splaver.* 1953.

 6 pages—50¢; special to students, 25¢.
Personnel Services, Inc.
Main St., Peapack, N. J.

Summarized in this "occupational abstract" are the nature of the work,
qualifications, preparation, registration,
entrance and advancement, supply and
demand, earnings, advantages and disadvantages, and opportunities for servicemen.

THE MEDICAL RECORDS
LIBRARIAN. 1953.

4 pages—free to high school principals
and guidance officers.

Simmons College
300 The Fenway, Boston 15, Mass.

This folder contains a description of the
work, personal qualifications, opportunities, educational and professional requirements, and rewards.

MEDICAL TECHNICIANS:

(D.O.T. No.: 0-50.01)

CAREER AS MEDICAL TECHNOL
OGIST. *R. Matthaei.* 1954.

12 pages—25¢.

B'nai B'rith Vocational Service Bureau
1129 Vermont Ave., N. W., Washington 5, D. C.

Discussed here are future prospects in
the field, nature of the work, personal
qualifications, preparation, certification,
remuneration, drawbacks, and sources of
further information.

EMPLOYMENT OPPORTUNITIES
FOR WOMEN MEDICAL TECHNOL
OGISTS AND LABORATORY TECH
NICIANS. M E D I C A L S E R I E S
BULLETIN NO. 203-4. *Women's Bureau, U. S. Dept. of Labor.* 1954.

54 pages—25¢.

*Supt. of Documents, Govt. Printing
Office*
Washington 25, D. C.

This bulletin describes the medical laboratory and its staff, preparation for the medical technologist's job, beginning jobs,
opportunities, places of employment,
earnings, qualifications for this work, nature of the work performed, and requirements for registration by the Registry of
Medical Technologists of the American
Society of Clinical Pathologists.

THE GIRL IN THE WHITE COAT.
H. Wells. 1953.

184 pages—$2.95.

Julian Messner, Inc.
8 West 40th St., New York 18, N. Y.

The heroine in this career novel is a
medical technologist. Included in the
book is information on the nature of the
work, qualifications, educational requirements, certification, getting started, and
typical places of employment. *(For teen-
age girls)*

MEDICAL LABORATORY TECH
NOLOGIST. Revised 1954.

4 pages—15¢ in Canada, 20¢ elsewhere.

Guidance Centre, Univ. of Toronto
371 Bloor St. W., Toronto 5, Ontario.

This "monograph" discusses the history
and nature of the work performed, working conditions, qualifications and preparation needed, advancement, remuneration,
advantages and disadvantages, and how to
get started.

MEDICAL TECHNICIAN. 1952.

4 pages—35¢; special to students, 25¢.
Chronicle Guidance Publications
Moravia, N. Y.

Reviewed in this "occupational brief" are
the history of the work, duties, working
conditions, wages, personal and training
requirements, opportunities for promotion, where employed, outlook, and methods of entry.

THE MEDICAL TECHNOLOGIST.
1956.

> 4 pages—free to high school principals
> and guidance officers.
> *Simmons College*
> 300 The Fenway, Boston 15, Mass.

This folder discusses the importance of the work, the urgent need for medical technologists, working conditions, qualifications, and preparation.

MORTICIANS:

(D.O.T. Nos.: 0-65.10, 0-65.20)

FUNERAL SERVICES AS A CAREER.
W. B. Belleau. 1956.

> 26 pages—75¢.
> *Park Publishing House*
> 4141 West Vliet St., Milwaukee 8,
> Wisc.

This pamphlet discusses the history and importance of the occupation, nature of the work, training, qualifications, entering the field, conditions of work, income, opportunities, advantages and disadvantages, opportunities for women, and licensing rules and regulations.

MORTICIAN. 1953.

> 4 pages—35¢; special to students, 25¢.
> *Chronicle Guidance Publications*
> Moravia, N. Y.

Reviewed in this "occupational brief" are the nature of the work performed, working conditions, wages, personal qualifications, training requirements, advantages and disadvantages, opportunities for women, where to find employment, methods of entry, and licensing. It also in-

cludes a list of accredited schools of mortuary science.

MORTICIAN AND EMBALMER.
1952.

> 4 pages—15¢ in Canada, 20¢ elsewhere.
> *Guidance Centre, Univ. of Toronto*
> 371 Bloor St. W., Toronto 5, Ontario.

This "monograph" discusses the history and nature of the work, working conditions, qualifications and preparation needed, advancement, remuneration, advantages and disadvantages, how to get started, and related occupations.

MORTICIANS. Revised 1954.

> 20 pages—25¢.
> *Michigan Employment Security Comm.*
> 7310 Woodward Ave., Detroit 2, Mich.

This "occupational guide" describes the history of mortuary operation, nature of the work of morticians, opportunities for employment, earnings, qualifications and training, working conditions, and advantages and disadvantages.

PHYSICIANS' ASSISTANTS:

(D.O.T. No.: 1-32.20)

IN THE DOCTOR'S OFFICE. *E. J. Parsons.* Revised 1956.

> 326 pages—$3.95.
> *J. B. Lippincott Co.*
> 227 So. 6th St., Philadelphia 5, Pa.

The nature of the work of the assistant, her qualifications for the job, specialized training desirable, and working conditions are presented in this book. (*For teen-age girls*)

THE PHYSICIAN'S ASSISTANT. Revised 1956.

4 pages—35¢; special to students, 25¢.
Chronicle Guidance Publications
Moravia, N. Y.

This "occupational brief" describes the history and nature of the work performed, working conditions, wages, personal qualifications, training requirements, advantages and disadvantages, advancement, opportunities for men, and methods of entering this occupation.

PHYSICIANS, MEDICAL:
(D.O.T. No.: 0-26.10)

PATHOLOGIST. *S. Splaver*. 1953.

6 pages—50¢; special to students, 25¢.
Personnel Services, Inc.
Main St., Peapack, N. J.

Summarized in this "occupational abstract" are the nature of the work, personal qualifications, preparation, licensing, entrance and advancement, opportunities for servicemen, supply and demand, earnings, and advantages and disadvantages.

PHYSICIAN. 1954.

4 pages—35¢; special to students, 25¢.
Chronicle Guidance Publications
Moravia, N. Y.

This "occupational brief" describes the history and nature of the profession, specialization, working conditions, earnings, personal and training requirements, opportunities for women, licensing, and related workers.

PHYSICIAN. Revised 1954.

4 pages—15¢ in Canada, 20¢ elsewhere.
Guidance Centre, Univ. of Toronto
371 Bloor St. W., Toronto 5, Ontario.

This "monograph" discusses the history and importance of the work, duties, working conditions, qualifications and preparation needed, opportunities for advancement, remuneration, advantages and disadvantages, how to get started, and related occupations.

SHOULD YOU BE A DOCTOR? *W. C. Alvarez*. 1955.

8 pages—free.
New York Life Insurance Co.
51 Madison Ave., New York 10, N. Y.

This authoritative public service booklet outlines the personal qualifications for entrance into this profession, training and costs, places of employment, income, women in this profession, and rewards.

WILLIAM CRAWFORD GORGAS: TROPIC FEVER FIGHTER. *B. Williams and S. Epstein*. 1953.

184 pages—$2.95.
Julian Messner, Inc.
8 West 40th St., New York 18, N. Y.

This is an inspirational biography of Dr. Gorgas, the Army doctor who conquered yellow fever, and is worthwhile reading for all young people who aspire to a medical career. (*For teen-agers*)

YOU AND YOUR DOCTOR. *M. S. Gumpert*. 1952.

258 pages—$3.00.
Bobbs-Merrill Co., Inc.
730 No. Meridian St., Indianapolis 7, Ind.

Described here is the nature of the work of the general practitioner. It has been prepared for the layman and presents worthwhile career information on the functions of the various medical specialists.

PHYSICIANS, OSTEOPATHIC:
(D.O.T. No.: 0-39.96)

OSTEOPATH. 1954.

4 pages—35¢; special to students, 25¢.
Chronicle Guidance Publications
Moravia, N. Y.

This pamphlet reviews the history and nature of the work performed, working conditions, earnings, personal and training requirements, opportunities for women, licensing, engaging in practice, and related jobs.

OSTEOPATHIC PHYSICIAN. Revised 1956.

4 pages—15¢ in Canada, 20¢ elsewhere.
Guidance Centre, Univ. of Toronto
371 Bloor St. W., Toronto 5, Ontario

This "monograph" includes a job defini-tion, discusses working conditions, quali-fications and preparation needed, advancement, remuneration, advantages and disadvantages, how to get started, and related jobs.

THE OSTEOPATHIC PHYSICIAN AND SURGEON. *W. E. Belleau.* 1951.

27 pages—60¢.
Park Publishing House
4141 West Vliet St., Milwaukee 8, Wisc.

Discussed in this pamphlet are the nature of the work, preparation and qualifications, licensure, how to enter the field, working conditions, earnings, employment prospects, and advantages and disadvantages.

SPEECH THERAPISTS:
(D.O.T. No.: 0-32.09)

CAREER AS SPEECH AND HEARING THERAPIST. *R. Shosteck.* Revised 1956.

12 pages—25¢.
B'nai B'rith Vocational Service Bureau
1129 Vermont Ave., N. W., Washington 5, D. C.

This booklet discusses the outlook in this field, nature of the work, personal requirements, training, certification, employment opportunities, and earnings.

SPEECH THERAPIST. *H. A. Robinson.* Revised 1956.

6 pages—50¢; special to students, 25¢.
Personnel Services, Inc.
Main St., Peapack, N. J.

Summarized in this "occupational abstract" are the nature of the work, future prospects, qualifications, preparation, entrance and advancement, earnings, and advantages and disadvantages.

X-RAY TECHNICIANS:

(D.O.T. No.: 0-50.04)

BEATRICE PERRY, X-RAY TECH-NICIAN. *D. Tooker.* 1952.

250 pages—$2.50.
Dodd, Mead and Co., Inc.
432 Fourth Ave., New York 16, N. Y.

This career novel includes information on the qualifications and preparation for entrance into this field. *(For teen-age girls)*

THE OUTLOOK FOR WOMEN AS MEDICAL X-RAY TECHNICIANS. BULLETIN NO. 203-8. *Women's Bureau, U. S. Dept. of Labor.* 1954.

53 pages—25¢.
Supt. of Documents, Govt. Printing Office
Washington 25, D. C.

Another of the bulletins in the Medical Services Series, it presents the history of the field, job specialization and job titles, hazards of the work, where x-ray technicians work, earnings, training, employment prospects, possibilities for advancement, qualifications for registration, and job descriptions.

X-RAY TECHNICIAN. 1952.

4 pages—35¢; special to students, 25¢.
Chronicle Guidance Publications
Moravia, N. Y.

Reviewed in this "occupational brief" are the history of the x-ray, duties of the x-ray technician, working conditions, wages, personal and training requirements, where to find employment, licensing, and related jobs.

X-RAY TECHNICIAN. Revised 1953.

4 pages—15¢ in Canada, 20¢ elsewhere.
Guidance Centre, Univ. of Toronto
371 Bloor St. W., Toronto 5, Ontario

This "monograph" describes the importance and nature of the work, working conditions, qualifications and preparation needed, opportunities for advancement, remuneration, advantages and disadvantages, how to get started, and related occupations.

MISCELLANEOUS:

CAREERS IN SERVICE TO THE HANDICAPPED. 1952.

53 pages—50¢.
National Society for Crippled Children and Adults, Inc.
11 So. LaSalle St., Chicago 3, Ill.

A thorough coverage of the rehabilitation profession is presented here, including the nature of the work in the different occupations, requirements, preparation, gratifications, opportunities available, and a list of colleges offering training in the rehabilitation specialties.

HEALTH CAREERS GUIDEBOOK. 1955.

156 pages—free to secondary schools and junior colleges.
National Health Council
1790 Broadway, New York 19, N. Y.

Prepared with the cooperation of the National Association of Secondary School Principals and the National Vocational Guidance Association, this book presents a preview of health careers, describes the teamwork aspects of the work performed in this field, suggests some pointers on post-high school planning, illustrates via a health careers calendar the length of time required for training for miscellaneous health occupations, and includes a section of health career briefings which highlights 156 such careers. (*For teachers, counselors and students*)

HOSPITAL CAREERS CALL FOR COURAGE. Revised 1955.

8 pages—10¢.
Glamour Magazine
420 Lexington Ave., New York 17, N. Y.

This magazine article reprint describes the nature of hospital work, training and earnings of the physician, professional nurse, practical nurse, nursing aide, med-ical technologist, x-ray technician, physical therapist, occupational therapist, medical social worker, dietitian, pharmacist, administrator, medical record librarian, and medical librarian. (*For female readers*)

PARTNERS FOR HEALTH. 1955.

40 pages—free to secondary schools and junior colleges.
National Health Council
1790 Broadway, New York 19, N. Y.

This booklet consists of the first thirty-nine pages of the *Health Careers Guidebook* and lacks only the section of health career briefings. (*For teachers, counselors and students*)

(also see fields of DENTISTRY, MENTAL HEALTH, NURSING, OCCUPATIONAL THERAPY, PHARMACY and PHYSICAL THERAPY)

For additional information, write to:

AMERICAN ASSOCIATION OF MEDICAL RECORD LIBRARIANS
510 No. Dearborn St., Chicago 10, Ill.

AMERICAN MEDICAL ASSOCIATION
535 No. Dearborn St., Chicago 10, Ill.

AMERICAN OSTEOPATHIC ASSOCIATION
212 East Ohio St., Chicago 11, Ill.

AMERICAN REGISTRY OF X-RAY TECHNICIANS
Metropolitan Bldg., Minneapolis 1, Minn.

NATIONAL ASSOCIATION OF CHIROPODISTS
3301 Sixteenth St., N. W.
Washington 10, D.C.

NATIONAL CHIROPRACTIC ASSOCIATION
National Bldg., Webster City, Iowa

REGISTRY OF MEDICAL TECHNOLOGISTS OF THE AMERICAN SOCIETY OF
CLINICAL PATHOLOGISTS
P. O. Box 1209, Muncie, Ind.

U. S. DEPT. OF HEALTH, EDUCATION AND WELFARE
Public Health Service, Washington 25, D. C.

MENTAL HEALTH

PSYCHIATRIC NURSES:
(D.O.T. Nos.: 0-33.36; 0-33.42)

CAREERS IN MENTAL HEALTH—
AS A PSYCHIATRIC NURSE. PUBLI-
CATION NO. 26. *Public Health Service,
U. S. Dept. of Health, Education, and
Welfare.* Revised 1954.

13 pages—10¢.
*Supt. of Documents, Govt. Printing
Office*
Washington 25, D. C.

This little booklet discusses the professional opportunities available in the field
of mental health, the specific job opportunities for psychiatric nurses, new chal-
lenges, personal qualifications, and
educational requirements.

PSYCHIATRIC SOCIAL WORKERS:
(D.O.T. No.: 0-27.20)

CAREERS IN MENTAL HEALTH—
AS A PSYCHIATRIC SOCIAL
WORKER. PUBLICATION NO. 28.
*Public Health Service, U. S. Dept. of
Health, Education, and Welfare.* Revised
1954.

14 pages—10¢.
*Supt. of Documents, Govt. Printing
Office*
Washington 25, D. C.

Discussed in this little booklet are the
nature of the work of the psychiatric social worker, places of employment,

personal qualifications, earnings, and
educational requirements.

PSYCHIATRIC SOCIAL WORKER.
H. A. Robinson. 1955.

6 pages—50¢; special to students, 25¢.
Personnel Services, Inc.
Main St., Peapack, N. J.

This pamphlet summarizes the importance and nature of the work, personal
qualifications, preparation, entrance and
advancement, earnings, opportunities for
servicemen, and advantages and disadvantages.

PSYCHIATRISTS:
(D.O.T. No.: 0-26.10)

CAREERS IN MENTAL HEALTH—
AS A PSYCHIATRIST. PUBLICATION
NO. 25. *Public Health Service, U. S.
Dept. of Health, Education, and Welfare.*
Revised 1954.

15 pages—10¢.
*Supt. of Documents, Govt. Printing
Office*
Washington 25, D. C.

This little booklet reviews the new frontiers in psychiatry, the nature of mental illness, what the psychiatrist does, the psychiatrist as a teamworker, need for research, where psychiatrists work, what they earn, and educational requirements.

PSYCHOLOGISTS:

(D.O.T. Nos.: 0-36.21 through 0-36.26)

CAREERS IN MENTAL HEALTH— AS A CLINICAL PSYCHOLOGIST. PUBLICATION NO. 27. *Public Health Service, U. S. Dept. of Health, Education, and Welfare.* Revised 1954.

 15 pages—10¢.
 Supt. of Documents, Govt. Printing Office
 Washington 25, D. C.

The importance of mental health services, the branches of psychology, applications of psychology, what the clinical psychologist does, typical places of employment, earnings, and educational requirements are included in this little booklet.

CLINICAL PSYCHOLOGIST. *G. J. Dudycha.* Revised 1956.

 6 pages—50¢; special to students, 25¢.
 Personnel Services, Inc.
 Main St., Peapack, N. J.

This "occupational abstract" summarizes future prospects in this field, it discusses the nature of the work, qualifications, training, certification, entrance, salaries, number and distribution, and advantages and disadvantages.

OPPORTUNITIES IN PSYCHOLOGY. *D. Super.* 1955.

 96 pages—$1.00.
 Vocational Guidance Manuals, Inc.

 1011 East Tremont Ave., New York 60, N. Y.

This "manual" presents a thorough coverage of the field; it discusses the nature of the work, growth and development of psychology, demand for services, financial and other rewards, typical places of employment, education and specialized training, getting started in the field, licensing, and professional organizations.

PSYCHOLOGISTS IN ACTION. PUBLIC AFFAIRS PAMPHLET NO. 229. *E. Ogg.* 1955.

 28 pages—25¢.
 Public Affairs Comm., Inc.
 22 East 38th St., New York 16, N. Y.

This pamphlet describes the nature of the activities of psychologists, specialties in this field, and importance of this work to society.

SCHOOL PSYCHOLOGIST. *G. J. Dudycha.* Revised 1956.

 6 pages—50¢; special to students, 25¢.
 Personnel Services, Inc.
 Main St., Peapack, N. J.

This pamphlet reviews the future prospects of the school psychologist, the nature of the work, qualifications, training, certification, entrance, salaries, number and distribution, and advantages and disadvantages.

MISCELLANEOUS:

CAREERS IN MENTAL HEALTH. PUBLICATION NO. 23. *Public Health Service, U. S. Dept. of Health, Education, and Welfare.* Revised 1956.

19 pages—20¢.

Supt. of Documents, Govt. Printing Office

Washington 25, D. C.

This booklet describes four branches in the field of mental health: psychiatry, psychiatric nursing, clinical psychology and psychiatric social work. Opportunities available, nature of the work, earnings, and requirements for the work are analyzed.

MIND WORK. *Mademoiselle's Jobs and Futures Dept.* 1954.

5 pages—25¢.

Alumnae Advisory Center, Inc.

541 Madison Ave., New York 22, N. Y.

The importance of their work to society, functions, educational preparation, qualifications, and earnings for psychiatric nurses, clinical psychologists, psychiatric social workers and psychiatrists are discussed in this magazine reprint. (*For female readers*)

(also see fields of MEDICAL AND HEALTH SERVICES, NURSING and SOCIAL SERVICE)

For additional information, write to:

AMERICAN ASSOCIATION OF PSYCHIATRIC SOCIAL WORKERS
1860 Broadway, New York 23, N. Y.

AMERICAN PSYCHIATRIC ASSOCIATION
1785 Massachusetts Ave., N. W.
Washington 6, D. C.

AMERICAN PSYCHOLOGICAL ASSOCIATION
1333 Sixteenth St., N. W., Washington 6, D. C.

NATIONAL ASSOCIATION FOR MENTAL HEALTH
1790 Broadway, New York 19, N. Y.

NATIONAL INSTITUTE OF MENTAL HEALTH
U. S. Dept. of Health, Education, and Welfare
Bethesda 14, Maryland

MERCHANDISING AND RETAILING

BUYERS:
(D.O.T. Nos.: 0-74.; 0-91.)

BUYER. 1954.

4 pages—35¢; special to students, 25¢.
Chronicle Guidance Publications
Moravia, N. Y.

This "occupational brief" reviews the history and nature of the work, working conditions, earnings, personal and educational requirements, chances for advancement, methods of obtaining employment, opportunities for women, and future prospects.

BUYER. 1954.

4 pages—15¢ in Canada, 20¢ elsewhere.
Guidance Centre, Univ. of Toronto
371 Bloor St. W., Toronto 5, Ontario

This "monograph" defines the job importance of this work to society, duties, personal qualifications, training, entrance into this field, earnings, related occupations, and advantages and disadvantages.

DEPARTMENT STORE BUYER. *S. Splaver.* Revised 1956.

6 pages—50¢; special to students, 25¢.
Personnel Services, Inc.
Main St., Peapack, N. J.

This pamphlet summarizes the nature of the work, qualifications, preparation, entrance and advancement, supply and demand, and advantages and disadvantages.

RETAILING—BUYER. 1954.

5 pages—10¢.
Glamour Magazine
420 Lexington Ave., New York 17, N. Y.

This "fact sheet" prepared by *Glamour's* Job Dept. reviews the nature of the work, how to get started in the field, advancement, salaries, training, and a partial list of schools offering courses in retailing. (*For female readers*)

THE YOUNG AMERICAN BUYER. *Mademoiselle's Jobs and Futures Dept.* 1954.

7 pages—25¢.
Alumnae Advisory Center, Inc.
541 Madison Ave., New York 22, N. Y.

The nature of the work of the store buyer, opportunities, earnings, qualifications, educational preparation, and chances for advancement are discussed in this magazine reprint. (*For female readers*)

DEPARTMENT STORE SALESCLERK:
(D.O.T. No.: 1-70.10)

DEPARTMENT STORE SALESCLERK. *S. Splaver.* 1954.

6 pages—50¢; special to students, 25¢.
Personnel Services, Inc.
Main St., Peapack, N. J.

Summarized in this "occupational abstract" are the nature of the work, qualifications, preparation, entrance and advancement, supply and demand, opportunities for servicemen, earnings, and advantages and disadvantages.

DISPLAY SPECIALISTS:

(D.O.T. No.: 0-43.30)

DISPLAY MAN. 1956.

4 pages—35¢; special to students, 25¢.
Chronicle Guidance Publications
Moravia, N. Y.

This "occupational brief" discusses the history and nature of the work performed, working conditions, wages, personal and training requirements, opportunities for women, outlook, where employed, methods of entry, and related jobs.

SHOWCASE FOR DIANE. *M. M. Freer.* 1951.

176 pages—$2.50.
Julian Messner, Inc.
8 West 40th St., New York 18, N. Y.

This career novel contains valuable information on the field of store display, nature of the work, training, how to get started, and advancement in this field. (*For teenage girls*)

MISCELLANEOUS:

CAREERS IN DEPARTMENT STORES. Revised 1956.

8 pages—25¢.
B'nai B'rith Vocational Service Bureau
1129 Vermont Ave., N. W., Washington 5, D. C.

This booklet discusses the future prospects in the field, nature of the job, opportunities available, how to get started in these careers, salaries, qualifications and training necessary for employment, and opportunities for advancement.

DEPARTMENT STORE JOBS. *Mademoiselle's Jobs and Futures Dept.* 1954.

3 pages—25¢.
Alumnae Advisory Center, Inc.
541 Madison Ave., New York 22, N. Y.

The nature of the work, qualifications, earnings, and how to enter upon the jobs as display artist, assistant buyer, layout artist, assistant fashion coordinator, assistant decorator, and copy writer are presented in this magazine reprint. (*For female readers*)

EMPLOYMENT OUTLOOK IN DEPARTMENT STORES. BULLETIN NO. 1020. *Bureau of Labor Statistics, U. S. Dept. of Labor.* 1951.

25 pages—20¢.
Supt. of Documents, Govt. Printing Office
Washington 25, D. C.

Another of the pamphlets in the employment outlook series, it presents the prospects for employment in the field, nature of the work opportunities, preparation for the work, working conditions, and salaries.

RETAIL BUSINESS PROPRIETOR. 1956.

4 pages—35¢; special to students, 25¢.
Chronicle Guidance Publications
Moravia, N. Y.

This "occupational brief" contains information on the kinds of retail businesses, choice of business, nature of work performed, working conditions, factors in success and failure, earnings, qualifications and training, and entry into business.

SHOULD YOU GO INTO FOOD RETAILING? *L. V. Eberhard*. 1957.

8 pages—free.
New York Life Insurance Co.
51 Madison Ave., New York 10, N. Y.

This public service pamphlet gives many statistics on expansion in food retailing and describes some of the 249 positions available. Also included is information on salary, hints for starting your own supermarket, personal qualifications for success, work conditions, and colleges offering special training and scholarships.

SHOULD YOU GO INTO RETAILING? *F. Lazarus, Jr.* 1956.

12 pages—free.
New York Life Insurance Co.
51 Madison Ave., New York 10, N. Y.

Five retailing executives have a roundtable discussion here and review opportunities in the field, advantages and disadvantages, salaries, preparation, and qualities for success.

(also see fields of BUSINESS ADMINISTRATION, CLOTHING AND FASHION, and PERSONNEL ADMINISTRATION)

For additional information, write to:

U. S. DEPT. OF COMMERCE
Washington 25, D. C.

PROSPECTORS:

(D.O.T. No.: 5-22.950)

PROSPECTOR. Revised 1955.

4 pages—15¢ in Canada, 20¢ elsewhere.

Guidance Centre, Univ. of Toronto
371 Bloor St. W., Toronto 5, Ontario

This "monograph" reviews the nature of the work performed, working conditions, personal qualifications, preparation for the work, advancement opportunities, earnings, how to get started, and related occupations.

MISCELLANEOUS:

OPPORTUNITIES IN CERAMICS.
S. R. Scholes. 1953.

96 pages—$1.00.
Vocational Guidance Manuals, Inc.
1011 East Tremont Ave., New York 60, N. Y.

This "manual" describes the growth and development of this field and its branches, the work of the ceramist, attributes necessary for success, demand, remuneration, ceramic education, and getting the job.

OPPORTUNITIES IN THE PETROLEUM INDUSTRY. *G. Patrick.* 1952.

95 pages—$1.00.
Vocational Guidance Manuals, Inc.
1011 East Tremont Ave., New York 60, N. Y.

Here is information on the scope of the industry, the nature of the varied opportunities, qualifications, educational requirements, and earnings.

OPPORTUNITIES IN PLASTICS. *D. A. Dearle.* 1953.

128 pages—$1.00.

Vocational Guidance Manuals, Inc.
1011 East Tremont Ave., New York 60, N. Y.

This "manual" discusses the history and nature of plastic materials, qualifications necessary for success in this industry, preparation, job and career opportunities, getting started, organizations in this industry, and a list of colleges offering plastics study.

SHOULD YOU GO INTO THE MINERAL INDUSTRY? *J. W. Vanderwilt.* 1956.

8 pages—free.
New York Life Insurance Co.
51 Madison Ave., New York 10, N. Y.

This career booklet describes the importance of this industry to society, nature of the work of varied personnel in this field, opportunities for employment, financial and other rewards, disadvantages, personal requirements, preparations, and outlook.

(also see fields of ENGINEERING, and SCIENCE)

For additional information, write to:

AMERICAN CERAMIC SOCIETY
2525 No. High St., Columbus 2, Ohio

AMERICAN INSTITUTE OF MINING AND METALLURGICAL ENGINEERS
29 West 39th St., New York 18, N. Y.

AMERICAN PETROLEUM INSTITUTE
50 West 50th St., New York 20, N. Y.

SOCIETY OF THE PLASTICS INDUSTRY
67 West 44th St., New York 18, N. Y.

NURSING

MALE NURSES:
(D.O.T. Nos.: 0-33.)

MAN NURSE. 1955.

4 pages—35¢; special to students, 25¢.
Chronicle Guidance Publications
Moravia, N. Y.

Included in this "occupational brief" are the history and nature of the work, working conditions, wages, qualifications, educational requirements, licensing, getting the job, future prospects, typical places of employment, and related jobs.

PRACTICAL NURSES:
(D.O.T. No.: 2-38.20)

NURSING ASSISTANT. Revised 1956.

4 pages—15¢ in Canada, 20¢ elsewhere.
Guidance Centre, Univ. of Toronto
371 Bloor St. W., Toronto 5, Ontario

This "monograph" describes the history and nature of the work, working conditions, qualifications and preparation needed, advancement, remuneration, advantages and disadvantages, and how to get started.

THE OUTLOOK FOR WOMEN AS PRACTICAL NURSES AND AUXILIARY WORKERS ON THE NURSING TEAM. MEDICAL SERVICES SERIES BULLETIN NO. 203-5. *Women's Bureau, U. S. Dept. of Labor.* 1953.

62 pages—40¢.
Supt. of Documents, Govt. Printing Office
Washington 25, D. C.

This pamphlet highlights the employment outlook for women in these occupations, the nature of the work, working conditions, training, and how to find employment.

PRACTICAL NURSE. 1952.

4 pages—35¢; special to students, 25¢.
Chronicle Guidance Publications
Moravia, N. Y.

Reviewed in this "occupational brief" are the history and nature of the work performed, working conditions, qualifications, training requirements, wages, where to find employment, opportunities for men, methods of entry, related jobs, and employment outlook.

PRACTICAL NURSE. *S. Splaver.* 1955.

6 pages—50¢; special to students, 25¢.
Personnel Services, Inc.
Main St., Peapack, N. J.

Described here are the history of the occupation, nature of the work, qualifications, preparation, licensing, entrance, supply and demand, opportunities for servicemen, earnings, and advantages and disadvantages.

TRAINED PRACTICAL NURSE. *H. M. Torrop.* 1954.

32 pages—$1.00.
Research Publishing Co., Inc.
P. O. Box 245, Boston 1, Mass.

The nature of the work, the beginnings of the field of practical nursing, employment opportunities, salaries, working conditions, qualifications and entrance requirements, training and licensing, getting the job, and typical places of employment are described in this booklet.

PUBLIC HEALTH NURSES:

(D.O.T. Nos.: 0-33.50 through 0-33.59)

THE PUBLIC HEALTH NURSE. 1954.

> 4 pages—free to high school principals and guidance officers.
> *Simmons College*
> 300 The Fenway, Boston 15, Mass.

Contained in this folder is information on the nature of the work of the public health nurse, need for these services in many areas, preparation, professional training in college and hospital, and the responsibilities and rewards in this field.

REGISTERED NURSES:

(D.O.T. Nos.: 0-33.)

A CAP FOR CORINNE. *Z. K. MacDonald.* 1952.

> 184 pages—$2.95.
> *Julian Messner, Inc.*
> 8 West 40th St., New York 18, N. Y.

Another of Messner's "romances for young moderns," this career novel incorporates information about the training and nature of the nurse's activities into the romance theme. *(For teen-age girls)*

HEALTH ABROAD—AN OPPORTUNITY FOR NURSES. *U. S. Dept. of Health, Education, and Welfare in cooperation with U. S. Foreign Operations Administration.* 1954.

> 20 pages—20¢.
> *Supt. of Documents, Govt. Printing Office*
> Washington 25, D. C.

The objectives of the U. S. Foreign Operations Administration's nursing program, typical programs in foreign countries, how to join the overseas health program, qualifications, salaries, and method of making application for these overseas positions are discussed in this booklet.

LINDA KENT, STUDENT NURSE. *D. Deming.* 1952.

> 274 pages—$2.50.
> *Dodd, Mead and Co., Inc.*
> 432 Fourth Ave., New York 16, N. Y.

Interwoven into the fictional tale of this career novel is a good deal of valuable information on the college and hospital training of registered nurses, the nature of their work, and the experiences which may await them. *(For teen-age girls)*

NURSE. 1954.

> 4 pages—35¢; special to students, 25¢.
> *Chronicle Guidance Publications*
> Moravia, N. Y.

This "occupational brief" reviews the history and nature of the work, working conditions, earnings, personal requirements, preparation, advancement, how to get started, typical places of employment, future prospects, licensing, and related occupations.

NURSE. Revised 1956.

4 pages—15¢ in Canada, 20¢ elsewhere.
Guidance Centre, Univ. of Toronto
371 Bloor St. W., Toronto 5, Ontario

Included in this "monograph" are the importance to society and nature of this work, working conditions, qualifications and preparation, methods of entry, advancement opportunities, earnings, advantages and disadvantages, and related jobs.

REGISTERED NURSE. *S. Splaver.* 1954.

6 pages—50¢; special to students, 25¢.
Personnel Services, Inc.
Main St., Peapack, N. J.

Summarized in this "occupational abstract" are the history of this occupation, nature of the work, qualifications, preparation, registration, entrance and advance-

ment, opportunities for servicemen, supply and demand, earnings, and advantages and disadvantages.

SHOULD YOU BE A NURSE? *R. Sleeper.* 1955.

8 pages—free.
New York Life Insurance Co.
51 Madison Ave., New York 10, N. Y.

This booklet discusses the gratification and importance of this work, number of registered nurses, demand for such services, typical places of employment, training and costs, earnings, and qualifications necessary for success in this field.

SUE MORRIS, SKY NURSE. *D. Deming.* 1953.

256 pages—$2.50.
Dodd, Mead and Co., Inc.
432 Fourth Ave., New York 16, N. Y.

This fictional tale of the experiences of an aviation nurse includes worthwhile occupational information on the nature of the work, qualifications and training, and job opportunities. *(For teen-age girls)*

MISCELLANEOUS:

CAREERS FOR NURSES. *D. Deming.* Reprinted 1952.

351 pages—$4.50.
McGraw-Hill Book Co., Inc.
330 West 42nd St., New York 36, N. Y.

A comprehensive presentation of the job opportunities available to nurses, this book describes the numerous branches of nursing, nature of the work of the nurses in these different areas, working conditions, earnings, qualifications and preparation necessary for success, and employment prospects.

NURSING. 1954.

10 pages—10¢.
Glamour Magazine
420 Lexington Ave., New York 17, N. Y.

This "fact sheet" discusses the growth of the nursing profession, qualifications, education and registration, salaries, advantages and disadvantages, opportunities for advancement, and overseas opportunities for professional nurses. It also includes information on the general qualifications, preparation, salaries, and opportunities for practical nurses.

OPPORTUNITIES IN NURSING. *E. P. Lewis*. 1952.

> 128 pages—$1.00.
> *Vocational Guidance Manuals, Inc.*
> 1011 East Tremont Ave., New York 60, N. Y.

This comprehensive "manual" discusses the growth and scope of the modern nursing profession, varied fields of nursing and allied fields, process of becoming a nurse and getting started in the profession, working conditions, advancement, and opportunities in practical nursing.

THE OUTLOOK FOR WOMEN IN PROFESSIONAL NURSING OCCUPATIONS. MEDICAL SERVICES SERIES BULLETIN NO. 203-3. *Women's Bureau, U. S. Dept. of Labor.* 1953.

> 80 pages—30¢.
> *Supt. of Documents, Govt. Printing Office*
> Washington 25, D. C.

This pamphlet discusses the major fields of nursing and the future prospects for women in the field, nature of the work opportunities, working conditions, qualifications and training requirements for Federal civil service employment as a nurse, and suggestions to the prospective nurse.

THE STORY OF NURSING. *B. S. Dodge*. 1954.

> 243 pages—$3.00.
> *Little, Brown and Co., Inc.*
> 34 Beacon St., Boston 6, Mass.

This book presents a thorough coverage of the history and growth of the nursing profession, the nurse's war-time role, the origin of the training schools, typical places of employment, gratifications of being a member of this profession, and the nature of nursing services.

(also see fields of MEDICAL AND HEALTH SERVICES, and MENTAL HEALTH)

For additional information, write to:

AMERICAN NURSES ASSOCIATION
2 Park Ave., New York 16, N. Y.

NATIONAL ASSOCIATION FOR PRACTICAL NURSE EDUCATION
654 Madison Ave., New York 21, N. Y.

NATIONAL LEAGUE FOR NURSING, COMMITTEE ON CAREERS
2 Park Ave., New York 16, N. Y.

OCCUPATIONAL THERAPY

OCCUPATIONAL THERAPISTS:

(D.O.T. No:. 0-32.04)

CAREERS IN OCCUPATIONAL THERAPY. *R. Wolozin.* 1955.

> 8 pages—25¢.
> *B'nai B'rith Vocational Service Bureau*
> 1129 Vermont Ave., N. W., Washington 5, D. C.

The importance to society, nature of the work, employment prospects, qualifications, certification, educational requirements, advancement, earnings, typical places of employment, and advantages and disadvantages of a career in occupational therapy are discussed in this pamphlet.

DO YOU BELONG IN THIS PROFESSION? OCCUPATIONAL THERAPY, PHYSICAL THERAPY, A CAREER FOR YOU. PAMPHLET 5-9. *U. S. Veterans Administration.* 1953.

> 8 pages—5¢.
> *Supt. of Documents, Govt. Printing Office*
> Washington 25, D. C.

The opportunities in these fields, qualifications, training, earnings, and employment prospects are discussed here.

OCCUPATIONAL THERAPIST. 1954.

> 4 pages—35¢; special to students, 25¢.
> *Chronicle Guidance Publications*
> Moravia, N. Y.

This "occupational brief" reviews the history and nature of the work performed, working conditions, wages, personal qualifications, preparation, opportunities for promotion, where to find employment, methods of entry, and related jobs.

OCCUPATIONAL THERAPIST. Revised 1954.

> 4 pages—15¢ in Canada, 20¢ elsewhere.
> *Guidance Centre, Univ. of Toronto*
> 371 Bloor St. W., Toronto 5, Ontario

This "monograph" discusses the history, importance, and nature of the work, working conditions, qualifications and preparation needed, opportunities for advancement, remuneration, advantages and disadvantages, how to get started, and related occupations.

OCCUPATIONAL THERAPY. *Women's Medical Specialist Corps, U. S. Army Medical Service.* 1952.

> 6 pages—5¢.
> *Supt. of Documents, Govt. Printing Office*
> Washington 25, D. C.

The nature of the work of the occupational therapist, qualifications, training opportunities, and opportunities for commissions in the U. S. Army are discussed in this pamphlet.

OCCUPATIONAL THERAPY AS A CAREER. *Women's Bureau, U. S. Dept. of Labor.* 1953.

> 8 pages—5¢.
> *Supt. of Documents, Govt. Printing Office*
> Washington 25, D. C.

This booklet sets forth the work involved in this field, training required, advancement opportunities, and job prospects. *(For high school and college girls)*

OPPORTUNITIES IN OCCUPA-
TIONAL THERAPY. *M. L. Franciscus.*
1952.

    112 pages—$1.00.
Vocational Guidance Manuals, Inc.
1129 Vermont Ave., N. W., Washing-
    ton 5, D. C.

This "manual" presents the development
and growth of the field of occupational
therapy, requirements for entering the
field, job descriptions, employment trends
and prospects, related fields, and a list
of schools offering courses in occupational
therapy.

THE OUTLOOK FOR WOMEN
AS OCCUPATIONAL THERAPISTS.
BULLETIN NO. 203-2. *Women's Bu-
reau, U. S. Dept. of Labor.* 1952.

    51 pages—20¢.
*Supt. of Documents, Govt. Printing
    Office*
Washington 25, D. C.

Reviewed in this bulletin are the duties
of occupational therapists, earnings, employment trends and outlook, advancement opportunities, qualifications for
admission to training schools, registration
requirements, and requirements for Federal civil service employment in this field.

*(also see fields of MEDICAL AND HEALTH SERVICES, MENTAL
HEALTH, and PHYSICAL THERAPY)*

For additional information, write to:

AMERICAN OCCUPATIONAL THERAPY ASSOCIATION
33 West 42nd St., New York 36, N. Y.

OPTICS

OPHTHALMOLOGISTS:

(D.O.T. No.: 0-26.10)

OPHTHALMOLOGIST. *W. Brackett and H. A. Robinson.* 1956.

  6 pages—50¢; special to students, 25¢.
  Personnel Services, Inc.
  Main St., Peapack, N. J.

This "occupational abstract" summarizes the growth of the profession; it discusses the nature of the work, qualifications, preparation, certification, entrance and advancement, earnings, number and distribution, future prospects, opportunities in military services, advantages and disadvantages, and related occupations.

OPTICIANS:

(D.O.T. Nos.: 5-08.)

OPTICIAN. 1955.

  4 pages—35¢; special to students, 25¢.
  Chronicle Guidance Publications
  Moravia, N. Y.

This "occupational brief" discusses the history and nature of work performed, working conditions, wages, personal and training requirements, outlook, opportunities for women, where to find employment, and methods of entry.

OPTICIANS. Revised 1955.

  16 pages—25¢.
  Michigan Employment Security Comm.
  7310 Woodward Ave., Detroit 2, Mich.

This guide contains information on the history and importance of the work, duties, future prospects, personal qualifications, educational requirements, advancement, earnings, working conditions, and advantages and disadvantages.

OPTOMETRISTS:

(D.O.T. No.: 0-39.92)

CAREER AS OPTOMETRIST. 1955.

  8 pages—25¢.
  B'nai B'rith Vocational Service Bureau
  1129 Vermont Ave., N. W., Washington 5, D. C.

The nature of the work, personal and educational requirements, costs of training, licensing, getting started in the field, earnings, and advantages and disadvantages are discussed in this booklet.

OPTOMETRIST. 1954.

  4 pages—35¢; special to students, 25¢.
  Chronicle Guidance Publications
  Moravia, N. Y.

This "occupational brief" reviews the importance and nature of the work performed, working conditions, earnings, qualifications and preparation, typical places of employment, methods of entering this field, outlook, and licensing.

OPTOMETRIST. Revised 1953.

4 pages—15¢ in Canada, 20¢ elsewhere.

Guidance Centre, Univ. of Toronto

371 Bloor St. W., Toronto 5, Ontario

This "monograph" defines the job, lists qualifications, training required, earnings, working conditions, advancement opportunities, advantages and disadvantages, how to get started, and related occupations.

OPTOMETRIST. Revised 1954.

20 pages—25¢.

Michigan Employment Security Comm.

7310 Woodward Ave., Detroit 2, Mich.

Contained in this pamphlet are the history of optometry, duties, future prospects for employment in the field, working conditions, earnings, qualifications for employment, preparation, opportunities for women in optometry, and advantages and disadvantages.

ORTHOPTIC TECHNICIANS:

(D.O.T. No.: 5-08.010)

ORTHOPTIC TECHNICIAN. *W. Brackett and H. A. Robinson.* 1953.

6 pages—50¢; special to students, 25¢.

Personnel Services, Inc.

Main St., Peapack, N. J.

This "occupational abstract" reviews the nature of the work, future prospects, qualifications, preparation, certification, entrance and advancement, earnings, number and distribution, and advantages and disadvantages.

MISCELLANEOUS:

OPPORTUNITIES IN OPTOMETRY AND OPTICS. *P. Pollack.* 1955.

95 pages—$1.00.

Vocational Guidance Manuals, Inc.

1011 East Tremont Ave., New York 60, N. Y.

The history and importance of optometry, number and distribution of optometrists and opticians, nature of the work, educational requirements, personal traits needed, incomes, getting started, and optical engineering as a career are described here.

(also see fields of MEDICAL AND HEALTH SERVICES)

For additional information, write to:

AMERICAN ASSOCIATION OF ORTHOPTIC TECHNICIANS
4753 Broadway, Chicago 40, Ill.

AMERICAN BOARD OF OPHTHALMOLOGY
Ivie Rd., Box 236, Cape Cottage Branch, Portland, Maine

AMERICAN OPTOMETRIC ASSOCIATION
707 Jenkins Bldg., Pittsburgh 22, Pa.

PERFORMANCE

ACTORS:
(D.O.T. Nos.: 0-02.)

OPPORTUNITIES IN ACTING. *F. Vreeland*. 1951.

128 pages—$1.00.
Vocational Guidance Manuals, Inc.
1011 East Tremont Ave., New York 60, N. Y.

This "manual" presents the art and rewards of acting, how to learn acting, types of acting positions, getting an acting job, and a list of colleges or institutions offering degrees in dramatic arts.

THE YOUNG ACTRESS IN NEW YORK. *Mademoiselle's College and Careers Dept.* 1956.

4 pages—25¢.
Alumnae Advisory Center, Inc.
541 Madison Ave., New York 22, N. Y.

This magazine reprint discusses the fierce competition for roles on the Broadway stage and offers some brief illustrations of girls who have come to New York hoping for success. *(For female college students)*

CIRCUS PERFORMERS:
(D.O.T. Nos.: 0-62.)

THE RINGLINGS; THE WIZARDS OF THE CIRCUS. *A. Harlow*. 1951.

181 pages—$2.95.
Julian Messner, Inc.
8 West 40th St., New York 18, N. Y.

This book relates the experience of the Ringling brothers and their circuses. Included in it is much information about the work of those who create and participate in circuses.

DANCERS:
(D.O.T. Nos.: 0-45.)

BALLET TEACHER. *L. Wyndham.* 1956.

192 pages—$2.95.
Julian Messner, Inc.
8 West 40th St., New York 18, N. Y.

This career novel presents occupational information about the field of ballet dancing as it unwinds the tale of the heroine's

attempts to develop ballet stars in her dancing school. *(For teen-age girls)*

DANCE TO THE PIPER. *A. G. deMille.* 1952.

342 pages—$3.50.
Little, Brown and Co.
34 Beacon St., Boston 6, Mass.

This is the autobiography of Agnes deMille, the famed choreographer. It is an inspiring tale for those who seek professional dancing careers and contains worthwhile occupational information on the work of the choreographer, entrance into this field, and progress in it.

DANCER. *S. Splaver.* 1952.

6 pages—50¢; special to students, 25¢.
Personnel Services, Inc.
Main St., Peapack, N. J.

Reviewed in this "occupational abstract" are the history of this form of expression, nature of the work of the professional dancer, qualifications, preparation, entrance and advancement, earnings, and advantages and disadvantages.

DANCERS OF THE BALLET. *M. F. Atkinson and M. Hillman.* 1955.

174 pages—$3.75.
Alfred A. Knopf, Inc.
501 Madison Ave., New York 22, N. Y.

The makings of a ballet star and a ballet are discussed here. Also included are tales of the careers of a number of outstanding dancers.

THE DANCING HEART. *L. G. Rosenheim.* 1951.

183 pages—$2.95.
Julian Messner, Inc.
8 West 40th St., New York 18, N. Y.

This career novel incorporates occupational information on the work of the ballet dancer into this romantic tale. *(For teen-age girls)*

FAMOUS BALLET DANCERS. *J. T. McConnell.* 1955.

176 pages—$2.75.
Thomas Y. Crowell Co.
432 Fourth Ave., New York 16, N. Y.

Valuable occupational information is incorporated into the biographical tales of such well-known dancers as Leslie Caron,

Alicia Markova, Moira Shearer and Maria Tallchief.

FOR DANCE MAJORS. *Mademoiselle's College and Careers Dept.* Revised 1954.

5 pages—25¢.
Alumnae Advisory Center, Inc.
541 Madison Ave., New York 22, N. Y.

Opportunities available in this field and valuable advice are presented in this magazine reprint. *(For female college students)*

PRIMA BALLERINA. *G. Malvern.* 1951.

179 pages—$2.95.
Julian Messner, Inc.
8 West 40th St., New York 18, N. Y.

The heroine of this career novel is a ballet dancer. Her adventures with a ballet company and her progress in this field are incorporated into the romantic tale. *(For teen-age girls)*

STAR PERFORMANCE. *W. Terry.* 1954.

224 pages—$2.95.
Doubleday and Co., Inc.
14 West 49th St., New York 20, N. Y.

This book relates the professional lives of some of the world's great ballerinas from Catherine de Medici to Alicia Markova. Much information about the nature of the work, qualifications, preparation, and working conditions is included.

STUDENT DANCER. *R. Woody.* 1951.

276 pages—$2.75.
Houghton-Mifflin Co.
2 Park St., Boston 7, Mass.

This is another career novel. Included in the fictional tale is a good bit of occupational information on the nature of the work of professional dancers and the career opportunities open to them. *(For teen-age girls)*

MODELS:

(D.O.T. Nos.: 2-43.40 through 2-43.49)

MODEL. 1953.

4 pages—35¢; special to students, 25¢.
Chronicle Guidance Publications
Moravia, N. Y.

This "occupational brief" reviews the nature of the work, working conditions, earnings, personal and training requirements, typical places of employment, how to get started, and opportunities for advancement.

MODELING. *Mademoiselle's College and Careers Dept.* Revised 1954.

5 pages—25¢.
Alumnae Advisory Center, Inc.
541 Madison Ave., New York 22, N. Y.

This magazine reprint answers questions regarding qualifications, how to get started, role of agencies, types of modeling, earnings, and what makes a successful model. *(For female readers)*

MODELING. *H. Conover.* Revised 1955.

22 pages—$1.00.
Bellman Publishing Co.
P. O. Box 172, Cambridge 38, Mass.

This authoritative pamphlet discusses who can become a model, preparation for becoming a model, various forms of modeling, how to secure a modeling position, model agencies and how they function, salaries, and related fields.

MODELING. 1955.

4 pages—10¢.
Glamour Magazine
420 Lexington Ave., New York 17, N. Y.

The modeling field, typical places of employment, types of models, how to get started in the field, earnings, opportunities in television, and training are presented in this "fact sheet." *(For female readers)*

SHOULD YOU BE A MODEL? *C. J. Conover.* 1956.

48 pages—$1.00.
Occu-Press
489 Fifth Ave., New York 17, N. Y.

Written by the famous model, Candy Jones Conover, this attractive pamphlet presents the history of modeling, opportunities today, classifications of modeling, TV model-actresses, what it takes to succeed in modeling, supply and demand, model agents, a typical working day, opportunities for males and children, earnings, advantages and disadvantages, and outlook.

MUSICIANS:

(D.O.T. Nos.: 0-24.)

INSTRUMENTAL MUSICIAN. 1954.

4 pages—35¢; special to students, 25¢.
Chronicle Guidance Publications
Moravia, N. Y.

Contained in this "occupational brief" is information on the history and nature of the work, working conditions, earnings, personal qualifications, preparation, future prospects, typical places of employment, methods of entry, and related jobs.

MUSICIAN. 1956.

4 pages—15¢ in Canada, 20¢ elsewhere.

Guidance Centre, Univ. of Toronto
371 Bloor St. W., Toronto 5, Ontario
This "monograph" describes the history and nature of the work, working conditions, qualifications and preparation, advancement, remuneration, advantages and disadvantages, how to get started, and related occupations.

MUSICIAN. *S. Splaver.* 1951.

6 pages—50¢; special to students, 25¢.
Personnel Services, Inc.
Main St., Peapack, N. J.
Summarized in this "occupational abstract" are the nature of the work, qualifications, preparation, entrance and advancement, supply and demand, earnings, and advantages and disadvantages.

OPPORTUNITIES IN MUSIC. *S. Spaeth.* 1951.

128 pages—$1.00.

Vocational Guidance Manuals, Inc.
1011 East Tremont Ave., New York 60, N. Y.
This "manual" describes the art and business of music, individual fields of performance, varied opportunities available in singing, conducting, composing, arranging, songwriting and teaching music, and qualifications and preparation.

PROFESSIONAL MUSICIANS. Revised 1955.

20 pages—25¢.
Michigan Employment Security Comm.
7310 Woodward Ave., Detroit 2, Mich.
This pamphlet describes the history and importance of this field, nature of the work performed by professional musicians, outlook for employment, qualifications for success, specialized training, how to get started, earnings, regularity of employment, and advantages and disadvantages.

PUPPETEERS:

(D.O.T. No.: 7-13.013)

RAGAMUFFIN ALLEY. *D. G. Butters.* 1951.

206 pages—$2.50.
Macrae-Smith Co.
225 So. 15th St., Philadelphia 2, Pa.
This career novel deals with the experiences of several young people who work together to create a puppet theater. There is worthwhile occupational information on the nature of the work of the puppeteer interwoven into the fictional tale. *(For teen-agers)*

SINGERS:

(D.O.T. Nos.: 0-24.00 through 0-24.09)

GETTING A START IN OPERA. *Mademoiselle's College and Careers Dept.* 1954.

5 pages—25¢.

Alumnae Advisory Center, Inc.
541 Madison Ave., New York 22, N. Y.
The difficulties encountered in attempting

128

to become an opera star, preparation and cost of training, when and where to make the formal debut, and amateur and professional opera companies are discussed here. *(For female readers)*

SINGER. *S. Splaver.* 1952.

 6 pages—50¢; special to students, 25¢.

Personnel Services, Inc.
Main St., Peapack, N. J.

This "occupational abstract" summarizes the nature of the work, qualifications, preparation, entrance and advancement, geographic distribution, opportunities for servicemen, supply and demand, earnings, and advantages and disadvantages.

MISCELLANEOUS:

JOBS IN THE RECORD INDUSTRY.
Mademoiselle's College and Careers Dept.
1956.

 5 pages—25¢.
 Alumnae Advisory Center, Inc.
 541 Madison Ave., New York 22, N. Y.

Music, art and English majors will find interesting job opportunities in the record industry according to this magazine reprint. *(For female college students)*

USHER. 1954.

 4 pages—35¢; special to students, 25¢.
 Chronicle Guidance Publications
 Moravia, N. Y.

This "occupational brief" defines the job, duties, working conditions, wages, qualifications and preparation, outlook, opportunities for women, typical places of employment, methods of entry, and related jobs.

(also see fields of COMMUNICATIONS AND ELECTRONICS)

For additional information, write to:

ACTORS EQUITY ASSOCIATION
45 West 47th St., New York 19, N. Y.

AMERICAN FEDERATION OF MUSICIANS
570 Lexington Ave., New York 22, N. Y.

AMERICAN GUILD OF VARIETY ARTISTS
1697 Broadway, New York 19, N. Y.

SCREEN ACTORS GUILD
7046 Hollywood Blvd., Hollywood 28, Calif.

PERSONNEL ADMINISTRATION

EMPLOYMENT INTERVIEWERS:
(D.O.T. No.: 0-68.71)

EMPLOYMENT INTERVIEWER. *V. F. Group.* 1955.

6 pages—50¢; special to students, 25¢.
Personnel Services, Inc.
Main St., Peapack, N. J.

This "occupational abstract" summarizes the history and nature of the work, future prospects, qualifications, preparation, entrance and advancement, earnings, and number and distribution of interviewers.

LABOR RELATIONS SPECIALISTS:
(D.O.T. No.: 0-68.76)

CAREERS IN LABOR RELATIONS. 1953.

6 pages—25¢.
B'nai B'rith Vocational Service Bureau
1129 Vermont Ave. N. W., Washington 5, D. C.

This booklet discusses the employment outlook in this field, nature of the work performed, personal qualifications, educational requirements, getting started, beginners' jobs and salaries.

LABOR RELATIONS SPECIALIST. 1953.

4 pages—35¢; special to students, 25¢.
Chronicle Guidance Publications
Moravia, N. Y.

Reviewed in this "occupational brief" are the nature of the work performed, working conditions, remuneration, qualifications and preparation, methods of obtaining such employment, typical places of employment, and future prospects.

TRAINING DIRECTORS:
(D.O.T. No.: 0-39.87)

TRAINING DIRECTOR. *V. F. Group.* 1955.

6 pages—50¢; special to students, 25¢.
Personnel Services, Inc.
Main St., Peapack, N. J.

Summarized in this "occupational abstract" are the history of the occupation, nature of the work, future prospects, qualifications, preparation, entrance and advancement, earnings, and number and distribution.

MISCELLANEOUS:

A FLAIR FOR PEOPLE. *H. A. Wells.*
1955.

> 192 pages—$2.95.
> *Julian Messner, Inc.*
> 8 West 40th St., New York 18, N. Y.

A good deal of valuable occupational information is included in this career novel. Incorporated into the fictional tale of the heroine's experiences in the personnel field is information on the nature of the work, qualifications, preparation, and advantages and disadvantages. *(For teen-age girls)*

PERSONNEL ADMINISTRATION. *C. C. Sorenson.* 1955.

> 18 pages—$1.00.
> *Bellman Publishing Co.*
> P. O. Box 172, Cambridge 38, Mass.

This "monograph" details the history and development of personnel administration, the functions in a personnel department, qualifications of a personnel director, scholastic training needed, employment opportunities, remuneration, opportunities for advancement, and advantages and disadvantages.

PERSONNEL WORK. 1955.

> 4 pages—10¢.
> *Glamour Magazine*
> 420 Lexington Ave., New York 17, N. Y.

The general functions of a personnel department are described in this "fact sheet," in addition to the jobs within a personnel department, qualifications, and training for such jobs. *(For female readers)*

SHOULD YOU GO INTO PERSONNEL WORK? *C. S. Ching.* 1955.

> 8 pages—free.
> *New York Life Insurance Co.*
> 51 Madison Ave., New York 10, N. Y.

This booklet highlights the importance of personnel work, functions of a personnel department, places of employment of personnel workers, specialized training, practical experience, opportunities for women, qualifications for success, and financial and other rewards.

STORE PERSONNEL JOBS: PICKING THE WINNERS. *Mademoiselle's Jobs and Futures Dept.* 1954.

> 5 pages—25¢.
> *Alumnae Advisory Center, Inc.*
> 541 Madison Ave., New York 22, N. Y.

The job opportunities in department store personnel administration, nature of the work, qualifications, preparation and earnings are discussed in this magazine reprint. *(For female readers)*

(also see fields of EDUCATION, and MERCHANDISING AND RETAILING)

For additional information, write to:

AMERICAN MANAGEMENT ASSOCIATION
330 West 42nd St., New York 36, N. Y.

AMERICAN PERSONNEL AND GUIDANCE ASSOCIATION
1535 "O" St., N. W., Washington 5, D. C.

PHARMACY

PHARMACISTS:

(D.O.T. Nos.: 0-25.)

PHARMACIST. 1954.

4 pages—35¢; special to students, 25¢.
Chronicle Guidance Publications
Moravia, N. Y.

This "occupational brief" reviews the importance and nature of the work performed, working conditions, remuneration, qualifications and preparation, advancement opportunities, how to enter this field, places of employment, future prospects, opportunities for women, and related jobs.

PHARMACIST. Revised 1953.

4 pages—15¢ in Canada, 20¢ elsewhere.
Guidance Centre, Univ. of Toronto
371 Bloor St. W., Toronto 5, Ontario

Included in this "monograph" are job definition, functions of the pharmacist, qualifications, specialized training, earnings, working conditions, methods of entry, advantages and disadvantages, and related occupations.

PHARMACISTS. Revised 1955.

20 pages—25¢.
Michigan Employment Security Comm.
7310 Woodward Ave., Detroit 2, Mich.

A thorough coverage of the field is presented in this pamphlet which includes a discussion of the history of pharmacy, nature of the work, employment outlook, number and distribution of pharmacists, qualifications and educational requirements, entering the field, remuneration, and opportunities for women.

SHOULD YOU BE A PHARMACIST?
W. P. Briggs. 1955.

12 pages—free.
New York Life Insurance Co.
51 Madison Ave., New York 10, N. Y.

This career booklet highlights the pharmacist's importance to society, history of pharmacy, places of employment and number of pharmacists, earnings, advantages and disadvantages, personal requisites for success, women pharmacists, preparation, and licensing. It also includes a list of pharmacy colleges.

(also see fields of MEDICAL AND HEALTH SERVICES, and SCIENCE)

For additional information, write to:

AMERICAN PHARMACEUTICAL ASSOCIATION
2215 Constitution Ave., N. W., Washington, D. C.

PHOTOGRAPHY

MOTION PICTURE PROJECTIONISTS:
(D.O.T. No.: 555.010)

MOTION PICTURE PROJECTIONIST.
1954.
> 4 pages—35¢; special to students, 25¢.
> *Chronicle Guidance Publications*
> Moravia, N. Y.

This "occupational brief" reviews the nature of the work, working conditions, earnings, personal qualifications, preparation, how to get started in this field, future prospects, and related jobs.

PHOTOGRAPHERS:
(D.O.T. Nos.: 0-56.)

COMMERCIAL PHOTOGRAPHER.
1952.
> 4 pages—35¢; special to students, 25¢.
> *Chronicle Guidance Publications*
> Moravia, N. Y.

Described in this "occupational brief" are the nature of the work, working conditions, earnings, other types of photographers, outlook, how to get started, qualifications and preparation, and related jobs.

KATIE AND HER CAMERA. *L. Hobart.* 1955.
> 192 pages—$2.95.
> *Julian Messner, Inc.*
> 8 West 40th St., New York 18, N. Y.

The photographic experiences of the heroine in this very readable career novel provide much valuable occupational information for young people aspiring to careers in photography. *(For teen-age girls)*

PHOTOGRAPHER. Revised 1954.
> 4 pages—15¢ in Canada, 20¢ elsewhere.
> *Guidance Centre, Univ. of Toronto*
> 371 Bloor St. W., Toronto 5, Ontario

This "monograph" contains information on the history and nature of the work performed, specialized areas of this field, working conditions, qualifications, training, income, methods of entry, advancement opportunities, and advantages and disadvantages.

PHOTOGRAPHER. *S. Splaver.* 1951.
> 6 pages—50¢; special to students, 25¢.
> *Personnel Services, Inc.*
> Main St., Peapack, N. J.

Summarized in this "occupational abstract" are the history of this field, nature of the work, qualifications, preparation, entrance and advancement, supply and demand, earnings, and advantages and disadvantages.

MISCELLANEOUS:

CAREERS IN PHOTOGRAPHY. 1953.

28 pages—free.
Rochester Institute of Technology
65 Plymouth Ave. So., Rochester 8,
N. Y.

This attractive pamphlet contains valuable information on the nature of varied career opportunities in such areas of photography as advertising, documentary, motion picture and newspaper photography.

OPPORTUNITIES IN PHOTOGRAPHY. *J. Deschin.* 1951.

112 pages—$1.00.
Vocational Guidance Manuals, Inc.
1011 East Tremont Ave., New York,
60, N. Y.

Included in this "manual" is information on the past and present of photography, educational preparation, getting started in this field, qualifications, nature of varied jobs, and related fields.

PHOTOGRAPHY. 1952.

10 pages—10¢.
Glamour Magazine
420 Lexington Ave., New York 17,
N. Y.

This "fact sheet" discusses the field of photography and the opportunities for professional photographers. It contains information on the qualifications and training for the professional photographer, getting started in this field, nature of the work, earnings, working conditions and equipment needed. *(For female readers)*

(also see field of ART)

For additional information, write to:

AMERICAN SOCIETY FOR CINEMATOGRAPHERS, INC.
1782 No. Orange Dr., Hollywood, Calif.

PHOTOGRAPHERS' ASSOCIATIONS OF AMERICA
520 Caxton Bldg., Cleveland 15, Ohio

PHYSICAL EDUCATION
AND RECREATION

BASEBALL PLAYERS:
(D.O.T. No.: 0-57.01)

BASEBALL IS THEIR BUSINESS. *Edited by H. Rosenthal. 1952.*

180 pages—$2.50.
Random House, Inc.
457 Madison Ave., New York 22, N. Y.

Authorities discuss the work of various persons who function in the field of baseball. In addition to the occupation of the baseball player, this book also includes information about the scout, the newspaperman, the radio announcer, the publicity man, the television producer, the umpire, the statistician, the administration man, and the manager.

BASEBALL PLAYER. *S. Splaver. 1953.*

6 pages—50¢; special to students, 25¢.
Personnel Services, Inc.
Main St., Peapack, N. J.

This "occupational abstract" presents a summary of available literature on the work of the baseball player, qualifications, preparation, entrance and advancement, earnings, number and distribution of players, and advantages and disadvantages.

BORN TO PLAY BALL. *W. Mays. 1955.*

168 pages—$2.50.
G. P. Putnam's Sons,
2 West 45th St., New York 19, N. Y.

This biography of the New York Giants' noted centerfielder is inspiring reading for all would-be baseball players. *(For teen-age boys)*

CASEY STENGEL — BASEBALL'S GREATEST MANAGER. *G. Schoor. 1953.*

185 pages—$2.95.
Julian Messner, Inc.
8 West 40th St., New York 18, N. Y.

An engrossing biography of the famed manager of the New York Yankees, this book contains worthwhile occupational information on baseball playing and management. *(For teen-age boys)*

JOE DiMAGGIO — THE YANKEE CLIPPER. *G. Schoor. 1956.*

192 pages—$2.95.
Julian Messner, Inc.
8 West 40th St., New York 18, N. Y.

This readable biography of one of the New York Yankees' most famous players provides valuable information on the field of professional baseball. *(For teen-age boys)*

THE STAN MUSIAL STORY. *G. Schoor. 1955.*

192 pages—$2.95.
Julian Messner, Inc.
8 West 40th St., New York 18, N. Y.

An inspiring biography written by the noted sports writer, this is an interesting and informative baseball tale containing valuable career material. *(For teen-age boys)*

THE STORY OF BOBBY SHANTZ. *R. C. Shantz. 1953.*

190 pages—$2.50.
J. B. Lippincott Co.
227 So. 6th St., Philadelphia 5, Pa.

This autobiography of the famous short-statured baseball player is an inspiring tale containing worthwhile occupational information of special interest to short young men who aspire to baseball careers. *(For teen-age boys)*

THE TED WILLIAMS STORY. *G. Schoor*. 1954.

188 pages—$2.95.
Julian Messner, Inc.
8 West 40th St., New York 18, N. Y.

The life of this famous Boston Red Sox player is a stimulating story containing a good bit of career information on the field of professional baseball. *(For teen-age boys)*

BOXERS:

(D.O.T. No.: 0-57.01)

THE JACK DEMPSEY STORY. *G. Schoor*. 1954.

186 pages—$2.95.
Julian Messner, Inc.
8 West 40th St., New York 18, N. Y.

This fascinating biography of one of the most famous heavyweight champions in the history of boxing contains valuable career information on the field of professional fighting. *(For teen-age boys)*

CAMP COUNSELORS:

(D.O.T. No.: 0-27.40)

CAMP COUNSELING. *Mademoiselle's Jobs and Futures Dept.* Revised 1952.

6 pages—25¢.
Alumnae Advisory Center, Inc.
541 Madison Ave., New York 22, N. Y.

This magazine reprint presents the working conditions of camp counselors, earnings, advantages and disadvantages, qualifications for the work, considerations in choice of a camp, and how to obtain positions. *(For female readers)*

CAMP COUNSELOR. *S. Splaver*. 1955.

6 pages—50¢; special to students, 25¢.
Personnel Services, Inc.
Main St., Peapack, N. J.

Summarized in this "occupational abstract" are the history of the occupation, nature of the work, qualifications, prepa-

ration, entrance and advancement, supply and demand, earnings, and advantages and disadvantages.

THE CAMP COUNSELOR. *R. A. Benson and J. A. Goldberg*. 1951.

337 pages—$4.50.
McGraw-Hill Book Co., Inc.
330 West 42nd St., New York 36, N. Y.

A thorough coverage of the occupation is presented here. It includes the functions of counselors, opportunities available to them, how to promote the well-being of campers, a counselor rating scale, an employment contract, and an application form.

SO YOU WANT TO BE A CAMP COUNSELOR. *E. Ott*. Reprinted 1951.

112 pages—75¢.

291 Broadway, New York 7, N. Y.

The nature of the work of the counselor is detailed in this book, which basically concerns Y.M.C.A. camps and their operation.

SUNNY, THE NEW CAMP COUNSELOR. *L. Rosenheim.* 1952.

179 pages—$2.95.
Julian Messner, Inc.
8 West 40th St., New York 18, N. Y.

The work of the heroine as a counselor in a summer camp makes this career novel stimulating and entertaining reading. *(For teen-age girls)*

HOCKEY PLAYERS:
(D.O.T. No.: 0-57.01)

HOCKEY PLAYER. 1955.

4 pages—15¢ in Canada, 20¢ elsewhere.
Guidance Centre, Univ. of Toronto
371 Bloor St. W., Toronto 5, Ontario

Included in this "monograph" are the history and nature of the work, working conditions, personal and training requirements, earnings, entering the field, advantages and disadvantages, and related occupations.

RECREATION DIRECTORS:
(D.O.T. Nos.: 0-27.06; 0-27.40; 0-98.57)

PLAYGROUND DIRECTOR. *S. Splaver.* 1955.

6 pages—50¢; special to students, 25¢.
Personnel Services, Inc.
Main St., Peapack, N. J.

This pamphlet summarizes the development of the occupation, nature of the work, qualifications, preparation, entrance and advancement, supply and demand, earnings, opportunities for servicemen, and advantages and disadvantages.

RECREATION DIRECTOR. 1954.

4 pages—35¢; special to students, 25¢.
Chronicle Guidance Publications
Moravia, N. Y.

This "occupational brief" reviews the nature of the work, working conditions, remuneration, personal requirements, preparation, future prospects, where to find employment, how to enter the field, and related jobs.

MISCELLANEOUS:

OPPORTUNITIES IN PHYSICAL ED-
UCATION, HEALTH AND RECREA-
TION. *J. B. Nash.* Revised 1953.

    128 pages—$1.00.
    Vocational Guidance Manuals, Inc.
    1011 East Tremont Ave., New York
      60, N. Y.

This "manual" analyzes the relationships
and opportunities existing in the fields of
physical education, health education and
recreation, requirements for entrance
and success in these fields, preparation,
duties, advantages and disadvantages, remuneration, how to get started, and path-
ways to advancement.

PHYSICAL EDUCATION MEANS
FUN FOR A LIVING. Revised 1954.

    5 pages—10¢.
    Glamour Magazine
    420 Lexington Ave., New York 17,
      N. Y.

This reprint discusses the rewards of this
work, nature of the different job opportunities, salaries, and typical places of
employment. *(For female readers)*

For additional information, write to:

AMERICAN ASSOCIATION FOR HEALTH, PHYSICAL EDUCATION
AND RECREATION
1201 Sixteenth St., N. W., Washington 6, D. C.

AMERICAN CAMPING ASSOCIATION
343 So. Dearborn St., Chicago 4, Ill.

NATIONAL RECREATION ASSOCIATION
8 West Eighth St., New York 11, N. Y.

PHYSICAL THERAPY

PHYSICAL THERAPISTS:

(D.O.T. No.: 0-52.22)

CAREER AS PHYSICAL THERAPIST. 1952.

4 pages—25¢.

B'nai B'rith Vocational Service Bureau
1129 Vermont Ave., N. W., Washington 5, D. C.

This booklet discusses the nature of the work, preparation, employment opportunities, earnings, and advantages and disadvantages.

DIARY OF A PHYSICAL THERAPIST. Revised 1954.

6 pages—10¢.

Glamour Magazine
420 Lexington Ave., New York 17, N. Y.

This magazine article reprint covers a typical day in the life of a physical therapist. It describes the qualifications, training, places of employment, duties, salaries, advantages, and future prospects for the job. *(For female readers)*

DO YOU BELONG IN THIS PROFESSION? OCCUPATIONAL THERAPY, PHYSICAL THERAPY, A CAREER FOR YOU. PAMPHLET 5-9. *U. S. Veterans Administration.* 1953.

8 pages—5¢.

Supt. of Documents, Govt. Printing Office
Washington 25, D. C.

The opportunities in these fields, qualifications, training, earnings, and employment prospects are discussed herein.

THE OUTLOOK FOR WOMEN AS PHYSICAL THERAPISTS. BULLETIN NO. 203-1. *Women's Bureau, U. S. Dept. of Labor.* 1952.

51 pages—20¢.

Supt. of Documents, Govt. Printing Office
Washington 25, D. C.

Contained in this pamphlet is information on the employment prospects in this field, places of employment, supply and demand, preparation for this work, earnings, working conditions, and requirements for Federal civil service positions.

PHYSICAL THERAPIST. Revised. 1956.

4 pages—35¢; special to students, 25¢.

Chronicle Guidance Publications
Moravia, N. Y.

This "occupational brief" reviews the nature of the work performed, working conditions, remuneration, personal and training requirements, where to find employment, methods of entry, licensure and registration, and related jobs.

PHYSICAL THERAPIST. Revised. 1954.

4 pages—15¢ in Canada, 20¢ elsewhere.

Guidance Centre, Univ. of Toronto
371 Bloor St. W., Toronto 5, Ontario

This "monograph" discusses the history and nature of the work, working conditions, qualifications and preparation needed, advancement opportunities, earnings, advantages and disadvantages, how to get started, and related occupations.

THE PHYSICAL THERAPIST. 1956.
  4 pages—free to high school principals
    and guidance officers.
Simmons College
300 The Fenway, Boston 15, Mass.
In this folder is information on the nature
of the job, rewards and opportunities,
necessary interests and aptitudes, and
preparation.

PHYSICAL THERAPY—A DEEPLY
REWARDING CAREER. *Women's*

*Specialist Corps, U. S. Army Medical
Service.* 1952.
  6 pages—5¢.
*Supt. of Documents, Govt. Printing
  Office*
Washington 25, D. C.
This booklet presents information on
training in the field of physical therapy,
opportunities available for therapists in
the U. S. Army medical service, nature
of the work, and earnings.

*(also see fields of MEDICAL AND HEALTH SERVICES, and
OCCUPATIONAL THERAPY)*

For additional information, write to:

AMERICAN PHYSICAL THERAPY ASSOCIATION
1790 Broadway, New York 19, N. Y.

140

PRINTING

COMPOSITORS:
(D.O.T. No.: 4-44.010)

COMPOSING-ROOM OCCUPATIONS.
Revised 1954.

24 pages—25¢.
Michigan Employment Security Comm.
7310 Woodward Ave., Detroit 2, Mich.

This pamphlet presents the employment prospects in Michigan. However, the information on the history and nature of the work in these occupations, typical places of employment, qualifications, wages, working conditions, how to get started, and advancement opportunities applies as well to the entire country.

COMPOSITOR. *S. Splaver.* 1956.

6 pages—50¢; special to students, 25¢.
Personnel Services, Inc.
Main St., Peapack, N. J.

This "occupational abstract" summarizes the development of this field, nature of the work, qualifications, preparation, entrance and advancement, supply and demand, earnings, and advantages and disadvantages.

HAND COMPOSITOR. 1953.

4 pages—35¢; special to students, 25¢.
Chronicle Guidance Publications
Moravia, N. Y.

This "occupational brief" describes the nature of the work, working conditions, wages, personal and training requirements, future prospects, typical places of employment, how to get started, and related jobs.

LINOTYPE OPERATORS:
(D.O.T. No.: 4-44.110)

LINOTYPE OPERATOR. Revised 1956.

4 pages—35¢; special to students, 25¢.
Chronicle Guidance Publications
Moravia, N. Y.

This "occupational brief" discusses the nature of the work of the linotype operator, employment opportunities, working conditions, qualifications and preparation, opportunities for women, where employed, methods of entry, and related jobs.

THE LINOTYPE OPERATOR. *O. R. Abel.* Revised 1956.

32 pages—$1.00.
Bellman Publishing Co.
P. O. Box 172, Cambridge 38, Mass.

This pamphlet describes the construction of the linotype machine, training necessary for a linotype operator, educational and physical requirements, working conditions, getting started, nature of the work, and employment outlook.

LITHOGRAPHERS:
(D.O.T. Nos.: 4-46.; 4-48.)

LITHOGRAPHIC OCCUPATIONS. Revised 1954.

24 pages—25¢.
Michigan Employment Security Comm.
7310 Woodward Ave., Detroit 2, Mich.

Thorough coverage of these occupations is presented here. It includes the history and nature of the work performed, qualifications, specialized preparation, earnings, working conditions, methods of entering these occupations, and advancement opportunities.

PHOTOENGRAVERS:
(D.O.T. No.: 4-47.100)

PHOTOENGRAVER. *L. Flader*. 1954.

44 pages—$1.00.
Research Publishing Co., Inc.
P. O. Box 245, Boston 1, Mass.

This little pamphlet presents the history of photoengraving, importance of this work, functions of photoengraver, working conditions, qualifications and special skills needed, training, opportunities for promotion, methods of obtaining employment, and related occupations.

PHOTOENGRAVING OCCUPATIONS. Revised 1954.

24 pages—25¢.
Michigan Employment Security Comm.
7310 Woodward Ave., Detroit 2, Mich.

Described here are the processes of photoengraving, the nature of the work performed by personnel employed in these occupations, qualifications and preparation necessary for entrance and success, apprenticeships, working conditions, and advancement opportunities.

PRESSMEN:
(D.O.T. Nos.: 4-48.)

JOB-PRINTING PRESSMAN. 1955.

4 pages—35¢; special to students, 25¢.
Chronicle Guidance Publications
Moravia, N. Y.

This "occupational brief" contains information on the history of this occupation, nature of the work, working conditions, wages, qualifications, training, getting started, places of employment, and future prospects.

OFFSET PRESSMAN. 1953.

4 pages—35¢; special to students, 25¢.
Chronicle Guidance Publications
Moravia, N. Y.

This "occupational brief" discusses the history and nature of the work performed, wages, personal and training requirements, methods of entering this occupation, future prospects, and related jobs.

PRESSMAN. *H. A. Robinson.* Revised 1956.

> 6 pages—50¢; special to students, 25¢.
> *Personnel Services, Inc.*
> Main St., Peapack, N. J.

This "occupational abstract" describes the nature of the work, future prospects, qualifications, preparation, entrance and advancement, earnings, number and distribution, related occupations, and advantages and disadvantages.

PRINTING PRESSMEN. Revised 1954.

> 20 pages—25¢.
> *Michigan Employment Security Comm.*
> 7310 Woodward Ave., Detroit 2, Mich.

This pamphlet discusses the history and importance of this work, duties of the pressman, typical places of employment, working conditions, wages, qualifications, training needed, methods of entry, advantages and disadvantages, and employment prospects in Michigan.

MISCELLANEOUS:

CAREERS IN PRINTING TRADES. Revised 1953.

> 8 pages—25¢.
> *B'nai B'rith Vocational Service Bureau*
> 1129 Vermont Ave., N. W., Washington 5, D. C.

Presented here are the opportunities in the field of printing, future prospects, nature of the work performed by printing personnel, preparation and qualifications for the work, wages, and advantages and disadvantages.

EMPLOYMENT OUTLOOK IN PRINTING OCCUPATIONS. BULLETIN NO. 1126. *Bureau of Labor Statistics, U. S. Dept. of Labor.* 1953.

> 34 pages—25¢.
> *Supt. of Documents, Govt. Printing Office*
> Washington 25, D. C.

This pamphlet reviews the scope of the printing industry, employment prospects, nature of the different work opportunities, qualifications, preparation, working conditions, and wages.

OPPORTUNITIES IN THE PRINTING TRADES. *P. F. Boughal.* 1951.

> 112 pages—$1.00.

> *Vocational Guidance Manuals, Inc.*
> 1011 East Tremont Ave., New York 60, N. Y.

This "manual" describes the work in various printing occupations, history of printing, apprenticeship training, qualifications, how to secure employment, and related fields. It also includes a list of schools offering printing and graphic arts courses.

PRINTER. Revised 1954.

> 4 pages—15¢ in Canada, 20¢ elsewhere.
> *Guidance Centre, Univ. of Toronto*
> 371 Bloor St. W., Toronto 5, Ontario

This "monograph" discusses the history and nature of the work performed, working conditions, qualifications, training, advancement opportunities, wages, methods of entering this occupation, and advantages and disadvantages.

SHOULD YOU GO INTO THE PRINTING INDUSTRY? *Wm. H. Walling.* 1955.

> 8 pages—free.
> *New York Life Insurance Co.*
> 51 Madison Ave., New York 10, N. Y.

This public service career booklet contains information on the importance of this industry to society, the eight major fields in the printing industry, supply and demand, earnings, opportunities for self employment, methods of entry, training, and personal qualifications.

STEREOTYPERS AND ELECTRO-TYPERS. Revised 1955.

16 pages—25¢.

Michigan Employment Security Comm.
7310 Woodward Ave., Detroit 2, Mich.

This "occupational guide" reviews the history and nature of the work, number and distribution of such workers, employment outlook, qualifications, educational requirements, apprenticeships, working conditions, typical places of employment, and advantages and disadvantages.

(also see field of PUBLISHING)

For additional information, write to:

Printing Industry of America, Inc.
719—15th St., N. W., Washington 5, D. C.

144

PROTECTIVE SERVICES

F.B.I. AGENTS:

(D.O.T. No.: 2-66.99)

THE F.B.I. *Q. Reynolds.* 1954.
  180 pages—$1.50.
  Random House, Inc.
  457 Madison Ave., New York 22, N. Y.

This educational and entertaining "landmark book" contains much valuable career information about the Federal Bureau of Investigation. (*For junior and senior high school students*)

THE F.B.I. STORY. *D. Whitehead.* 1956.
  368 pages—$4.95.
  Random House, Inc.
  457 Madison Ave., New York 22, N. Y.

A profoundly engrossing book for all who aspire to careers in the F.B.I., this volume is packed with the hair-raising experiences of F.B.I. men and the nature of their daily activities in protecting the American citizenry. A foreword by J. Edgar Hoover is included.

OUR F.B.I., AN INSIDE STORY. *J. J. Floherty.* 1951.
  192 pages—$2.75.
  J. B. Lippincott Co.
  227 So. 6th St., Philadelphia 5, Pa.

Teen-age boys will be fascinated by this book, which describes the special activities of F.B.I. men, functions of the F.B.I., training for positions with this Federal agency, and some of the investigations in which these special agents have participated. (*For teen-age boys*)

THE STORY OF THE F.B.I. *Editors of Look.* 1954.
  286 pages—$3.95.
  E. P. Dutton and Co., Inc.
  300 Fourth Ave., New York 10, N. Y.

This beautifully illustrated book describes the history of the F.B.I., its importance to society, the nature of the work of F.B.I. men including the role of the F.B.I. during World War II, personal qualifications and specialized training needed to obtain such positions, and methods of obtaining employment with the F.B.I.

FIREMEN:

(D.O.T. Nos.: 2-63.)

FIREMAN. 1953.
  4 pages—35¢; special to students, 25¢.
  Chronicle Guidance Publications
  Moravia, N. Y.

This "occupational brief" reviews the history and nature of the work performed, working conditions, qualifications and training requirements, earnings, typical places of employment, getting started in this occupation, and future prospects.

FIREMAN. Revised 1953.
  4 pages—15¢ in Canada, 20¢ elsewhere.

Guidance Centre, Univ. of Toronto
371 Bloor St. W., Toronto 5, Ontario

This "occupational monograph" reviews the history and nature of the work performed, working conditions, qualifications and preparation needed for entrance and success, methods of entry, remuneration, and advantages and disadvantages.

MUNICIPAL FIRE FIGHTERS. 1954.
20 pages—25¢.
Michigan Employment Security Comm.
7310 Woodward Ave., Detroit 2, Mich.

Contained here is information on the importance and nature of the work, typical places of employment, working conditions, employment outlook, requirements for obtaining such positions, and advantages and disadvantages.

POLICE OFFICERS:
(D.O.T. No.: 2-66.01)

POLICE OFFICERS. *B. S. Fischer.*
1955.
24 pages—25¢.
Michigan Employment Security Comm.
7310 Woodward Ave., Detroit 2, Mich.

This "occupational guide" reviews the history and importance of this work, duties of police officers, qualifications and educational requirements, typical places of employment, and opportunities for women.

POLICEMAN—POLICEWOMAN.
1956.
4 pages—35¢; special to students, 25¢.
Chronicle Guidance Publications
Moravia, N. Y.

This "occupational brief" reviews the nature of the work, qualifications and training for the job, working conditions, earnings, employment outlook, and opportunities for promotion.

POLICEMAN (ROYAL CANADIAN MOUNTED). Revised 1954.
4 pages—15¢ in Canada, 20¢ elsewhere.
Guidance Centre, Univ. of Toronto
371 Bloor St. W., Toronto 5, Ontario

This "monograph" reviews the nature of the work performed, qualifications and preparation, advancement opportunities, salaries, methods of entering this occupation, and advantages and disadvantages.

PROBATION OFFICERS:
(D.O.T. No.: 0-27.20)

CAREERS IN PROBATION AND PAROLE. 1953.
8 pages—25¢.
B'nai B'rith Vocational Service Bureau
1129 Vermont Ave., N. W., Washington 5, D. C.

This career booklet contains information on the history and nature of this work, future prospects, typical places of employment, educational requirements, salaries, methods of obtaining these jobs, working conditions, and advancement opportunities.

MINING AND METALLURGY

METALLURGISTS:
(D.O.T. Nos.: 0-14.)

METALLURGICAL ENGINEER. *H. A. Robinson.* 1955.

6 pages—50¢; special to students, 25¢.
Personnel Services, Inc.
Main St., Peapack, N. J.

This "occupational abstract" summarizes the history of the occupation, nature of the work, future prospects, opportunities for servicemen, qualifications, preparation, entrance and advancement, earnings, number and distribution, advantages and disadvantages, and related occupations.

METALLURGIST. 1953.

4 pages—35¢; special to students, 25¢.
Chronicle Guidance Publications
Moravia, N. Y.

This "occupational brief" discusses the nature and importance of the work, working conditions, personal and training requirements, advancement opportunities, typical places of employment, how to enter the field, earnings, and related jobs.

METALLURGIST (METALLURGICAL ENGINEER). 1956.

4 pages—15¢ in Canada, 20¢ elsewhere.
Guidance Centre, Univ. of Toronto
371 Bloor St. W., Toronto 5, Ontario

Job definition, working conditions, qualifications and preparation needed, advancement, remuneration, advantages and disadvantages, how to get started, and related occupations are discussed here.

METALLURGY. *A. S. Cohan.* 1955.

20 pages—$1.00.
Bellman Publishing Co.
P. O. Box 172, Cambridge 38, Mass.

This "vocational and professional monograph" discusses the history and development of the metallurgical profession, training and education required, description of the work, employment opportunities, remuneration, chances for advancement, advantages and disadvantages, trends, and a list of professional organizations and trade associations.

MINERS:
(D.O.T. Nos.: 5-21.; 5-32.)

MINER (METAL). Revised 1953.

4 pages—15¢ in Canada, 20¢ elsewhere.
Guidance Centre, Univ. of Toronto
371 Bloor St. W., Toronto 5, Ontario

This "monograph" discusses the history, importance and nature of the work, working conditions, qualifications and preparation, earnings, getting started, and advantages and disadvantages.

MISCELLANEOUS:

OPPORTUNITIES IN LAW EN-
FORCEMENT (MUNICIPAL). *J. J.
O'Connor, Jr. and J. J. O'Connor, Sr.*
1955.

   96 pages—$1.00.
Vocational Guidance Manuals, Inc.
1011 East Tremont Ave., New York
   60, N. Y.

This "manual" reviews the personal qualifications for a law enforcement career,
educational preparation, employment opportunities, police department organization, conditions of employment, nature of
the work, advantages and disadvantages,
and opportunities for women.

(also see field of PUBLIC SERVICE)

For additional information, write to:

154 FEDERAL BUREAU OF INVESTIGATION, U. S. DEPT. OF JUSTICE
Washington 25, D. C.

155 NATIONAL PROBATION AND PAROLE ASSOCIATION
1790 Broadway, New York 19, N. Y.

147

PUBLIC SERVICE

CITY PLANNERS:
(D.O.T. No.: 0-16.01)

CITY PLANNER. *H. A. Robinson.* Revised 1956.

  6 pages—50¢; special to students, 25¢.
  Personnel Services, Inc.
  Main St., Peapack, N. J.

Summarized in this "occupational abstract" are the nature of the work, future prospects, qualifications, preparation, entrance and advancement, earnings, opportunities, and advantages and disadvantages.

FOREIGN SERVICE PERSONNEL:
(D.O.T. Nos.: 0-39.99; 0-94.70)

NEW OPPORTUNITIES IN THE U. S. FOREIGN SERVICE. *U. S. Dept. of State.* Revised 1956.

  20 pages—15¢.
  Supt. of Documents, Govt. Printing Office
  Washington 25, D. C.

This attractive pamphlet discusses Foreign Service opportunities, history of the Service, work and training of an officer, the three different groups in the Foreign Service, eight classes of officers, pay, promotion, allowances, leaves and other benefits, and the nature of the examination given to the officer candidates.

THE U. S. FOREIGN SERVICE; A CAREER FOR YOUNG AMERICANS. *U. S. Dept. of State.* 1952.

  79 pages—25¢.
  Supt. of Documents, Govt. Printing Office
  Washington 25, D. C.

This is a comprehensive presentation of the opportunities available in the Foreign Service, the regulations of the Board of Examiners for the various career opportunities, and the personal requirements and educational qualifications for such employment.

MAIL CARRIERS AND CLERKS:
(D.O.T. No.: 1-27.20)

LETTER CARRIER. Revised 1953.

  4 pages—15¢ in Canada, 20¢ elsewhere.
  Guidance Centre, Univ. of Toronto
  371 Bloor St. W., Toronto 5, Ontario

This "monograph" discusses the importance and nature of the work, working conditions, qualifications necessary for entry and success, preparation, earnings, advantages and disadvantages, getting started, and related occupations.

POST OFFICE CLERK. 1953.

4 pages—35¢; special to students, 25¢.
Chronicle Guidance Publications
Moravia, N. Y.

This "occupational brief" describes the nature of the work performed, working conditions, salaries, qualifications, training requirements, advancement, outlook, methods of entry, and related jobs.

POLITICIANS:

(D.O.T. Nos.: 0-83.; 0-94.)

BREAKING INTO POLITICS. *Mademoiselle's College and Careers Dept.* 1956.

7 pages—25¢.
Alumnae Advisory Center, Inc.
541 Madison Ave., New York 22, N. Y.

Discussed in this magazine reprint are the paid and volunteer, full-time and part-time opportunities in politics with examples of women who have succeeded in this field. *(For female readers)*

LET'S GO INTO POLITICS. *R. E. Baldwin.* 1952.

179 pages—$2.75.
Macmillan Co., Inc.
60 Fifth Ave., New York 11, N. Y.

Raymond Earl Baldwin, former Governor and Senator from the state of Connecticut, suggests that young people give thought to careers in politics. He tells of his political experiences and offers advice on how to go about entering politics.

WORKING IN POLITICS. 1956.

12 pages—10¢.
Glamour Magazine
420 Lexington Ave., New York 17, N. Y.

This "fact sheet" highlights the activities of the major committees of the political parties, job opportunities available to volunteer and paid workers, qualifications, preparation, and sources of further information. *(For female readers)*

MISCELLANEOUS:

AFTER COLLEGE—WHAT? 1955.

24 pages—free.
U. S. Civil Service Comm.
Washington 25, D. C.

This pamphlet suggests that college graduates consider "Uncle Sam as an employer." It discusses how jobs are filled via the new Federal Service Entrance Examination, the career service, salary schedule, promotions, training programs, and government job benefits. *(For college students)*

THE CIVIL SERVICE APPOINTMENT SYSTEM, THE GATEWAY TO A GOVERNMENT CAREER. *U. S. Civil Service Comm.* 1955.

12 pages—5¢.
Supt. of Documents, Govt. Printing Office
Washington 25, D. C.

This booklet discusses the Career-Conditional Appointment System, how it works, employee rights under this system, and how the new system affects present employees.

FEDERAL CAREERS, A DIRECTORY FOR COLLEGE STUDENTS. *U. S. Civil Service Comm.* 1956.

> 79 pages—60¢.
> *Supt. of Documents, Govt. Printing Office*
> Washington 25, D. C.

This comprehensive reference manual has been prepared in three parts as follows: Part I presents general information regarding Federal employment, Part II discusses government agencies and the opportunities which they offer to college men and women, and Part III describes the nature of the work, qualifications required and career opportunities in major Federal government occupations. *(For college students)*

FEDERAL JOBS OUTSIDE THE CONTINENTAL UNITED STATES. PAMPHLET 29. *U. S. Civil Service Commission.* Revised 1956.

> 8 pages—5¢.
> *Supt. of Documents, Govt. Printing Office*
> Washington 25, D. C.

In this leaflet is information on how jobs are filled, conditions of employment, and some of the agencies employing overseas personnel.

FEDERAL WHITE-COLLAR WORKERS, THEIR OCCUPATIONS AND SALARIES. BULLETIN NO. 1117. *Bureau of Labor Statistics, U. S. Dept. of Labor.* 1953.

> 43 pages—15¢.
> *Supt. of Documents, Govt. Printing Office*
> Washington 25, D. C.

Discussed herein are the types of positions available, number of persons employed in each of these occupations, the agencies where they are employed, and earnings.

FUTURES IN THE FEDERAL GOVERNMENT. PAMPHLET 30. 1955.

> 28 pages—free.
> *U. S. Civil Service Comm.*
> Washington 25, D. C.

This pamphlet presents the career opportunities offered through the new Federal Service Entrance Examination, nature of the examination and how to apply for it, and addresses for further information from specific Federal agencies.

SHOULD YOU BE A PUBLIC SERVANT? *R. Moses.* 1955.

> 8 pages—free.
> *New York Life Insurance Co.*
> 51 Madison Ave., New York 10, N. Y.

This career booklet highlights the importance of the public servant to society, the three chief kinds of public service posts, opportunities in public service, advantages and disadvantages, salaries, and educational preparation.

THINKING ABOUT YOUR FIRST JOB? REMEMBER—UNCLE SAM. PAMPHLET 5. 1956.

> 14 pages—free.
> *U. S. Civil Service Comm.*
> Washington 25, D. C.

This leaflet reviews some of the opportunities available to young people in government agencies. *(For high school students)*

WASHINGTON JOB HUNT. *Mademoiselle's College and Careers Dept.* 1955.

> 7 pages—25¢.
> *Alumnae Advisory Center, Inc.*
> 541 Madison Ave., New York 22, N. Y.

The nature of some of the job opportunities with government agencies, the Civil Service Commission's new college recruiting program, how to obtain employment, and salary scales are discussed in this magazine reprint. *(For female college students)*

THE WAY TO A JOB IN GOVERN-MENT. *U. S. Civil Service Comm.* 1954.

   6 pages—5¢.

   Supt. of Documents, Govt. Printing Office

Washington 25, D. C.

This folder presents general information regarding the procedures to follow in seeking Federal civil service employment.

WORKING FOR THE U.S.A. *U. S. Civil Service Comm.* Revised 1955.

   24 pages—10¢.

   Supt. of Documents, Govt. Printing Office

Washington 25, D. C.

Included in this pamphlet is information on how to apply for a civil service job, what is expected of a government worker, and general points on working for the government.

(see also field of PROTECTIVE SERVICES)

For additional information, write to:

U. S. CIVIL SERVICE COMMISSION
Washington 25, D. C.

PUBLISHING

BOOKBINDERS:
(D.O.T. No.: 4-49.010)

BOOKBINDING OCCUPATIONS. Revised 1954.

20 pages—25¢.
Michigan Employment Security Comm.
7310 Woodward Ave., Detroit 2, Mich.

This "occupational guide" describes the history and importance of these occupations, nature of the work performed, working conditions, earnings, opportunities for handicapped persons, qualifications, unions, and advantages and disadvantages of the work.

EDITORS:
(D.O.T. Nos.: 0-06.40 through 0-06.59)

EDITOR. *S. Schuman.* Revised 1956.

6 pages—50¢; special to students, 25¢.
Personnel Services, Inc.
Main St., Peapack, N. J.

This "occupational abstract" summarizes the nature of the work, qualifications, preparation, entrance and advancement in this occupation, number and distribution of editors, remuneration, and advantages and disadvantages.

IN THE MINK. *A. Scott-James.* 1952.

255 pages—$3.00.
E. P. Dutton and Co., Inc.
300 Fourth Ave., New York 10, N. Y.

Occupational information on the work of the editor of the English edition of an American fashion magazine is contained in this career novel. *(For teen-age girls)*

WEEKLY NEWSPAPER EDITOR. 1956.

4 pages—35¢; special to students, 25¢.
Chronicle Guidance Publications
Moravia, N. Y.

Discussed in this "occupational brief" are the history and nature of the work performed, working conditions, earnings, personal and training requirements, how to enter this field, and national outlook.

PROOFREADERS:
(D.O.T. No.: 1-10.07)

PROOF-READER. 1952.

4 pages—15¢ in Canada, 20¢ elsewhere.
Guidance Centre, Univ. of Toronto
371 Bloor St. W., Toronto 5, Ontario

This "monograph" reviews the history and nature of the work, working conditions, qualifications and preparation, advancement, earnings, and related occupations.

MISCELLANEOUS:

BOOK PUBLISHING. *Mademoiselle's Jobs and Futures Dept.* 1952.

    5 pages—25¢.
    Alumnae Advisory Center, Inc.
    541 Madison Ave., New York 22, N. Y.

The competition in this field, nature of job opportunities, how to get started, qualifications, earnings for beginners, and tips for advancement are included in this magazine reprint. *(For female readers)*

CAREERS IN BOOK PUBLISHING. *D. Melcher.* 1952.

    8 pages—25¢.
    B'nai B'rith Vocational Service Bureau
    1129 Vermont Ave., N. W., Washington 5, D. C.

This booklet discusses future prospects in the industry, the nature of the opportunities available and the work performed, working conditions, remuneration, opportunities for promotion, and unions.

DO YOU WANT A JOB IN PUBLISHING? Revised 1954.

    6 pages—10c.
    Glamour Magazine
    420 Lexington Ave., New York 17, N. Y.

This is a reprint of an article which appeared in *Glamour*. It describes the three branches of publishing (magazine, book, and newspaper) and the editorial and non-editorial opportunities for women. *(For female readers)*

SO YOU WANT A JOB IN PUBLISHING? *D. Melcher.* Revised 1956.

    16 pages—25¢.
    R. R. Bowker and Co.
    62 West 45th St., New York 36, N. Y.

The size and nature of the book publishing industry, educational preparation, opportunities for men, methods of job hunting, landing a job in publishing, salaries, advancement, and miscellaneous job opportunities are discussed in this pamphlet.

(see also fields of PRINTING, and WRITING AND LINGUISTICS)

For additional information, write to:

AMERICAN BOOK PUBLISHERS COUNCIL
2 West 46th St., New York 36, N. Y.

AMERICAN NEWSPAPER GUILD
99 University Place, New York 3, N. Y.

RELIGION

CLERGYMEN:

(D.O.T. No.: 0-08.10)

CLERGYMAN. Revised 1953.

　4 pages—15¢ in Canada, 20¢ elsewhere.

Guidance Centre, Univ. of Toronto
371 Bloor St. W., Toronto 5, Ontario

This "monograph" reviews the history and nature of the work performed, its importance to society, qualifications and preparation, earnings, working conditions, advantages and disadvantages, and related occupations.

MISCELLANEOUS:

CAREERS IN JEWISH COMMUNITY SERVICE. 1955.

　1 kit—$1.50.

B'nai B'rith Vocational Service Bureau
1129 Vermont Ave., N. W., Washington 5, D. C.

This kit consists of nine booklets pertaining to careers in cantorial work, community organization, community relations, group work, Jewish education, the rabbinate, social casework, synagogue administration and vocational service, and an illustrated chart summarizing the basic facts in these booklets.

OPPORTUNITIES IN CATHOLIC RELIGIOUS VOCATIONS. *G. Poage.* 1952.

　144 pages—$1.00.

Vocational Guidance Manuals, Inc.
1011 East Tremont Ave., New York 60, N. Y.

Here is a thorough coverage of the field which includes information on qualifications, nature of the opportunities in the priesthood, in the brotherhood and in the sisterhood, and a directory of communities.

OPPORTUNITIES IN JEWISH RELIGIOUS VOCATIONS. *W. Duckat.* 1952.

　128 pages—$1.00.

Vocational Guidance Manuals, Inc.
1011 East Tremont Ave., New York 60, N. Y.

This "manual" contains information on synagogue vocations, communal vocations, dietary vocations, the nature of the work, preparation required, qualifications, and future prospects.

OPPORTUNITIES IN PROTESTANT RELIGIOUS VOCATIONS. *J. O. Nelson.* 1952.

　128 pages—$1.00.

Vocational Guidance Manuals, Inc.
1011 East Tremont Ave., New York 60, N. Y.

This "manual" reviews the nature of these vocations, training required, the meaning of a "call," the varied opportunities available, educational preparation, factors to consider in selecting a seminary, and how to get started.

RELIGION. *J. A. Nichols, Jr.* 1955.

　24 pages—$1.00.

Bellman Publishing Co.
P. O. Box 172, Cambridge 38, Mass.
A discussion of the meaning and functions of religion, personal qualifications for success in religious work, advantages and disadvantages, positions held by religious workers, women in religion, remuneration, and a list of religious colleges and seminaries is contained in this booklet.

For additional information, write to:

NATIONAL COUNCIL OF CHURCHES
297 Fourth Ave., New York 10, N. Y.

SYNAGOGUE COUNCIL OF AMERICA
110 West 42nd St., New York 36, N. Y.

SALESMANSHIP

AUCTIONEERS:
(D.O.T. No.: 1-51.10)

AUCTIONEER. 1954.

    4 pages—35¢; special to students, 25¢.
Chronicle Guidance Publications
Moravia, N. Y.

This "occupational brief" reviews the history and nature of the work performed, working conditions, personal qualifications, remuneration, opportunities for advancement, typical places of employment, and future prospects.

AUCTIONEER. Revised 1954.

    4 pages—15¢ in Canada, 20¢ elsewhere.
Guidance Centre, Univ. of Toronto
371 Bloor St. W., Toronto 5, Ontario

Presented in this "monograph" is information on the history of the occupation, nature of the work, working conditions, qualifications and preparation, earnings, advantages and disadvantages, methods of entering this field, and related occupations.

HOUSE-TO-HOUSE SALESMEN:
(D.O.T. No.: 1-55.10)

CAREERS IN HOUSE-TO-HOUSE
SELLING. Revised 1956.

    8 pages—25c.
B'nai B'rith Vocational Service Bureau
1129 Vermont Ave., N. W., Washington 5, D. C.

This booklet describes the work of the house-to-house salesman, personal qualifications necessary for success, future prospects, how to get started, earnings, and advantages and disadvantages.

HOUSE-TO-HOUSE SALESMAN.
1956.

    4 pages—35¢; special to students, 25¢.
Chronicle Guidance Publications
Moravia, N. Y.

This "occupational brief" reviews the history and nature of the work performed, working conditions, earnings, personal and training requirements, outlook, and opportunities for women.

SALESPEOPLE:
(D.O.T. Nos.: 1-75.; 1-85.; 1-86.; 1-87.)

PHIL STERLING, SALESMAN. *M. Gross.* 1951.

    200 pages—$2.50.
Dodd, Mead and Co.
432 Fourth Ave., New York 16, N. Y.

This career novel includes information on the techniques of salesmanship and the nature of a successful sales career. *(For teen-agers)*

SALES CLERKS AND SALESPER-
SONS. 1952.

> 4 pages—35¢; special to students, 25¢.
> *Chronicle Guidance Publications*
> Moravia, N. Y.

This "occupational brief" defines the job, working conditions, wages, qualifications, entry into jobs, outlook, and where to find employment.

SALESMAN. 1956.

> 4 pages—15¢ in Canada, 20¢ else-where.
> *Guidance Centre, Univ. of Toronto*
> 371 Bloor St. W., Toronto 5, Ontario

This "monograph" reviews the history and nature of the work, working conditions, qualifications and preparation needed, employment and advancement, remuneration, advantages and disadvantages, and related occupations.

SALESMEN AND SALESWOMEN.
1952.

> 4 pages—35¢; special to students, 25¢.
> *Chronicle Guidance Publications*
> Moravia, N. Y.

This "occupational brief" reviews the history and nature of the work, working conditions, personal qualifications needed for success, earnings, and how to get started in the profession.

SHOULD YOU BE A SALESMAN?
R. A. Whitney. 1955.

> 8 pages—free.
> *New York Life Insurance Co.*
> 51 Madison Ave., New York 10, N. Y.

This career booklet highlights the importance of this vocation, employment prospects, qualifications for success, and financial and other rewards.

(also see fields of MERCHANDISING AND RETAILING)

For additional information, write to:

NATIONAL SALES EXECUTIVES, INC.
136 East 57th St., New York 22, N. Y.

SCIENCE

ATOMIC SCIENTISTS:

(D.O.T. Nos.: 0-35.)

OPPORTUNITIES IN ATOMIC EN-
ERGY. *K. D. Hartzell.* 1951.

    144 pages—$1.00.

    Vocational Guidance Manuals, Inc.

    1011 East Tremont Ave., New York
      60, N. Y.

This comprehensive "manual" reviews the
importance of atomic energy and explains
what atomic energy is, discusses the personnel of the Atomic Energy Commission,
various scientists and engineers employed in the field of atomic energy, qualifications for the work, preparation, and
specialized training requirements.

SHOULD YOU BE AN ATOMIC SCI-
ENTIST? *L. R. Hafstad.* 1956.

    12 pages—free.

    New York Life Insurance Co.

    51 Madison Ave., New York 10, N. Y.

This attractive career booklet highlights
the growth of the field and its importance
to society, future prospects, places of employment, nature of the work, personal
qualifications, financial rewards, advantages and disadvantages, and educational
requirements.

BIOLOGICAL SCIENTISTS:

(D.O.T. Nos.: 0-35.)

ADVENTURES WITH REPTILES:
THE STORY OF ROSS ALLEN. *C. J.
Hylander.* 1951.

    174 pages—$2.95.

    Julian Messner, Inc.

    8 West 40th St., New York 18, N. Y.

Ross Allen, an outstanding authority on
alligators, crocodiles and snakes, operates
the Reptile Institute in Silver Springs,
Florida. This stimulating biography
traces the development of a boy's nature
study hobby into a man's vocation and
offers worthwhile career information on
the work of the naturalist, his importance
to society, working conditions, hazards,
and progress in the field. *(For young
people)*

BACTERIOLOGIST. 1956.

    4 pages—35¢; special to students, 25¢.

    Chronicle Guidance Publications

    Moravia, N. Y.

This "occupational brief" reviews the history and nature of the work performed,
working conditions, earnings, personal
and training requirements, opportunities
for women, where to find employment,
and related occupations.

BACTERIOLOGIST. *H. A. Robinson.*
Revised 1956.

    6 pages—50¢; special to students, 25¢.

    Personnel Services, Inc.

    Main St., Peapack, N. J.

This "occupational abstract" summarizes
the nature of the work, future prospects,
qualifications, preparation, entrance and

advancement, earnings, advantages and disadvantages, and related occupations.

BIOLOGICAL SCIENTISTS—EDUCATIONAL REQUIREMENTS FOR EMPLOYMENT OF. V.A. PAMPHLET 7-8.2. *Veterans Administration in cooperation with the Bureau of Labor Statistics, U. S. Dept. of Labor. 1955.*

21 pages—15¢.
Supt. of Documents, Govt. Printing Office
Washington 25, D. C.

This is one of a series of pamphlets prepared for use in the Veterans Administration rehabilitation program. It discusses employment opportunities, qualifications and preparation for such specialized vocations as agricultural scientists, animal scientists, plant scientists, microbiologists and bacteriologists, pharmacologists, geneticists and biophysicists. *(For counselors)*

CAREERS IN THE NATURAL SCIENCES. Revised 1954.

8 pages—25¢.
B'nai B'rith Vocational Service Bureau
1129 Vermont Ave., N. W., Washington 5, D. C.

Reviewed in this booklet are the outlook for specialists in this field, nature of the work, training required, personal qualifications, earnings, and advantages and disadvantages.

CHEMICAL SCIENTISTS:

(D.O.T. Nos.: 0-07.)

ASSISTANT CHEMIST. 1953.

4 pages—35¢; special to students, 25¢.
Chronicle Guidance Publications
Moravia, N. Y.

This "occupational brief" reviews the nature of the work performed, working conditions, salaries, qualifications, training requirements, opportunities for promotion, opportunities for women, where to find employment, methods of entry, and related jobs.

BIOCHEMIST. 1956.

4 pages—35¢; special to students, 25¢.
Chronicle Guidance Publications
Moravia, N. Y.

This "occupational brief" reviews the history of biochemistry, work performed, working conditions, wages, personal and training requirements, advancement, outlook, where to find employment, and methods of entry into the field.

CAREERS IN CHEMISTRY. *R. Shosteck.* Revised 1956.

12 pages—25¢.
B'nai B'rith Vocational Service Bureau
1129 Vermont Ave., N. W., Washington 5, D. C.

This booklet reviews job prospects for chemists, nature of the work, educational requirements, college expenses, personal qualifications, beginning jobs, women in chemistry, sources of employment, earnings, and working conditions.

CHEMIST. Revised 1956.

4 pages—15¢ in Canada, 20¢ elsewhere.
Guidance Centre, Univ. of Toronto
371 Bloor St. W., Toronto 5, Ontario

This "monograph" describes the history, importance and nature of the work, working conditons, qualifications and preparation necessary, remuneration, advantages and disadvantages, how to get started, and related occupations.

CHEMISTS — EDUCATIONAL REQUIREMENTS FOR EMPLOYMENT OF. V.A. PAMPHLET 7-8.3. *Veterans Administration in cooperation with Bureau of Labor Statistics, U. S. Dept. of Labor.* 1955.

11 pages—15¢.
Supt. of Documents, Govt. Printing Office
Washington 25, D. C.

This is another one of the series of pamphlets prepared for use in the Veterans Administration rehabilitation program and includes the nature of the work, places of employment, qualifications, and educational requirements. *(For counselors)*

EMPLOYMENT OUTLOOK IN THE INDUSTRIAL CHEMICAL INDUSTRY. BULLETIN NO. 1151. *Bureau of Labor Statistics, U. S. Dept. of Labor.* 1954.

37 pages—30¢.
Supt. of Documents, Govt. Printing Office
Washington 25, D. C.

This pamphlet, part of the employment outlook series, reviews the development of this industry, varied employment opportunities, nature of the work, number of workers, training requirements, earnings, working conditions, and future prospects.

OPPORTUNITIES FOR WOMEN IN CHEMISTRY. 1955.

4 pages—free to high school principals and guidance officers
Simmons College
300 The Fenway, Boston 15, Mass.

Reviewed in this folder are some of the accomplishments of chemistry, need for chemists, opportunities for women, personal qualifications, and preparation.

SHOULD YOU BE A CHEMIST? *I. Langmuir.* 1955.

8 pages—free.
New York Life Insurance Co.
51 Madison Ave., New York 10, N. Y.

This public service career booklet highlights the importance of chemistry to society, opportunities available, qualifications for success, areas of employment, preparation, and future prospects.

SOAP AND DETERGENT INDUSTRY. *O. M. Gale.* 1955.

19 pages—$1.00.
Bellman Publishing Co.
P. O. Box 172, Cambridge 38, Mass.

This pamphlet discusses the importance of the soap industry, development of soap making, employment opportunities in this industry, future trends, professional organization, and trade publications.

EARTH SCIENTISTS:

(D.O.T. Nos.: 0-35.)

ASTRONOMY. *F. D. Miller.* 1955.

32 pages—$1.00.
Bellman Publishing Co.
P. O. Box 172, Cambridge 38, Mass.

This pamphlet discusses the history of astronomy, attraction of an astronomical career, personal qualifications desirable in an astronomer, scholastic training, employment opportunities, advantages and disadvantages, and places of employment.

EMPLOYMENT OUTLOOK FOR
EARTH SCIENTISTS. BULLETIN NO.
1050. *Bureau of Labor Statistics, U. S.
Dept. of Labor.* 1952.

> 38 pages—30¢.
> *Supt. of Documents, Govt. Printing
> Office*
> Washington 25, D. C.

The development of this field, employment opportunities for various types of earth scientists, nature of the work, earnings, places of employment, preparation, methods of entry into this field, and future prospects are included in this pamphlet.

GEOLOGIST. 1956.

> 4 pages—35¢; special to students, 25¢.
> *Chronicle Guidance Publications*
> Moravia, N. Y.

This "occupational brief" reviews the nature of the work, its importance to society, specialization in the profession, working conditions, earnings, qualifications, preparation, and outlook.

GEOLOGIST. *W. Brackett and H. A.
Robinson.* 1956.

> 6 pages—50¢; special to students, 25¢.
> *Personnel Services, Inc.*
> Main St., Peapack, N. J.

This "occupational abstract" reviews the development of this profession, nature of the work, future prospects, opportunities for women, opportunities for servicemen, qualifications, preparation, entrance and advancement, earnings, number and distribution of geologists, advantages and disadvantages, and related occupations.

GEOLOGISTS—EDUCATIONAL REQUIREMENTS FOR EMPLOYMENT OF. V.A. PAMPHLET 7-8.5. *Veterans Administration in cooperation with Bureau of Labor Statistics, U. S. Dept. of Labor.* 1955.

> 11 pages—15¢.
> *Supt. of Documents, Govt. Printing
> Office*
> Washington 25, D. C.

Another of the pamphlets in the series prepared for use in the Veterans Administration rehabilitation program, it includes the nature of the work, qualifications, places of employment, and educational requirements. *(For counselors)*

METEOROLOGIST. Revised 1954.

> 4 pages—15¢ in Canada, 20¢ elsewhere.
> *Guidance Centre, Univ. of Toronto*
> 371 Bloor St. W., Toronto 5, Ontario

This "monograph" discusses the history and importance, nature of the work, working conditions, qualifications and preparation necessary, advancement, advantages and disadvantages, and related occupations.

METEOROLOGIST. *A. V. Carlin.* 1955.

> 39 pages—$1.00.
> *Research Publishing Co., Inc.*
> P. O. Box 245, Boston 1, Mass.

This little pamphlet presents the history of meteorology, the sub-divisions in this field and the nature of the work, places of employment, salaries, advantages and disadvantages, personal and educational requirements, training centers, and related occupations.

PHYSICAL SCIENTISTS:

(D.O.T. Nos.: 0-35.)

CAREERS IN GEOPHYSICS. *D. R. Frifield.* 1955.

> 8 pages—25¢.
> *B'nai B'rith Vocational Service Bureau*
> 1129 Vermont Ave., N. W. Washington 5, D. C.

This booklet reviews the history and nature of the work performed in this field, outlook, personal and educational requirements, specialized training, methods of entry, advancement, salaries, and places of employment.

DO WOMEN BELONG IN PHYSICS? *Mademoiselle's College and Careers Dept.* 1955.

> 5 pages—25¢.
> *Alumnae Advisory Center, Inc.*
> 541 Madison Ave., New York 22, N. Y.

This magazine reprint analyzes the reasons why so few women have become physicists and presents examples of the nature of the work of some female physicists who have succeeded. *(For female college students)*

EMPLOYMENT OUTLOOK FOR PHYSICISTS. BULLETIN NO. 1144. *Bureau of Labor Statistics, U. S. Dept. of Labor.* 1953.

> 24 pages—25¢.
> *Supt. of Documents, Govt. Printing Office*
> Washington 25, D. C.

The areas of specialization in this field, history, places of employment for physicists, future prospects, supply and demand, earnings, and training requirements are discussed in this booklet.

GEOPHYSICISTS—EDUCATION REQUIREMENTS FOR EMPLOYMENT

OF. V.A. PAMPHLET 7-8.6. *Veterans Administration in cooperation with Bureau of Labor Statistics, U. S. Dept. of Labor.* 1955.

> 10 pages—15¢.
> *Supt. of Documents, Govt. Printing Office*
> Washington 25, D. C.

Prepared for use in the Veterans Administration rehabilitation program, this pamphlet contains information on the nature of the work, training requirements, fields of specialization, and places of employment. *(For counselors)*

MICHAEL FARADAY: FROM ERRAND BOY TO MASTER PHYSICIST. *H. Sootin.* 1954.

> 180 pages—$2.95.
> *Julian Messner, Inc.*
> 8 West 40th St., New York 18, N. Y.

This biography contains stimulating occupational information and traces the professional growth of this prominent physicist. It describes his many accomplishments. *(For teen-age boys)*

OCCUPATIONAL GOALS FOR COLLEGE STUDENTS. PART I: ARCHITECTURE, ENGINEERING, AND THE PHYSICAL SCIENCES. *Edited by M. Hammond.* 1951.

> 96 pages—75¢.
> *Ohio State University Press*
> Columbus 10, Ohio

College students who aspire to careers in the physical sciences will find valuable information here on the opportunities available, nature of the work, qualifications, specialized training required, and future prospects. *(For college students)*

OPPORTUNITIES FOR WOMEN IN THE FIELD OF PHYSICS. 1952.

> 4 pages—free to high school principals and guidance officers
> *Simmons College*
> 300 The Fenway, Boston 15, Mass.

This folder reviews the field of physics, opportunities for female physicists, salaries, qualifications, and training for this work.

PHYSICISTS—EDUCATIONAL REQUIREMENTS FOR EMPLOYMENT OF. V.A. PAMPHLET 7-8.7. *Veterans Administration in cooperation with Bureau of Labor Statistics, U. S. Dept. of Labor.* 1955.

> 11 pages—15¢.
> *Supt. of Documents, Govt. Printing Office*
> Washington 25, D. C.

This pamphlet, which has been prepared for use in the Veterans Administration rehabilitation program reviews the nature of the work, places of employment, and educational requirements. *(For counselors)*

YOUR CAREER IN PHYSICS. *P. Pollack*. 1955.

> 127 pages—$2.75.
> *H. P. Dutton and Co., Inc.*
> 300 Fourth Ave., New York 10, N. Y.

This book presents the history and importance of this field, progress in various specialties, employment opportunities, demand and supply, typical places of employment, personal qualifications, training, earnings, and prospects.

SOCIAL SCIENTISTS:
(D.O.T. Nos.: 0-36.)

ANTHROPOLOGISTS. *Mademoiselle's College and Careers Dept.* 1956.

> 7 pages—25¢.
> *Alumnae Advisory Center, Inc.*
> 541 Madison Ave., New York 22, N. Y.

This magazine reprint describes the work of anthropologists, opportunities for women, qualifications, and educational preparation. *(For female college students)*

EMPLOYMENT OUTLOOK IN THE SOCIAL SCIENCES. BULLETIN NO. 1167. *Bureau of Labor Statistics, U. S. Dept. of Labor.* 1954.

> 66 pages—30¢.
> *Supt. of Documents, Govt. Printing Office*
> Washington 25, D. C.

This pamphlet describes the nature of the work of specialists in this field, such as the anthropologists, historians, political scientists, sociologists and statisticians. It also lists the necessary preparation for these vocations, methods of entry, earnings, and employment outlook.

SOCIOLOGISTS — EDUCATIONAL REQUIREMENTS FOR EMPLOYMENT OF. V.A. PAMPHLET 7-8.8. *Veterans Administration in cooperation with Bureau of Labor Statistics, U. S. Dept. of Labor.* 1955.

> 11 pages—15¢.
> *Supt. of Documents, Govt. Printing Office*
> Washington 25, D. C.

This is another one of the pamphlets prepared for use in the Veterans Administration rehabilitation program. It includes educational requirements, nature of the work, and places of employment. *(For counselors)*

STATISTICIANS — EDUCATIONAL REQUIREMENTS FOR EMPLOYMENT OF. V.A. PAMPHLET 7-8.9. *Veterans Administration in cooperation with Bureau of Labor Statistics, U. S. Dept. of Labor.* 1955.

8 pages—15¢.
Supt. of Documents, Govt. Printing Office
Washington 25, D. C.

This pamphlet was prepared for use in the Veterans Administration rehabilitation program. It reviews the nature of the work, places of employment, and educational requirements. *(For counselors)*

MISCELLANEOUS:

CAREERS AND OPPORTUNITIES IN SCIENCE. *P. Pollack.* 1954.

> 252 pages—$3.75.
> *E. P. Dutton and Co., Inc.*
> 300 Fourth Ave., New York 10, N. Y.

Described here are the miscellaneous opportunities for employment in scientific occupations, nature of the work of various scientists, places of employment, personal qualifications, preparation, and earnings.

RESEARCH JOBS FOR COLLEGE GRADUATES. *Mademoiselle's Jobs and Futures Dept.* 1952.

> 5 pages—25¢.
> *Alumnae Advisory Center, Inc.*
> 541 Madison Ave., New York 22, N. Y.

This magazine reprint presents examples of various research activities performed by women scientists. It also includes information about the educational preparation, earnings, places of employment, and qualifications for scientific research positions. *(For female college students)*

TECHNICAL ASSISTANT. 1955.

> 4 pages—35¢; special to students, 25¢.
> *Chronicle Guidance Publications*
> Moravia, N. Y.

This "occupational brief" reviews the history and nature of the work performed, working conditions, remuneration, personal and training requirements, opportunities for promotion, employment outlook, opportunities for women, and methods of entry.

YOUR OPPORTUNITIES IN SCIENCE AND ENGINEERING. Revised 1956.

> 30 pages—free.
> *National Association of Manufacturers*
> 2 East 48th St., New York 17, N. Y.

This well-illustrated pamphlet outlines the new frontiers available in scientific work, the nature of the work of various scientific personnel, qualifications and preparation, techniques for developing "success qualities," and future prospects. *(For young people)*

(also see fields of ENGINEERING, and MEDICAL AND HEALTH SERVICES)

For additional information, write to:

AMERICAN ASSOCIATION FOR THE ADVANCEMENT OF SCIENCE
1515 Massachusetts Ave., N. W., Washington 5, D. C.

SOCIAL SERVICE

SOCIAL WORKERS:
(D.O.T. Nos.: 0-27.)

CAREER AS MEDICAL SOCIAL WORKER. *D. Frifield.* 1955.

8 pages—25¢.
B'nai B'rith Vocational Service Bureau
1129 Vermont Ave., N. W., Washington 5, D. C.

This booklet reviews the history and nature of the work, future prospects, qualifications, educational requirements, earnings, places of employment, and advantages and disadvantages.

FIND YOUR CAREER IN FAMILY SOCIAL WORK. 1954.

12 pages—free.
Family Service Assoc. of America
192 Lexington Ave., New York 16, N. Y.

The nature of the family caseworker's activities, importance, qualifications and preparation, earnings, advancement, and opportunities for men and for women in the field of social work are discussed in this pamphlet.

OPPORTUNITIES IN SOCIAL WORK. *J. P. Anderson.* 1952.

112 pages—$1.00.
Vocational Guidance Manuals, Inc.
1011 East Tremont Ave., New York 60, N. Y.

This "manual" reviews the history and development of the field of social work, nature of the work, working conditions, personal qualifications, educational preparation, typical jobs, and a list of schools which are members of the American Association of Schools of Social Work.

THE OUTLOOK FOR WOMEN IN SOCIAL WORK. BULLETIN NO. 235-8. *Women's Bureau, U. S. Dept. of Labor.* 1952.

93 pages—30¢.
Supt. of Documents, Govt. Printing Office
Washington 25, D. C.

Social work specializations (social case work, group work, community organization, social work administration, teaching, and research), the employment outlook in these areas, nature of the work, and supply and demand are discussed here.

SOCIAL WORK. 1955.

3 pages—10¢.
Glamour Magazine
420 Lexington Ave., New York 17, N. Y.

This "fact sheet" from *Glamour's* Job Dept. discusses the nature of the work, qualifications and training, advantages, and salaries. *(For female readers)*

SOCIAL WORKER. 1954.

4 pages—35¢; special to students, 25¢.
Chronicle Guidance Publications
Moravia, N. Y.

This "occupational brief" reviews the history and nature of the work performed, working conditions, wages, personal and training requirements, licensing, and where to find employment.

SOCIAL WORKER. Revised 1954.

4 pages—15¢ in Canada, 20¢ elsewhere.
Guidance Centre, Univ. of Toronto
371 Bloor St. W., Toronto 5, Ontario

This "monograph" discusses the importance and nature of the work, working conditions, qualifications and preparation, advancement opportunities, remuneration, advantages and disadvantages, how to get started, and related occupations.

SOCIAL WORKERS. 1956.

20 pages—25¢.
Michigan Employment Security Comm.
7310 Woodward Ave., Detroit 2, Mich.

This "occupational guide" reviews the nature of the work, working conditions, location of jobs, earnings, qualifications, and disadvantages and advantages.

MISCELLANEOUS:

A CAREER IN COMMUNITY WORK. 1954.

4 pages—free to high school principals and guidance officers.
Simmons College
300 The Fenway, Boston 15, Mass.

This folder explains the nature of this work, opportunities available, qualifications, earnings, and educational preparation.

BIG BROTHER WORK AS A CAREER. *R. J. Fornwalt*. 1954.

6 pages—25¢.
Big Brother Movement
33 Union Sq. W., New York 3, N. Y.

Information is provided here on the history of the Big Brother Movement, various employment opportunities, nature of the work, and earnings.

PROFESSIONAL OPPORTUNITIES IN GIRL SCOUTING. 1952.

40 pages—free.
Girl Scouts of the U.S.A.
155 East 44th St., New York 17, N. Y.
The miscellaneous professional employment opportunities, nature of the work performed, qualifications and preparation for work with the Girl Scouts, and working conditions are discussed in this booklet.

THE RIGHT JOB FOR JUDITH. *E. Johnson*. 1951.

184 pages—$2.95.
Julian Messner, Inc.
8 West 40th St., New York 18, N. Y.

This career novel incorporates into the romantic theme worthwhile occupational information on the functions of the settlement house worker. *(For teen-age girls)*

(also see field of MENTAL HEALTH)

For additional information, write to:

AMERICAN ASSOCIATION OF GROUP WORKERS
129 East 52nd St., New York 22, N. Y.

AMERICAN ASSOCIATION OF SOCIAL WORKERS
One Park Ave., New York 16, N. Y.

TRANSPORTATION AND TRAVEL

MERCHANT MARINE PERSONNEL:
(D.O.T. Nos.: 0-88.; 5, 7, 9-48.)

ABLE SEAMAN. 1956.

    4 pages—35¢; special to students, 25¢.
Chronicle Guidance Publications
Moravia, N. Y.

This "occupational brief" reviews the history of the merchant marine, work performed by able seamen, working conditions, wages, personal and training requirements, opportunities for promotion, where to find employment, and methods of entry.

EMPLOYMENT OUTLOOK IN THE MERCHANT MARINE. BULLETIN NO. 1054. *Bureau of Labor Statistics, U. S. Dept. of Labor.* 1952.

    38 pages—30¢.
Supt. of Documents, Govt. Printing Office
Washington 25, D. C.

This pamphlet reviews the role of the merchant marine and its importance to society, nature of the job opportunities, qualifications and training requirements, earnings, working conditions, and future prospects.

OPPORTUNITIES IN THE MERCHANT MARINE. *J. J. O'Connor, Jr.* 1953.

    160 pages—$1.00.
Vocational Guidance Manuals, Inc.
1011 East Tremont Ave., New York 60, N. Y.

This comprehensive "manual" describes the nature and meaning of the merchant marine, ship's organization, current conditions in the industry, future prospects, working conditions at sea, earnings, entering the merchant marine, duties of various types of personnel, maritime schools, personal qualifications, opportunities ashore, and advantages and disadvantages.

MOTOR TRANSPORT PERSONNEL:
(D.O.T. Nos.: 5, 7, 9-49.200)

THE AMERICAN MOTOR TRANSPORT INDUSTRY. *N. Curry.* 1956.

    40 pages—$1.00.
Bellman Publishing Co.
P. O. Box 172, Cambridge 38, Mass.

This "vocational and professional monograph" tells the history of the industry, its importance to society, education suggested, employment opportunities, related occupations, nature of the work, earnings, and the national associations in this industry.

BUS DRIVER. 1953.

    4 pages—35¢; special to students, 25¢.
Chronicle Guidance Publications
Moravia, N. Y.

This "occupational brief" reviews the history and nature of the work, working conditions, wages, qualifications and training needed, opportunities for advancement, how to get started, and related jobs.

OPPORTUNITIES IN MOTOR TRANSPORTATION. *C. B. Rawson.* 1951.

> 112 pages—$1.00.
> *Vocational Guidance Manuals, Inc.*
> 1011 East Tremont Ave., New York 60, N. Y.

This comprehensive "manual" describes the scope of the industry and the truck driver's job, the bus driver, the truck and bus mechanic, and other miscellaneous opportunities. It includes information on getting started, the outlook, earnings, educational opportunities, and related fields.

ROUTEMAN. 1954.

> 4 pages—35¢; special to students, 25¢.
> *Chronicle Guidance Publications*
> Moravia, N. Y.

This "occupational brief" reviews the history and importance of the work, nature of the work performed, working conditions, wages, personal and training requirements, methods of entry, and related jobs.

STREET CAR OPERATOR AND BUS DRIVER. Revised 1955.

> 4 pages—15¢ in Canada, 20¢ elsewhere.
> *Guidance Centre, Univ. of Toronto*
> 371 Bloor St. W., Toronto 5, Ontario

This "monograph" defines the job, describes personal and educational requirements, entrance and advancement, earnings, working conditions, related occupations, and advantages and disadvantages.

TAXI DRIVER. 1954.

> 4 pages—35¢; special to students, 25¢.
> *Chronicle Guidance Publications*
> Moravia, N. Y.

This "brief" reviews the history of the occupation, duties on the job, working conditions, wages, qualifications and preparation, advancement, future prospects, methods of entry, and licensing.

TRUCK DRIVER. 1953.

> 4 pages—35¢; special to students, 25¢.
> *Chronicle Guidance Publications*
> Moravia, N. Y.

This pamphlet reviews the history and nature of the work performed, working conditions, wages, personal and training requirements, tells how to get started, and lists related jobs.

RAILWAY PERSONNEL:
(D.O.T. Nos.: 0-98.7; 5, 7, 9-38. through 9-44.)

THE AMERICAN RAILWAY INDUSTRY. *C. J. Corliss.* 1955.

> 26 pages—$1.00.
> *Bellman Publishing Co.*
> P. O. Box 172, Cambridge 38, Mass.

This pamphlet discusses the development and size of the railroad business in the United States, the railway organization and its many departments, railroad employees and their duties, earnings, qualifications of a railroad man, opportunities for advancement, advantages and disadvantages, opportunities for women, and how to seek a railroad job.

LOCOMOTIVE FIREMAN. Revised 1951.

> 4 pages—15¢ in Canada, 20¢ elsewhere.
> *Guidance Centre, Univ. of Toronto*
> 371 Bloor St. W., Toronto 5, Ontario

The history and nature of the work performed, working conditions, qualifications and preparation needed, advancement, earnings, advantages and disadvantages, how to get started, and related occupations are reviewed in this "monograph."

RAILROAD CONDUCTOR. Revised 1956.

4 pages—15¢ in Canada, 20¢ elsewhere.
Guidance Centre, Univ. of Toronto
371 Bloor St. W., Toronto 5, Ontario

This "monograph" includes information on the history, importance, and nature of the work, working conditions, qualifications and preparation needed, advancement, remuneration, advantages and disadvantages, getting started, and related occupations.

RAILWAY BRAKEMAN. 1954.

4 pages—15¢ in Canada, 20¢ elsewhere.
Guidance Centre, Univ. of Toronto
371 Bloor St. W., Toronto 5, Ontario

This "monograph" contains information on the history of this occupation, nature of the work of train, freight and yard brakemen, working conditions, qualifications and preparation, promotion opportunities, earnings, methods of entry, advantages and disadvantages, and related occupations.

TRAFFIC PERSONNEL:
(D.O.T. No.: 0-97.66)

CAREERS IN TRAFFIC ENGINEERING. *E. Zach.* 1954.

8 pages—25¢.
B'nai B'rith Vocational Service Bureau
1129 Vermont Ave., N. W., Washington 5, D. C.

This career booklet contains a history of the field, and discusses future prospects, nature of the work performed, qualifications and education necessary for entrance, places of employment, advancement opportunities, and earnings.

TRAFFIC MANAGER. 1955.

4 pages—35¢; special to students, 25¢.
Chronicle Guidance Publications
Moravia, N. Y.

This "occupational brief" reviews the history and nature of the work performed, working conditions, wages, personal and training requirements, where employed, outlook, opportunities for women, related jobs, and methods of entry.

TRAVEL PERSONNEL:
(D.O.T. Nos.: 1-87.69; 1-18.42)

JOBS IN TRAVEL. 1955.

7 pages—10¢.
Glamour Magazine
420 Lexington Ave., New York 17, N. Y.

This "fact sheet" presents the qualifications and company requirements for jobs in this field, types of travel agencies, where to inquire for employment, varied opportunities, duties, salaries, and advancement possibilities. *(For female readers)*

OPPORTUNITIES IN TRAVEL. *D. Short.* Revised 1953.

  96 pages—$1.00.
Vocational Guidance Manuals, Inc.
1011 East Tremont Ave., New York
    60 N. Y.

This is a comprehensive presentation of the principal divisions of the travel industry and the varied opportunities in this field. It also discusses salaries, training, prospects for employment, and how to get started.

(also see field of AVIATION)

For additional information, write to:

AMERICAN TRUCKING ASSOCIATIONS, INC.
1424—16th St., N. W., Washington 6, D. C.

ASSOCIATION OF AMERICAN RAILROADS
Transportation Bldg., Washington 6, D. C.

NATIONAL ASSOCIATION OF MOTOR BUS OPERATORS
839—17th St., N. W., Washington 6, D. C.

NATIONAL MARITIME UNION
346 West 17th St., New York 11, N. Y.

VETERINARY MEDICINE

VETERINARIANS:

(D.O.T. No.: 0-34.10)

VETERINARIAN. 1954.

4 pages—35¢; special to students, 25¢.
Chronicle Guidance Publications
Moravia, N. Y.

This "occupational brief" reviews the history and nature of the work performed, working conditions, remuneration, personal and training requirements, future prospects, opportunities for women, where to find employment, and licensing.

VETERINARIAN. Revised 1954.

4 pages—15¢ in Canada, 20¢ elsewhere.
Guidance Centre, Univ. of Toronto
371 Bloor St. W., Toronto 5, Ontario

The importance of this profession to society, nature of the work, working conditions, qualifications and preparation, promotional opportunities, earnings, advantages and disadvantages, getting started, and related occupations are discussed in this pamphlet.

VETERINARIAN. Reprinted 1954.

20 pages—25¢.
Michigan Employment Security Comm.
7310 Woodward Ave., Detroit 2, Mich.

This "guide" reviews the history and importance of this profession, nature of the work, employment prospects, personal and educational qualifications, licensing, remuneration, and advantages and disadvantages of the work.

VETERINARIAN. *T. J. Jones.* 1954.

32 pages—$1.00.
Research Publishing Co., Inc.
P. O. Box 245, Boston 1, Mass.

This little pamphlet tells of the history of the field of veterinary medicine, duties of the veterinarian, personal qualifications, earnings, advantages and disadvantages, preparation, training centers, licenses, obtaining employment in this field, typical places of employment, and professional associations.

(also see fields of AGRICULTURE, and MEDICAL AND HEALTH SERVICES)

For additional information, write to:

AMERICAN VETERINARY MEDICAL ASSOCIATION
600 So. Michigan Ave., Chicago 5, Ill.

WRITING AND LINGUISTICS

JOURNALISTS:
(D.O.T. Nos.: 0-06.)

CAREERS IN JOURNALISM. *R. Shosteck*. 1953.

12 pages—25¢.
B'nai B'rith Vocational Service Bureau
1129 Vermont Ave., N. W., Washington 5, D. C.

Described in this booklet are the future prospects in this field, nature of the work, methods of entry, number of journalists, preparation and qualifications, opportunities for women, salaries, working conditions, and related jobs.

DEADLINE. *Wm. Corbin*. 1952.

244 pages—$2.75.
Coward-McCann, Inc.
210 Madison Ave., New York 16, N. Y.

This career novel tells the tale of a newspaper cub reporter, the fictional on-the-job adventures, the nature of the work, qualifications, and advantages and disadvantages of this occupation. *(For teenagers)*

GET THAT STORY—JOURNALISM, ITS LORE AND THRILLS. *J. J. Floherty*. 1952.

150 pages—$2.75.
J. B. Lippincott Co.
227 So. 6th St., Philadelphia 5, Pa.

This well-illustrated book narrates the history and development of newspapers, the processes in the production and distribution of a large city newspaper, and the work of various newspaper personnel. *(For teen-agers)*

INDUSTRIAL JOURNALIST. *S. Menne*. 1956.

32 pages—$1.00.

Research Publishing Co., Inc.
P. O. Box 245, Boston 1, Mass.

This little pamphlet presents the history and definition of the occupation, it describes its importance to society, salaries, personal qualifications, aptitudes and special skills needed, advantages and disadvantages, educational requirements, methods of securing jobs, typical places of employment, and a list of training centers.

JOBS WITH THE PRESS. *Mademoiselle's Jobs and Futures Dept*. 1951.

8 pages—25c.
Alumnae Advisory Center, Inc.
541 Madison Ave., New York 22, N. Y.

This magazine reprint presents the qualifications for success in journalism, typical places of employment, nature of job opportunities, earnings, future prospects, and tells how to get started. *(For female readers)*

JOURNALISM. 1953.

4 pages—35¢; special to students, 25¢.
Chronicle Guidance Publications
Moravia, N. Y.

Another of the "occupational briefs" in this series, it defines the job, working conditions, wages, personal and training requirements, training opportunities, methods of entering this field, and future prospects.

JOURNALISTS. *F. P. Gill*. 1956.

24 pages—25¢.
Michigan Employment Security Comm.
7310 Woodward Ave., Detroit 2, Mich.

This "occupational guide" reviews the history and nature of the work, future prospects, personal qualifications, educational requirements, tells how to get started, earnings, places of employment, and advantages and disadvantages.

NELLIE BLY—FIRST WOMAN REPORTER. *I. Noble.* 1956.

192 pages—$2.95.
Julian Messner, Inc.
8 West 40th St., New York 18, N. Y.

This true story of Elizabeth Cochrane's adventures as a reporter for the old *New York World* is inspirational career reading for young people who aspire to a career in journalism. *(For teen-agers)*

REPORTER. Revised 1954.

4 pages—15¢ in Canada, 20¢ elsewhere.
Guidance Centre, Univ. of Toronto
371 Bloor St. W., Toronto 5, Ontario

This "monograph" discusses the history and nature of the work, working conditions, qualifications and preparation, advancement opportunities, earnings, how to get started, and advantages and disadvantages.

OPPORTUNITIES IN JOURNALISM. *E. E. Sugarman.* 1951.

126 pages—$1.00.
Vocational Guidance Manuals, Inc.
1011 East Tremont Ave., New York 60, N. Y.

This comprehensive "manual" analyzes many writing and editorial jobs on newspapers, jobs in related fields, and other writing opportunities. It also includes information on wages, training, qualifications, how to get started, and a list of colleges and universities offering degrees in journalism.

SHOULD YOU BE A NEWSPAPERMAN? *G. C. Biggers.* 1955.

8 pages—free.
New York Life Insurance Co.
51 Madison Ave., New York 10, N. Y.

Another of the public service career booklets in this series, it reviews the incomes of newspapermen, the atmosphere in a newspaper office, the nature of the work of the newspaperman, importance to society, college preparation, opportunities for women, personal qualifications, gratifications of the work, and related fields.

LINGUISTS:

(D.O.T. No.: 0-68.39)

JOBS FOR LANGUAGE MAJORS. *Mademoiselle's College and Careers Dept.* 1956.

5 pages—25¢.
Alumnae Advisory Center, Inc.
541 Madison Ave., New York 22, N. Y.

This magazine reprint reviews the nature of opportunities in this field with illustrations of young women who have succeeded. *(For female college students)*

INTERPRETER. 1952.

4 pages—35¢; special to students, 25¢.
Chronicle Guidance Publications
Moravia, N. Y.

This "occupational brief" reviews the nature of the work performed, working conditions, wages, personal and training requirements, opportunities for advancement, job prospects, typical places of employment, related jobs, and advantages and disadvantages.

TRANSLATOR. 1953.

2 pages—35¢; special to students, 25¢.
Chronicle Guidance Publications
Moravia, N. Y.

This "occupational brief" defines the job, outlines the duties, wages, personal and training requirements, advantages and disadvantages, and tells where to find employment.

LITERARY AGENTS:
(D.O.T. No.: 1-48.03)

DO YOUNG WRITERS NEED AGENTS? *Mademoiselle's College and Careers Dept.* 1954.

6 pages—25¢.
Alumnae Advisory Center, Inc.
541 Madison Ave., New York 22, N. Y.

The role which literary agents play in selling the works of young writers is detailed here. The viewpoints of writers, editors and literary agents are expressed. *(For female students)*

WRITERS:
(D.O.T. Nos.: 0-06.)

OPPORTUNITIES IN FREE LANCE WRITING. *H. C. Maxon.* 1951.

106 pages—$1.00.
Vocational Guidance Manuals, Inc.
1011 East Tremont Ave., New York 60, N. Y.

This "manual" discusses the ability necessary for writing success, market for free lance writers, earnings, opportunities, training, working conditions, breaking into the field, writing the story, and working with editors and agents.

SHOULD YOU BE A WRITER? *S. Schuman.* 1956.

48 pages—$1.00.
Occu-Press
489 Fifth Ave., New York 17, N. Y.

This authoritative pamphlet describes the history of the writing profession, what it takes to be a writer, markets for manuscripts, preparation for entrance into this field, preparation of manuscripts, working conditions, rewards and disadvantages, earnings, writers' associations, and future prospects.

MISCELLANEOUS:

CAREERS FOR ENGLISH MAJORS. *L. R. Middlebrook.* 1954.

27 pages—25¢.
New York University Press
Washington Square, New York 3, N. Y.

An authoritative, comprehensive presentation of the career opportunities available to college graduates who have majored in English, this pamphlet highlights the job possibilities in editing, writing and teaching.

175

OPPORTUNITIES IN BUSINESS
PAPERS. *J. L. Morrison.* 1955.
>96 pages—$1.00.
>*Vocational Guidance Manuals, Inc.*
>1011 East Tremont Ave., New York
>60, N. Y.

Included in this "manual" is information on the growth and scope of this field, qualifications and educational preparation for entrance, how to get started, job classifications, related fields, and organizations in this field.

OPPORTUNITIES IN FOREIGN
LANGUAGES. *T. Huebener.* 1955.
>96 pages—$1.00.
>*Vocational Guidance Manuals, Inc.*
>1011 East Tremont Ave., New York
>60, N. Y.

Another of the "manuals" in this series, it describes the field of foreign languages, attributes necessary for success, educational preparation, finding your job, types of positions, duties, and the numerous opportunities in foreign trade, industry, government and teaching.

(also see field of PUBLISHING)

For additional information, write to:

AUTHORS LEAGUE OF AMERICA
6 East 39th St., New York 16, N. Y.

SOCIETY OF MAGAZINE WRITERS
520 Fifth Ave., New York 18, N. Y.

CAREER GUIDANCE

CAREER CONFERENCES:

HOW TO CONDUCT A CAREER CONFERENCE. 1956.

19 pages—free.
National Association of Manufacturers
2 East 48th St., New York 17, N. Y.

Reviewed here are the purposes of a career conference, how to initiate such a conference in your community, planning this conference, suggested guide for vocational speakers, vocational questionnaire for senior students, and the career conference program. *(For high school officials and businessmen)*

HOW TO CONDUCT A VOCATIONAL GUIDANCE CONFERENCE FOR HIGH SCHOOL STUDENTS. 1956.

4 pages—free.
National Association of Manufacturers
2 East 48th St., New York 17, N. Y.

This folder includes the planning of a vocational guidance forum, its sponsors, participants and program. *(For counselors and local industry leaders)*

HOW TO PLAN AND ORGANIZE A SCHOOL PROGRAM OF TV AND RADIO DISCUSSIONS ON CAREER OPPORTUNITIES. 1956.

7 pages—free.
National Association of Manufacturers
2 East 48th St., New York 17, N. Y.

This indicates the nature of the career opportunities program, the panel and how it works, the details of programming, and publicity and promotion. *(For educators and industrial leaders)*

PLANNING A CAREER CONFERENCE. 1952.

4 pages—10¢.
Glamour Magazine
420 Lexington Ave., New York 17, N. Y.

This "fact sheet" outlines the purposes of a career conference, details of organizing or planning a career conference, length and type of conference, attendance, selection of career fields to be covered, guest speakers, schedule of speakers, publicity and entertainment, and miscellaneous factors of importance. *(For counselors and community leaders)*

CAREER PLANNING:

AFTER HIGH SCHOOL—WHAT? *S. Splaver*. Reprinted 1954.

12 pages—50¢.
Occu-Press
489 Fifth Ave., New York 17, N. Y.

This guidance playlet for classroom, P.T.A., assembly, youth club, and church young people's fellowship use presents the problem of post-high school career choice. *(For young people, parents and counselors)*

CAN I GET THE JOB—LET'S FIND OUT. 1954.

32 pages—free.
General Motors Corp.
Dept. of Public Relations, Detroit 2, Mich.

This attractive public service pamphlet discusses your interests, selecting the right job, what you have to offer, what employers are looking for, where to start your entry into the working world, how to get an interview, and personal characteristics for success on the job. *(For young people)*

CAREER COUNSELING GUIDE FOR ENGINEERS. 1956.

36 pages—free.
General Electric Co.
Cincinnati 15, Ohio

This authoritative pamphlet aims to aid young engineers and would-be engineers to plan for their future growth and progress. It includes facts about the eight major engineering activities and the means of evaluating personal attributes, and provides for an overall evaluation of the readers' qualifications for these activities. *(For engineering students and graduates)*

THE COST OF FOUR YEARS AT COLLEGE. 1956.

13 pages—free.
New York Life Insurance Co.
51 Madison Ave., New York 10, N. Y.

Canadian and United States colleges and universities are listed here, including their locations, nature and size of their enrollments, tuition fees, costs of room and board and general comments. *(For young people, parents and counselors)*

EMPLOYMENT AFTER COLLEGE: REPORT ON WOMEN GRADUATES, CLASS OF 1955. *Women's Bureau, U. S. Dept. of Labor in cooperation with Na-*

tional Vocational Guidance Association. 1956.

33 pages—25¢.
Supt. of Documents, Govt. Printing Office
Washington 25, D. C.

The findings of a survey of the employment status of women college graduates of June 1955 are presented here. Included are the graduates' comments on the need for guidance, their first jobs, their earnings, and their views on their college education. *(For female college students and college advisers)*

FROM SCHOOL TO JOB: GUIDANCE FOR MINORITY YOUTH. *A. Tanneyhill.* 1953.

28 pages—25¢.
Public Affairs Comm., Inc.
22 East 38th St., New York 16, N. Y.

This pamphlet highlights the past and present patterns of employment, counseling, and the accomplishments of programs aimed at guiding young members of minority groups. *(For counselors and community leaders)*

HOW TO CHOOSE A CAREER. *Mademoiselle's College and Careers Dept.* Revised 1956.

5 pages—25¢.
Alumnae Advisory Center, Inc.
541 Madison Ave., New York 22, N. Y.

The importance of self-analysis, self-discovery, and exploration of the job world in the process of career choice are discussed here. *(For female college students)*

HOW TO CHOOSE THAT CAREER—CIVILIAN AND MILITARY. *S. N. Feingold.* 1954.

52 pages—$1.00.
Bellman Publishing Co.
P. O. Box 172. Cambridge 38, Mass.

Among the topics which this pamphlet

178

highlights are charting one's course, education, preparation for service, educational opportunities in service, developing a sense of values, abilities and interests, and choosing that career—civilian and military. *(For young people, parents and counselors)*

HOW TO CHOOSE THAT COLLEGE. *C. C. Dunsmoor and O. C. Davis.* Reprinted 1955.

> 52 pages—$1.00.
> *Bellman Publishing Co.*
> P. O. Box 172, Cambridge 38, Mass.

Here is valuable information on how to choose a college wisely, who should go to college, the types of institutions of higher learning, college admission requirements, ten "tips" on planning your high school program, how colleges choose their students, considerations in your choice of college, making application for admission to college, meeting the costs, and making good at college. *(For young people and parents)*

HOW TO CREATE YOUR CAREER. 1956.

> 32 pages—30¢.
> *National Vocational Guidance Association*
> 1534 "O" St., N. W., Washington 5, D. C.

This very readable pamphlet stresses the importance of career planning, figuring out the real "you," learning about the working world, and using the help available to make a wise career choice. *(For young people)*

HOW TO VISIT COLLEGES. 1954.

> 24 pages—25¢.
> *National Vocational Guidance Association,*
> 1534 "O" St., N. W., Washington 5, D. C.

A practical guide for prospective college students, this pamphlet presents valuable information on the importance of visiting colleges before making the final choice, when to visit, what to look for, and what to do after the visit. *(For young people and parents)*

I FIND MY VOCATION. *H. Kitson.* 1954.

> 282 pages—$2.80.
> *McGraw-Hill Book Co., Inc.*
> 330 West 42nd St., New York 36, N. Y.

This authoritative vocational guidance volume is used as a textbook in high school classes and aids students in the process of intelligent career planning. *(For high school students)*

MIKE, THE MECHANIC. *S. Splaver.* 1954.

> 12 pages—50¢.
> *Occu-Press*
> 489 Fifth Ave., New York 17, N. Y.

This is another of the playlets in the socio-guidrama series. *(For young people, parents and counselors)*

OCCUPATIONAL PLANNING AND COLLEGE. *U. S. Dept. of Labor in cooperation with U. S. Dept. of Health, Education, and Welfare.* 1954.

> 19 pages—10c.
> *Supt. of Documents, Govt. Printing Office*
> Washington 25, D. C.

Pertinent suggestions are offered to young men regarding their plans for the future. Employment opportunities, location of work, type of employer, cost of training, earnings, and college subjects and activities are among the topics discussed. *(For male college students)*

PLANNING YOUR FUTURE. *G. E. Myers, G. M. Little, and S. A. Robinson.* Revised 1953.

526 pages—$3.60.

McGraw-Hill Book Co., Inc.

330 West 42nd St., New York 36, N. Y.

This highly readable volume is packed with valuable information to aid high school students in planning for their future careers intelligently. *(For young people)*

PLANNING YOUR JOB FUTURE. *E. Stoops and L. Rosenheim. 1953.*

40 pages—40¢.

Science Research Associates

57 West Grand Ave., Chicago 10, Ill.

This "junior life adjustment" booklet discusses the process of career planning for pre-teen agers. *(For upper elementary and junior high school students)*

YOU AND YOUR FUTURE. *R. N. Hatch and M. D. Parmenter.* Revised 1955.

56 pages—90¢.

Arthur C. Croft Publications

100 Garfield Ave., New London, Conn.

This is a "text-notebook" prepared for use in Grade 9 Occupations classes. It deals with such subjects as planning your vocation, taking stock of yourself, improving yourself, and exploring occupations. *(For ninth grade classes)*

YOUR FUTURE IS WHAT YOU MAKE IT. Revised 1954.

30 pages—free.

National Association of Manufacturers

2 East 48th St., New York 17, N. Y.

This public service pamphlet discusses the process of choosing a vocation, preparing for it, landing it, and progressing in it. *(For young people)*

YOUR INTERESTS AND YOUR CAREER. 1955.

7 pages—25¢.

B'nai B'rith Vocational Service Bureau

1129 Vermont Ave., N. W., Washington 5, D. C.

This booklet highlights the discovery of one's interests, the development of new interests, and the relationships between interests, careers and school planning. *(For students and counselors)*

JOB HUNTING:

HOW TO FIND A JOB. *M. E. Campbell. 1954.*

6 pages—10¢.

Glamour Magazine

420 Lexington Ave., New York 17, N. Y.

The Personnel Director of Conde Nast Publications offers some pertinent advice on the process of job hunting and presents six steps in a successful job hunt. *(For job hunters)*

HOW TO WRITE A LETTER OF APPLICATION. *Mademoiselle's Jobs and Futures Dept. 1953.*

4 pages—25¢.

Alumnae Advisory Center, Inc.

541 Madison Ave., New York 22, N. Y.

Helpful advice on writing job application letters and resumes of experience are offered here. *(For job hunters)*

JOB GETTING GUIDANCE FOR YOUNG PEOPLE. *R. J. Fornwalt. 1955.*

5 pages—10¢.

Big Brother Movement

33 Union Sq. W., New York 3, N. Y.

Here are tips to young people seeking their first jobs. Included are such items as how to prepare for the interview, how to complete the application form, and how to write a letter of job application. *(For high school and college students)*

MA AND SUE—ON A JOB INTERVIEW. S. *Splaver*. Reprinted 1955.

12 pages—50¢.
Occu-Press
489 Fifth Ave., New York 17, N. Y.
This guidance playlet, for use in classrooms, P.T.A.s, assemblies, youth clubs and young people's fellowship meetings, presents a mother accompanying her daughter for a job interview. *(For young people, parents and counselors)*

PICK YOUR JOB AND LAND IT. S. and M. *Edlund*. Revised 1954.

320 pages—$3.95.
Prentice-Hall, Inc.
70 Fifth Ave., New York 11, N. Y.
The authors, the well-known founders of the Man Marketing Clinics, present suggestions for analyzing one's talents, choosing career goals, and landing the job via varied job hunting campaigns. *(For young people and adults)*

SUCCESS IN THE WORLD OF WORK. R. F. *Cromwell*, R. N. *Hatch* and M. D. *Parmenter*. Revised 1953.

56 pages—90¢.
Arthur C. Croft Publications
100 Garfield Ave., New London, Conn.
This "text-notebook" presents material on finding the job, letters of application, application forms and special tests, and the employment interview. *(For ninth and tenth grade classes)*

TIPS FOR THE JOB INTERVIEW. *Mademoiselle's College and Careers Dept.* 1955.

4 pages—25¢.
Alumnae Advisory Center, Inc.
541 Madison Ave., New York 22, N. Y.
This is an interesting view of the discussions taking place at job interviews. *(For female college students)*

TIPS ON THE TECHNIQUE OF JOB HUNTING. 1952.

9 pages—10¢.
Glamour Magazine
420 Lexington Ave., New York 17, N. Y.
Valuable job hunting tips are presented in this "fact sheet." A suggested form for a personal data sheet and various sources of help for job hunters are included. *(For job hunters)*

MILITARY GUIDANCE:

CAREERS FOR WOMEN IN THE ARMED SERVICES. 1955.

8 pages—25¢.
B'nai B'rith Vocational Service Bureau
1129 Vermont Ave., N. W., Washington 5, D. C.
The various career opportunities for women in the Army, Navy, Air Corps and Marines, personal and physical qualifications, and training requirements are in-

cluded in this booklet. *(For young women and counselors)*

HOW TO GET AHEAD IN THE ARMED FORCES. R. *Horchow*. 1951.

96 pages—$1.00.
Doubleday and Co., Inc.
Garden City, N. Y.
Valuable information is presented here on the job opportunities in the armed

services, what to expect upon entrance, advancement, commission requirements, and opportunities for further training. *(For young people and counselors)*

JILL AND PERRY GO MILITARY. *S. Splaver.* 1955.

  12 pages—50¢.
  Occu-Press
489 Fifth Ave., New York 17, N. Y.

This is another of the playlets in the socio-guidrama series. The problem concerns a high school senior who wishes to leave school and enter the armed forces. *(For young people, parents and counselors)*

SHOULD YOU MAKE A CAREER IN THE ARMED FORCES? *Admiral Arthur W. Radford.* 1957.

  12 pages—free.
  New York Life Insurance Co.
51 Madison Ave., New York 10, N. Y.

Nearly every civilian occupation has its counterpart in the Armed Forces. This authoritative and fully-illustrated public service pamphlet lists scores of opportunities for men and women in combat units, exploration, engineering, research, scholarship, and administration. There are ample details on aptitudes, preparation, entry, promotion, and earnings.

YOU AND THE DRAFT. *Wm. S. Vincent and J. R. Russell.* 1952.

48 pages—40¢.
Science Research Associates
57 West Grand Ave., Chicago 10, Ill.

This pamphlet discusses why young men must plan their futures, enlistment versus waiting to be drafted, procedures for entering the armed forces, and the career and training opportunities available in the services. *(For young men)*

YOUR LIFE PLANS AND THE ARMED FORCES. 1955.

  149 pages—$2.00.
  American Council on Education
1785 Massachusetts Ave., N. W., Washington 6, D. C.

Prepared for use in high school Orientation classes, this book presents information on the vocational and educational opportunities in the armed forces, military obligations, and the specific career training programs in the various branches of the services. *(For young people and counselors)*

(Counselors are advised to write directly to the U.S. Dept. of Defense and to the individual branches of the armed forces for the latest copies of the U. S. ARMY OCCUPATIONAL HANDBOOK, U. S. NAVY OCCUPATIONAL HANDBOOK, and other recent publications on opportunities in the military services.)

MISCELLANEOUS CAREERS:

AFTER HIGH SCHOOL WHAT? *Women's Bureau, U. S. Dept. of Labor.* 1954.

  12 pages—10¢.
  Supt. of Documents, Govt. Printing Office
Washington 25, D. C.

This is in the form of a reply to a high school girl's questions. It discusses choos-

ing a career, importance of finishing high school, and includes a list of some job opportunities for girls. *(For high school girls)*

THE COLLEGE GIRL LOOKS AHEAD TO HER CAREER OPPORTUNITIES. *M. Zapoleon.* 1956.

272 pages—$3.75.
Harper and Brothers
49 East 33rd St., New York 16, N. Y.

A most comprehensive presentation, this book surveys the many career opportunities available to the college girl after her graduation. *(For female college students, parents and counselors)*

DIRECTORY OF PROFESSIONAL OPPORTUNITIES. *R. Shosteck. 1954.*

81 pages—75¢.

B'nai B'rith Vocational Service Bureau
1129 Vermont Ave., N. W., Washington 5, D. C.

This directory presents the specific opportunities available in some twenty professional and semi-professional occupations. *(For high school and college students)*

ESTIMATES OF WORKER TRAIT REQUIREMENTS FOR 4,000 JOBS AS DEFINED IN THE DICTIONARY OF OCCUPATIONAL TITLES. *U. S. Dept. of Labor. 1956.*

158 pages—$2.25.

Supt. of Documents, Govt. Printing Office
Washington 25, D. C.

Aptitudes, physical capacities, interests, working conditions and training time are indicated for 4,000 jobs. *(For counselors)*

EXPLORING OCCUPATIONS. *R. F. Cromwell, R. N. Hatch and M. D. Parmenter. Revised 1953.*

56 pages—90¢.

Arthur C. Croft Publications
100 Garfield Ave., New London, Conn.

This "text-notebook" introduces students to the job opportunities in ten occupational families. *(For ninth and tenth grade classes)*

EXPLORING THE WORLD OF JOBS. *D. E. Kitch. 1952.*

40 pages—40¢.

Science Research Associates
57 West Grand Ave., Chicago 10, Ill.

Another of their "junior life adjustment" booklets, it discusses a variety of jobs and the abilities and preparation necessary for success on these jobs. *(For upper elementary and junior high school students)*

GLAMOUR'S JOB CHART: 9 VITAL JOBS FOR WOMEN IN BUSINESS. 1956.

4 pages—10¢.

Glamour Magazine
420 Lexington Ave., New York 17, N. Y.

Basic information is presented here on the jobs of the mail girl, receptionist, clerk, typist, office machine operator, stenographer, secretary, telephone operator and salesgirl. *(For female job hunters)*

GUIDE TO EARNING A LIVING. *E. Cunningham and L. Reed. 1955.*

116 pages—$3.95.

Simon and Schuster, Inc.
630 Fifth Ave., New York 20, N. Y.

More than 100 occupations are described here. Information is included on the qualifications necessary for entry, nature of the work, opportunities, and advancement. *(For job hunters)*

JOB GUIDE FOR YOUNG WORKERS —1956-57 EDITION. *U. S. Dept. of Labor. 1956.*

64 pages—40¢.

Supt. of Documents, Govt. Printing Office
Washington 25, D. C.

Information is presented on beginning jobs for young people, employment prospects, qualifications necessary, duties, opportunities for advancement, and how and where to obtain these jobs. *(For young people)*

JOBS FOR THE GIRL WITH COMPLETE HIGH SCHOOL TRAINING OR LESS. 1954.

> 17 pages—10¢.
> *Glamour Magazine*
> 420 Lexington Ave., New York 17, N. Y.

This "fact sheet" reviews numerous job opportunities open to the high school graduate and to the girl who has not completed high school. For each job opportunity, duties, training personal qualifications, where to apply, and general comments are included. *(For girls with a high school education or less)*

JOBS FOR THE LIBERAL ARTS GRADUATE. *Mademoiselle's College and Careers Dept.* 1953.

> 7 pages—25¢.
> *Alumnae Advisory Center, Inc.*
> 541 Madison Ave., New York 22, N. Y.

The following beginning jobs for girls with liberal arts background and no experience are charted here: continuity writer, group leader, museum aid, research trainee, language specialist, elementary school teacher, airline hostess, ensign-second lieutenant (WAC, WAVES, Women Marines), department store trainee, telephone representative, lab technician, personnel assistant, library assistant, engineering aid, junior copywriter, airline agent, secretary, cub reporter, editorial assistant, case aid, and junior underwriter. *(For female liberal arts students)*

OCCUPATIONAL OUTLOOK HANDBOOK. BULLETIN NO. 998. *Bureau of Labor Statistics, U. S. Dept. of Labor.* Revised 1951.

> 574 pages—$3.00.
> *Supt. of Documents, Govt. Printing Office*
> Washington 25, D. C.

This is a compendium of occupational information including reports on 433 major occupations. These reports review the nature of the work, where to find employment, training and other qualifications, outlook, earnings, and where to go for more information. *(For counselors, teachers of Occupations, and students)* *J. Greenleaf.* 1955.

OCCUPATIONS AND CAREERS. *W.*

> 605 pages—$4.20.
> *McGraw-Hill Book Co., Inc.*
> 330 West 42nd St., New York 36, N. Y.

This is an exceptionally comprehensive textbook for high school Occupations courses. It has been prepared in three parts as follows: Part I concerns itself with the individual and his evaluation of self and community; Part II presents analyses of occupations by major groups; and Part III presents miscellaneous typical industries and occupations therein. *(For high school students and counselors)*

SRA OCCUPATIONAL BRIEFS. Annually.

> 70 briefs—$28.25 (by annual subscription).
> *Science Research Associates*
> 57 West Grand Ave., Chicago 10, Ill.

Seven packets of occupational briefs are sent to those who subscribe to this service. Each packet contains ten briefs, each concerned with a different occupation. (These briefs are not available for individual occupations and for this reason have not been referred to by individual occupational title.)

VOCATIONS FOR GIRLS. *M. R. Lingenfelter and H. D. Kitson.* Revised 1951.

> 364 pages—$3.00.
> *Harcourt, Brace and Co.*

383 Madison Ave., New York 17, N. Y.

This very readable book is divided into eight sections of occupational information. The sections are as follows: guardians of health, women who mean business, people are their business, scientists and engineers, literary and artistic workers, farm and home workers, workers for Uncle Sam, new horizons for women. *(For female students and counselors)*

APPENDIX

CAREER MATERIALS

available without charge from:

NEW YORK LIFE INSURANCE COMPANY
Public Relations Department
51 Madison Avenue, New York 10, N. Y.

GENERAL BOOKLET:

1. *The Cost of Four Years at College.* Lists a representative group of colleges with cost of attendance.

BOOKLETS ON INDIVIDUAL CAREERS:

1. *Should You Be A Doctor?* by Walter C. Alvarez, M.D., as told to Morton Sontheimer.
2. *Should You Be A Lawyer?* by Roscoe Pound, as told to Donald Robinson.
3. *Should You Be An Aeronautical Engineer?* by Igor Sikorsky, as told to Phil Gustafson.
4. *Should You Be A Teacher?* by William F. Russell, as told to Llewellyn Miller.
5. *Should You Become A Public Servant?* by Robert Moses, as told to Donald Robinson.
6. *Should You Be A Farmer?* by R. I. Throckmorton, as told to Andre Fontaine.
7. *Should You Be A Newspaperman?* by George C. Biggers as told to Morton Sontheimer.
8. *Should You Be An Architect?* by Pietro Belluschi, as told to Donald Robinson.
9. *Should You Be An Accountant?* by John L. Carey, as told to Donald Robinson.
10. *Should You Be A Chemist?* by Dr. Irving Langmuir, as told to Clive Howard.
11. *Should You Be A Salesman?* by Robert A. Whitney, as told to Oscar Schisgall.
12. *Should You Be A Nurse?* by Ruth Sleeper, as told to Llewellyn Miller.
13. *Should You Be An Electronic Engineer?* by Mervin J. Kelly, as told to Donald Robinson.
14. *Should You Go Into Business For Yourself?* by Morton Sontheimer.
15. *Should You Be A Pharmacist?* by W. Paul Briggs, as told to Donald Robinson.
16. *Should You Be A Dentist?* by Philip E. Blackerby, Jr., D.D.S., as told to Morton M. Hunt.
17. *Should You Be A Banker?* by Fred F. Florence, as told to Morton Sontheimer.
18. *Should You Be A Home Economist?* by Catherine T. Dennis, as told to Llewellyn Miller.
19. *Should You Go Into The Printing Industry?* by William H. Walling, as told to Roger Dakin.
20. *Should You Go Into The Mineral Industry?* by John W. Vanderwilt, as told to Donald Robinson.

187

INDEX

INDEX

192

194

197

Soap and Detergent Industry Scientist, 160
Social Service, 166-167
  (See also *Mental Health*)
  Big Brother, 167
  Girl Scout Worker, 167
  Social Worker, 167-168
    Administrator, 167-168
    Case Worker, 167-168
    Community Organizer, 167-168
    Family Worker, 167-168
    Group Worker, 167-168
    Research Worker, 167-168
    Teacher, 167-168
Social Scientist, 163
Social Worker,
  Jewish, 154
  Medical, 105-106, 166-167
  Psychiatric, 107
Sociologist, 163-164
Soil Conservationist, 48-49
Songwriter, 128
Sound Effects Man, Radio, 44
  Television, 44
Special Events, Television, 43
Specialist, Labor Relations, 130
Specialized Teacher, 62
Speech Therapist, 104
Stage Setting Designer, 18
Statistician, 164
  Baseball, 135
Steam Fitter, 54, 55, 56
Stenographer, 33-34
Stereotyper, 144
Steward, Airline, 21, 23
Stewardess, Airline, 21, 23
Stock and Bond Broker, 26, 27
Stock Broker, 26, 27
Stock Clerk, 32, 34
Stonemason, 50
Street Car Driver, 169
Student Personnel Worker, 60
Summer Work, 77-78
Surveyor, 69
Synagogue Administrator, 154
Synagogue Vocational Guidance, 154

Tailor, 38
Taxi Driver, 169
Teacher,
  Adult Education, 60
  Audio-Visual Aids, 60
  of the Blind, 62
  College, 60-61
  Elementary School, 61
  English, 175
  Foreign Language, 174-176

Teacher—*Cont.*
  Home Economics, 63, 73-74
  Jewish Education, 154
  Music, 127-128
  Nursery School, 61
  Overseas, 64
  Secondary School, 62
  Social Work, 167-168
  Specialized, 62
  Vocational, 63
Technical Agriculture, 14
Technical Assistant, 164
Technician,
  Communications, 41, 42, 44
  Dental, 58
  Electronic, 41, 42, 44
  Food, 74
  Laboratory, 164, 184
  Medical, 101-102
  Orthoptic, 123
  Radio, 41, 42, 44
  Telephone, 41, 42, 44
  Television, 41, 42, 44
  Textile, 39
  X-Ray, 105-106
Telephone,
  Operator, 42-43
  Opportunities, 42-43
  Representative, 184
  Technician, 42
Television,
  Actor, 43-44
  Advertising Worker, 11
  Director, 43-44
  Engineer, 41, 42-44
  Installation, 42, 43-44
  Model, 127
  News Announcer, 43
  Operator, 41
  Personnel, 43-44, 127
  Producer, 43-44
  Producer, Baseball, 135
  Programming, 43
  Promotion Worker, 43-44
  Repairman, 42, 43-44
  Research Worker, 43
  Salesperson, 43-44
  Sound Effects Man, 43-44
  Special Events, 43
  Technician, 42
  Writer, 43-44
  Writer, Continuity, 184
Teller, Bank, 25, 27
Textile Designer, 39
Textile Technician, 39
Therapist,
  Occupational, 120-121

202

Set in Times Roman
Format by Robert Cheney
Manufactured by The Haddon Craftsmen, Inc.
Published by HARPER & BROTHERS, *New York*